CLYMER®

KAWASAKI

EX500, GPZ500S and Ninja 500R • 1987-2002

D1609408

The world's finest publisher of mechanical how-to manuals

PRIMEDIA
Business Directories & Books

P.O. Box 12901, Overland Park, Kansas 66282-2901

Copyright ©2002 PRIMEDIA Business Magazines & Media Inc.

FIRST EDITION
First Printing November, 1991

SECOND EDITION
Updated to include 1992-1993 models
First Printing January, 1994
Second Printing November, 1996
Third Printing July, 1999

THIRD EDITION
Updated by Ed Scott to include 1994-2002 models
First Printing January, 2003
Second Printing June, 2004

Printed in U.S.A.

CLYMER and colophon are registered trademarks of PRIMEDIA Business Magazines & Media Inc.

ISBN: 0-89287-842-8

Library of Congress: 2002115452

TECHNICAL PHOTOGRAPHY: David Harter and Ron Wright.

TOOLS AND EQUIPMENT: K & L Supply at www.klsupply.com.

COVER: Mark Clifford Photography, Los Angeles, California.

CLYMER®

Publisher Shawn Etheridge

EDITORIAL

Managing Editor
James Grooms

Associate Editor
Jason Beaver
Lee Buell

Technical Writers
Jay Bogart
Michael Morlan
George Parise
Mark Rolling
Ed Scott
Ron Wright

Editorial Production Manager
Dylan Goodwin

Senior Production Editor
Greg Araujo

Production Editors
Holly Messinger
Darin Watson

Associate Production Editor
Susan Hartington
Julie Jantzer
Justin Marciniak

Technical Illustrators
Steve Amos
Errol McCarthy
Mitzi McCarthy
Bob Meyer
Mike Rose

MARKETING/SALES AND ADMINISTRATION

Advertising & Promotions Manager
Elda Starke

Advertising & Promotions Coordinators
Melissa Abbott
Wendy Stringfellow

Art Director
Chris Paxton

Sales Managers
Ted Metzger, Manuals
Dutch Sadler, Marine
Matt Tusken, Motorcycles

Business Manager
Ron Rogers

Customer Service Manager
Terri Cannon

Customer Service Representatives
Shawna Davis
Courtney Hollars
Susan Kohlmeyer
April LeBlond
Jennifer Lassiter
Ernesto Suarez

Warehouse & Inventory Manager
Leah Hicks

PRIMEDIA
Business Magazines & Media
P.O. Box 12901, Overland Park, KS 66282-2901 • 800-262-1954 • 913-967-1719

The following books and guides are published by PRIMEDIA Business Directories & Books.

More information available at *primediabooks.com*

CONTENTS

QUICK REFERENCE DATA

MOTORCYCLE INFORMATION

MODEL:_____ YEAR:_____

VIN NUMBER:_____

ENGINE SERIAL NUMBER:_____

CARBURETOR SERIAL NUMBER OR I.D. MARK:_____

TUNE-UP SPECIFICATIONS

Spark plug (standard heat range)	
1987-1993	NGK DR8ES or ND X27ESR-U
1994-on	
U.S.	NGK D9EA or ND X27ES-U
Canada	NGK DR9EA or ND X27ESR-U
Other than U.S. & Canada	NGK D9EA or ND X27ES-U
Gap	0.6-0.7 mm (0.024-0.028 in.)
Valve clearance	
Intake	0.13-0.18 mm (0.005-0.007 in.)
Exhaust	0.18-0.23 mm (0.007-0.009 in.)
Idle speed	1150-1250 rpm
Compression-standard	128-196 psi (9.0-13.8 kg/cm2)

TIRES AND TIRE PRESSURE

Tire Size	Pressure @ load 0-215 lb. (0-97.5 kg)	Over 215 lb. (Over 97.5 kg)
Front-100/90-16 54H Tubeless	28 psi (196 kPa)	32 psi (221 kPa)
Rear-120/90-16 63H Tubeless	32 psi (221 kPa)	36 psi (245 kPa)

RECOMMENDED LUBRICANTS AND FUEL

Engine oil	Rated SE or SF; 10W-40, 10W-50 or 20W-50
Front fork oil	SAE 10W20
Brake fluid	DOT 3
Fuel	87 pump octan (RON + MON/2)
	91 research octane (RON)
Battery	Distilled water
Cooling system	Permanent type antifreeze compounded for aluminum engines and radiator

ENGINE OIL CAPACITY

	Liter	U.S. Quart
Without filter change	2.8	2.9
With filter change	3.4	3.59

FRONT FORK OIL CAPACITY

	Oil capacity	Oil level
Oil change capacity		
1987-1993	245 mL	131 mm (5.1 in.)
1994-on	300 mL	115-118 mm (4.53-4.65 in.)
Rebuild capacity		
1987-1993	284-289 mL	131 mm (51 in.)
1994-on	348-356 mL	115-118 mm (4.53-4.65 in.)

COOLING SYSTEM SPECIFICATIONS

Capacity	1.8 L (1.90 qt.)
Coolant type	Antifreeze suited for aluminum engines
Coolant ratio	50% purified water/50% coolant
Radiator cap	11-15 psi (0.75-1.05 kg/cm^2)
Thermostat	
Opening temperature	176.9-182.3° F
	(80.5-83.5° C)
Valve opening lift	Not less than 8 mm (5/16 in.)
	(203° F (95° C)

DRIVE CHAIN SPECIFICATIONS

Manufacturer	Enuma endless
Size	EK520 MV-O 104 links
20 link length	
Standard	317.5-318.4 mm (12.50 –12.54 in.)
Service limit	323 mm (12.72 in.)
Chain slack	35-40 mm (1.37-1.57 in.)

ELECTRICAL SPECIFICATIONS

Charging system	
Regulator/rectifier	
output voltage	14-15 volts
Alternator output test	60 volts AC @ 4,000 rpm
Resistance check	0.3-0.6 volts
Ignition system	
Ignition coil	
Primary	2.2-3.9 ohms
Secondary	10-16 K ohms
Pickup coil resistance	400-490 ohms
Starter motor	
Brush wear limit	6.0 mm (0.236 in.)

BMW

M308	500 & 600 CC Twins, 55-69
M309	F650, 1994-2000
M500-3	BMW K-Series, 85-97
M502-3	BMW R50/5-R100 GSPD, 70-96
M503	R850 & R1100, 93-98

HARLEY-DAVIDSON

M419	Sportsters, 59-85
M428	Sportster Evolution, 86-90
M429-4	Sportster Evolution, 91-03
M418	Panheads, 48-65
M420	Shovelheads,66-84
M421-3	FLS/FXS Evolution,84-99
M423	FLS/FXS Twin Cam 88B, 2000-2003
M422	FLH/FLT/FXR Evolution, 84-94
M430-2	FLH/FLT Twin Cam 88, 1999-2003
M424-2	FXD Evolution, 91-98
M425	Dyna Glide Twin Cam, 99-01

HONDA

ATVs

M316	Odyssey FL250, 77-84
M311	ATC, TRX & Fourtrax 70-125, 70-87
M433	Fourtrax 90 ATV, 93-00
M326	ATC185 & 200, 80-86
M347	ATC200X & Fourtrax 200SX, 86-88
M455	ATC250 & Fourtrax 200/ 250, 84-87
M342	ATC250R, 81-84
M348	TRX250R/Fourtrax 250R & ATC250R, 85-89
M456-2	TRX250X 87-92; TRX300EX 93-03
M446	TRX250 Recon 97-02
M346-3	TRX300/Fourtrax 300 & TRX300FW/Fourtrax 4x4, 88-00
M200	TRX350 Rancher, 00-03
M459-2	Fourtrax Foreman 95-01
M454-2	TRX400EX 99-03

Singles

M310-13	50-110cc OHC Singles, 65-99
M319	XR50R-XR70R, 97-03
M315	100-350cc OHC, 69-82
M317	Elsinore, 125-250cc, 73-80
M442	CR60-125R Pro-Link, 81-88
M431-2	CR80R, 89-95, CR125R, 89-91
M435	CR80, 96-02
M457-2	CR125R & CR250R, 92-97
M464	CR125R, 1998-2002
M443	CR250R-500R Pro-Link, 81-87
M432-3	CR250R, 88-91 & CR500R, 88-01
M437	CR250R, 97-01
M312-13	XL/XR75-100, 75-03
M318-4	XL/XR/TLR 125-200, 79-03
M328-2	XL/XR250, 78-00; XL/XR350R 83-85; XR200R, 84-85; XR250L, 91-96
M320	XR400R, 96-00
M339-7	XL/XR 500-650, 79-03

Twins

M321	125-200cc, 65-78
M322	250-350cc, 64-74
M323	250-360cc Twins, 74-77
M324-5	Twinstar, Rebel 250 & Nighthawk 250, 78-03
M334	400-450cc, 78-87
M333	450 & 500cc, 65-76
M335	CX & GL500/650 Twins, 78-83
M344	VT500, 83-88
M313	VT700 & 750, 83-87
M440	Shadow 1100cc, 85-96
M460-2	VT1100C2 A.C.E. Shadow, 95-99

Fours

M332	CB350-550cc, SOHC, 71-78
M345	CB550 & 650, 83-85
M336	CB650,79-82
M341	CB750 SOHC, 69-78
M337	CB750 DOHC, 79-82
M436	CB750 Nighthawk, 91-93 & 95-99
M325	CB900, 1000 & 1100, 80-83
M439	Hurricane 600, 87-90
M441-2	CBR600, 91-98
M445	CBR600F4, 99-03
M434	CBR900RR Fireblade, 93-98
M329	500cc V-Fours, 84-86
M438	Honda VFR800, 98-00
M349	700-1000 Interceptor, 83-85
M458-2	VFR700F-750F, 86-97
M327	700-1100cc V-Fours, 82-88
M340	GL1000 & 1100, 75-83
M504	GL1200, 84-87
M508	ST1100/PAN European, 90-02

Sixes

M505	GL1500 Gold Wing, 88-92
M506-2	GL1500 Gold Wing, 93-00
M507	GL1800 Gold Wing, 01-04
M462-2	GL1500C Valkyrie, 97-03

KAWASAKI

ATVs

M465-2	KLF220 & KLF250 Bayou, 88-03
M466-2	KLF300 Bayou, 86-98
M467	KLF400 Bayou, 93-99
M470	KEF300 Lakota, 95-99
M385	KSF250 Mojave, 87-00

Singles

M350-9	Rotary Valve 80-350cc, 66-01
M444-2	KX60, 83-02; KX80 83-90
M448	KX80/85/100, 89-03
M351	KDX200, 83-88
M447-2	KX125 & KX250, 82-91 KX500, 83-02
M472-2	KX125, 92-00
M473-2	KX250, 92-00
M474	KLR650, 87-03

Twins

M355	KZ400, KZ/Z440, EN450 & EN500, 74-95
M360-3	EX500, GPZ500S, Ninja R, 87-02
M356-3	700-750 Vulcan, 85-02
M354-2	VN800 Vulcan 95-04
M357-2	VN1500 Vulcan 87-99
M471-2	VN1500 Vulcan Classic, 96-04

Fours

M449	KZ500/550 & ZX550, 79-85
M450	KZ, Z & ZX750, 80-85
M358	KZ650, 77-83
M359-3	900-1000cc Fours, 73-81
M451-3	1000 &1100cc Fours, 81-02
M452-3	ZX500 & 600 Ninja, 85-97
M453-3	Ninja ZX900-1100 84-01
M468	ZX6 Ninja, 90-97
M469	ZX7 Ninja, 91-98
M453-3	900-1100 Ninja, 84-01
M409	Concours, 86-04

POLARIS

ATVs

M496	Polaris ATV, 85-95
M362	Polaris Magnum ATV, 96-98
M363	Scrambler 500, 4X4 97-00
M365-2	Sportsman/Xplorer, 96-03

SUZUKI

ATVs

M381	ALT/LT 125 & 185, 83-87
M475	LT230 & LT250, 85-90
M380	LT250R Quad Racer, 85-88
M343	LTF500F Quadrunner, 98-00
M483-2	Suzuki King Quad/ Quad Runner 250, 87-98

Singles

M371	RM50-400 Twin Shock, 75-81
M369	125-400cc 64-81
M379	RM125-500 Single Shock, 81-88
M476	DR250-350, 90-94
M384-2	LS650 Savage, 86-03
M386	RM80-250, 89-95
M400	RM125, 96-00
M401	RM250, 96-02

Twins

M372	GS400-450 Twins, 77-87
M481-3	VS700-800 Intruder, 85-02
M482-2	VS1400 Intruder, 87-01
M484-3	GS500E Twins, 89-02
M361	SV650, 1999-2002

Triple

M368	380-750cc, 72-77

Fours

M373	GS550, 77-86
M364	GS650, 81-83
M370	GS750 Fours, 77-82
M376	GS850-1100 Shaft Drive, 79-84
M378	GS1100 Chain Drive, 80-81
M383-3	Katana 600, 88-96 GSX-R750-1100, 86-87
M331	GSX-R600, 97-00
M478-2	GSX-R750, 88-92 GSX750F Katana, 89-96
M485	GSX-R750, 96-99
M338	GSF600 Bandit, 95-00
M353	GSF1200 Bandit, 96-03

YAMAHA

ATVs

M499	YFM80 Badger, 85-01
M394	YTM/YFM200 & 225, 83-86
M488-4	Blaster, 88-02
M489-2	Timberwolf, 89-00
M487-4	Warrior, 87-03
M486-4	Banshee, 87-02
M490-2	YFM350 Moto-4 & Big Bear, 87-98
M493	YFM400FW Kodiak, 93-98
M280	Raptor 660R, 01-03

Singles

M492-2	PW50 & PW80, BW80 Big Wheel 80, 81-02
M410	80-175 Piston Port, 68-76
M415	250-400cc Piston Port, 68-76
M412	DT & MX 100-400, 77-83
M414	IT125-490, 76-86
M393	YZ50-80 Monoshock, 78-90
M413	YZ100-490 Monoshock, 76-84
M390	YZ125-250, 85-87 YZ490, 85-90
M391	YZ125-250, 88-93 WR250Z, 91-93
M497-2	YZ125, 94-01
M498	YZ250, 94-98 and WR250Z, 94-97
M406	YZ250F & WR250F, 01-03
M491	YZ400F, YZ426F & WR400F, 98-00
M417	XT125-250, 80-84
M480-3	XT/TT 350, 85-00
M405	XT500 & TT500, 76-81
M416	XT/TT 600, 83-89

Twins

M403	650cc, 70-82
M395-9	XV535-1100 Virago, 81-99
M495-2	V-Star 650, 98-03
M281	V-Star 1100, 99-04

Triple

M404	XS750 & 850, 77-81

Fours

M387	XJ550, XJ600 & FJ600, 81-92
M494	XJ600 Seca II, 92-98
M388	YX600 Radian & FZ600, 86-90
M396	FZR600, 89-93
M392	FZ700-750 & Fazer, 85-87
M411	XS1100 Fours, 78-81
M397	FJ1100 & 1200, 84-93
M375	V-Max, 85-03
M374	Royal Star, 96-03

VINTAGE MOTORCYCLES

Clymer® Collection Series

M330	Vintage British Street Bikes, BSA, 500-650cc Unit Twins; Norton, 750 & 850cc Commandos; Triumph, 500-750cc Twins
M300	Vintage Dirt Bikes, V. 1 Bultaco, 125-370cc Singles; Montesa, 123-360cc Singles; Ossa, 125-250cc Singles
M301	Vintage Dirt Bikes, V. 2 CZ, 125-400cc Singles; Husqvarna, 125-450cc Singles; Maico, 250-501cc Singles; Hodaka, 90-125cc Singles
M305	Vintage Japanese Street Bikes Honda, 250 & 305cc Twins; Kawasaki, 250-750cc Triples; Kawasaki, 900 & 1000cc Fours

MAINTENANCE LOG

Date	Miles	Type of Service

INTRODUCTION

The EX500 (known as the GPZ500S in Europe) was introduced in 1987 as an inexpensive beginner's bike. Kawasaki hit their mark and more since the EX's unveiling. This motorcycle quickly established a reputation as one of the most reliable and low maintenance machines available. Basically unchanged for 15 years, the EX remains one of Kawasaki's best selling motorcycles.

The parallel twin engine is based on the 454 LTD entry-level cruiser. The overhead cam 8-valve twin displaces 498cc. Fuel and air are mixed by two 34mm constant velocity (CV) carburetors. A tight-ratio six-speed transmission makes the most of the engine's predictable power.

A half fairing, perfect for providing modest protection during commutes, covers the EX's double-cradle steel box frame. This ridged frame design is ideal, as the light-weight sectional steel tubing resists flexing inputs from the engine and road. Once the rider gets going the disc brake units on the front and rear (a rear drum was upgraded in 1997) are up to the task of stopping the 388-pound EX. With simple design features and quality construction it is little wonder that the EX is a first choice for first time riders and those seeking a low cost alternative to motorcycle exotica.

CHAPTER ONE

NOTE: If you own a 1994 or later model EX500, first check the Supplement at the back of this book for any new service information.

GENERAL INFORMATION

This detailed, comprehensive manual covers the Kawasaki EX500, GPZ500S and Ninja 500R models from 1987 to 2002.

Information unique to 1994-2002 models is covered in the Supplement at the end of the manual.

This manual is written simply and clearly enough for owners who have never worked on a motorcycle, but is complete enough for use by experienced mechanics.

Troubleshooting, tune-up, maintenance and repair are not difficult if you know what tools and equipment to use and what to do. Anyone with some mechanical ability can perform most of the procedures in this manual.

Some of the procedures require the use of special tools. Using an inferior substitute tool for a special tool is not recommended as it can be dangerous to you and may damage the part.

Metric and U.S. standards are used throughout this manual. Metric to U.S. conversion is given in **Table 2**.

MANUAL ORGANIZATION

This chapter provides general information and discusses equipment and tools useful both for preventive maintenance and troubleshooting.

Chapter Two provides methods and suggestions for quick and accurate diagnosis and repair of problems. Troubleshooting procedures discuss typical symptoms and logical methods to pinpoint the trouble.

Chapter Three explains all periodic lubrication and routine maintenance necessary to keep your Kawasaki operating well. Chapter Three also includes recommended tune-up procedures, eliminating the need to consult other chapters constantly on the various assemblies.

Subsequent chapters describe specific systems such as the engine, clutch, primary drive, transmission, fuel, exhaust, suspension, steering and brakes. Each chapter provides disassembly, repair and assembly procedures in simple step-by-step form. If a repair is impractical for a home mechanic, it is so indicated. It is usually faster and less expensive to take such repairs to a dealer or competent repair shop. Specifications concerning a particular system are included at the end of the appropriate chapter.

NOTES, CAUTIONS AND WARNINGS

The terms NOTE, CAUTION and WARNING have specific meanings in this manual. A NOTE provides additional information to make a step or procedure easier or more clear. Disregarding a NOTE could cause some inconvenience, but would not cause damage or personal injury.

A CAUTION emphasizes areas where equipment damage could occur. Disregarding a CAUTION could cause permanent mechanical damage; however, personal injury is unlikely.

A WARNING emphasizes areas where personal injury or even death could result from negligence. Mechanical damage may also occur. WARNINGS *are to be taken seriously.* In some cases, serious injury and death have resulted from disregarding similar warnings.

SAFETY FIRST

Professional mechanics can work for years and never sustain a serious injury. If you observe a few rules of common sense and safety, you can enjoy many safe hours servicing your own machine. If you ignore these rules you can hurt yourself or damage the equipment.

1. Never use gasoline as a cleaning solvent.

2. Never smoke or use a torch in the vicinity of flammable liquids, such as cleaning solvent, in open containers.

3. If welding or brazing is required on the machine, remove the fuel tank and rear shock to a safe distance, at least 50 feet away. Welding on a gas tank requires special safety precautions and must be performed by someone skilled in the process. Do not attempt to weld or braze a leaking gas tank.

4. Use the proper sized wrenches to avoid damage to fasteners and injury to yourself.

5. When loosening a tight or stuck nut, be guided by what would happen if the wrench should slip. Be careful; protect yourself accordingly.

6. When replacing a fastener, make sure to use one with the same measurements and strength as the old one. Incorrect or mismatched fasteners can result in damage to the vehicle and possible personal injury. Beware of fastener kits that are filled with cheap and poorly made nuts, bolts, washers and cotter pins. Refer to *Fasteners* in this chapter for additional information.

7. Keep all hand and power tools in good condition. Wipe greasy and oily tools after using them. They are difficult to hold and can cause injury. Replace or repair worn or damaged tools.

8. Keep your work area clean and uncluttered.

9. Wear safety goggles during all operations involving drilling, grinding, the use of a cold chisel or anytime you feel unsure about the safety of your eyes. Safety goggles should also be worn anytime compressed air is used to clean a part.

10. Keep an approved fire extinguisher nearby. Be sure it is rated for gasoline (Class B) and electrical (Class C) fires.

11. When drying bearings or other rotating parts with compressed air, never allow the air jet to rotate the bearing or part; the air jet is capable of rotating them at speeds far in excess of those for which they were designed. The bearing or rotating part is very likely to disintegrate and cause serious injury and damage.

SERVICE HINTS

Most of the service procedures covered are straightforward and can be performed by anyone reasonably handy with tools. It is suggested, however, that you consider your own capabilities carefully before attempting any operation involving major disassembly of the engine or transmission.

1. "Front," as used in this manual, refers to the front of the motorcycle; the front of any component is the end closest to the front of the motorcycle. The "left-" and "right-hand" sides refer to the position of the parts as viewed by a rider sitting on the seat facing forward. For example, the throttle control is on the right-hand side. These rules are simple, but confusion can cause a major inconvenience during service.

2. Whenever servicing the engine or transmission, or when removing a suspension component, the bike should be secured in a safe manner. If the bike is to be parked on its sidestand, check the stand to make sure it is secure and not damaged. Block the front and rear wheels if they remain on the ground. A small hydraulic jack and a block of wood can be used to raise the chassis. If the transmission is not going to be worked on and the drive chain is connected to the rear wheel, shift the transmission into first gear.

3. Disconnect the negative battery cable when working on or near the electrical, clutch or starter systems and before disconnecting any wires. On most batteries, the negative terminal will be marked with a minus (–) sign and the positive terminal with a plus (+) sign.

4. When disassembling a part or assembly, it is a good practice to tag the parts for location and mark all parts which mate together. Small parts, such as bolts, can be identified by placing them in plastic sandwich bags. Seal the bags and label them with masking tape and a marking pen. When reassembly will take place immediately, an accepted practice is to place nuts and bolts in a cupcake tin or egg carton in the order of disassembly.

5. Finished surfaces should be protected from physical damage or corrosion. Keep gasoline and brake fluid off painted surfaces.

6. Use penetrating oil on frozen or tight bolts, then strike the bolt head a few times with a hammer and punch (use a screwdriver on screws). Avoid the use of heat where possible, as it can warp, melt or affect the temper of parts. Heat also ruins finishes, especially paint and plastics.

7. Keep flames and sparks away from a charging battery or flammable fluids and do not smoke near them. It is a good idea to have a fire extinguisher handy in the work area. Remember that many gas appliances in homes or garages (water heater, clothes drier, etc.) have pilot lights.

8. No parts removed or installed (other than bushings and bearings) in the procedures given in this manual should require unusual force during disassembly or assembly. If a part is difficult to remove or install, find out why before proceeding.

9. Cover all openings after removing parts or components to prevent dirt, small tools, etc. from falling in.

10. Read each procedure *completely* while looking at the actual parts before starting a job. Make sure you *thoroughly* understand what is to be done and then carefully follow the procedure, step by step.

11. Recommendations are occasionally made to refer service or maintenance to a Kawasaki dealer or a specialist in a particular field. In these cases, the work will be done more quickly and economically than if you performed the job yourself.

12. In procedural steps, the term "replace" means to discard a defective part and replace it with a new or exchange unit. "Overhaul" means to disassemble, inspect, measure, repair or replace defective parts and reassemble.

13. Some operations require the use of a hydraulic press. It would be wiser to have these operations performed by a shop equipped for such work, rather than to try to do the job yourself with makeshift equipment that may damage your machine.

14. Repairs go much faster and easier if your machine is clean before you begin work. There are many special cleaners on the market, like Bel-Ray Degreaser, for washing the engine and related parts. Follow the manufacturer's directions on the container for the best results. Clean all oily or greasy parts with cleaning solvent as you remove them.

WARNING
Never use gasoline as a cleaning agent. It presents an extreme fire hazard. Be sure to work in a well-ventilated area when using cleaning solvent. Keep a fire extinguisher, rated for gasoline fires, handy in any case.

15. Much of the labor charged for by dealers is to remove, disassemble, assemble and reinstall other parts in order to reach the defective part. It is frequently possible to perform the preliminary operations yourself and then take the defective unit to the dealer for repair at considerable savings.

16. If special tools are required, make arrangements to get them before you start. It is frustrating and time-consuming to get partly into a job and then be unable to complete it.

17. Make diagrams (or take a Polaroid picture) wherever similar-appearing parts are found. For instance, crankcase bolts are often not the same length. You may think you can remember where everything came from—but mistakes are costly. There is also the possibility that you may be sidetracked and not return to work for days or even weeks—in which time carefully laid out parts may have become disturbed.

18. When assembling parts, be sure all shims and washers are replaced exactly as they came out.

19. Whenever a rotating part butts against a stationary part, look for a shim or washer. Use new gaskets if there is any doubt about the condition of the old ones. A thin coat of oil on non-pressure type gaskets may help them seal more effectively.

20. If it is necessary to make a gasket, and you do not have a suitable old gasket to use as a guide, apply engine oil to the gasket surface of the part. Then place the part on the new gasket material and press the part slightly. The oil will leave a very accurate outline on the gasket material that can be cut around.

Be sure to use the same gasket material thickness as the original gasket.

21. Heavy grease can be used to hold small parts in place if they tend to fall out during assembly. However, keep grease and oil away from electrical and brake components.

22. A carburetor is best cleaned by disassembling it and soaking the parts in a commercial carburetor cleaner. Never soak gaskets and rubber parts in these cleaners. Never use wire to clean out jets and air passages unless otherwise instructed to do so in Chapter Seven. They are easily damaged. Use compressed air to blow out the carburetor only if the float has been removed first.

23. Take your time and do the job right. Do not forget that a newly rebuilt engine must be broken in just like a new one.

TORQUE SPECIFICATIONS

Torque specifications throughout this manual are given in Newton Meters (N•m) and foot-pounds (ft.-lb.).

Table 3 lists general torque specifications for nuts and bolts that are not listed in the respective chapters. To use the table, first determine the size of the nut or bolt. **Figure 1** and **Figure 2** show how this is done.

FASTENERS

The materials and designs of the various fasteners used on your Kawasaki are not arrived at by chance or accident. Fastener design determines the type of tool required to work the fastener. Fastener material is carefully selected to decrease the possibility of physical failure.

Threads

Nuts, bolts and screws are manufactured in a wide range of thread patterns. To join a nut and bolt, the diameter of the bolt and diameter of the hole in the nut must be the same. It is just as important that the threads on both be properly matched. The best way to tell if the threads on 2 fasteners are matched is to turn the nut on the bolt (or the bolt into the threaded hole in a piece of equipment) with fingers only. Be sure both pieces are clean. If much force is required, check the thread condition on each fastener. If the

thread condition is good but the fasteners jam, the threads are not compatible. A thread pitch gauge can also be used to determine pitch. Kawasaki manufactures using metric standard fasteners. The threads are cut differently from those of American fasteners (**Figure 3**).

Most threads are cut so that the fastener must be turned clockwise to tighten it. These are called right-hand threads. Some fasteners have left-hand threads; they must be turned counterclockwise to be tightened. Left-hand threads are used in locations where normal rotation of the equipment would tend to loosen a right-hand threaded fastener.

Machine Screws

There are many different types of machine screws. **Figure 4** shows a number of screw heads requiring different types of turning tools. Heads are also designed to protrude above the metal (round) or to be slightly recessed in the metal (flat). See **Figure 5**.

Bolts

Commonly called bolts, the technical name for these fasteners is cap screw. Metric bolts are described by the diameter and pitch (or the distance between each thread). For example, a M8 - 1.25 bolt is one that has a diameter of 8 millimeters with a distance of 1.25 millimeters between each thread. The measurement across 2 flats on the head of the

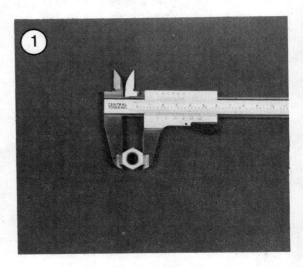

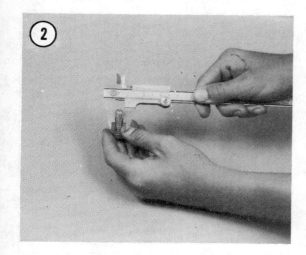

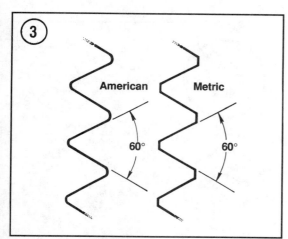

bolt indicates the proper wrench size to be used. **Figure 2** shows how to determine bolt diameter.

Nuts

Nuts are manufactured in a variety of types and sizes. Most are hexagonal (6-sided) and fit on bolts, screws and studs with the same diameter and pitch. **Figure 6** shows several types of nuts. The common nut is generally used with a lockwasher. Self-locking nuts have a nylon insert which prevents the nut from loosening; no lockwasher is required. Wing nuts are designed for fast removal by hand. Wing nuts are used for convenience in non-critical locations.

To indicate the size of a nut, manufacturers specify the diameter of the opening and the threads per inch. This is similar to bolt specifications, but without the length dimension. The measurement across 2 flats on the nut (**Figure 1**) indicates the proper wrench size to be used.

Prevailing Torque Fasteners

Several types of bolts, screws and nuts incorporate a system that develops an interference between the bolt, screw, nut or tapped hole threads. Interference is achieved in various ways: by distorting threads, coating threads with dry adhesive or nylon, distorting the top of an all-metal nut, using a nylon insert in the center or at the top of a nut, etc.

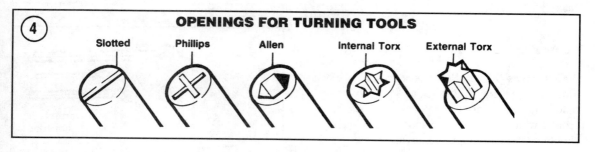

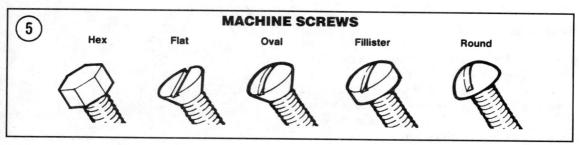

Prevailing torque fasteners offer greater holding strength and better vibration resistance. Some prevailing torque fasteners can be reused if in good condition. Others, like the nylon insert nut, form an initial locking condition when the nut is first installed; the nylon forms closely to the bolt thread pattern, thus reducing any tendency for the nut to loosen. When the nut is removed, the locking efficiency is greatly reduced. For greatest safety, it is recommended that you install new prevailing torque fasteners whenever they are removed.

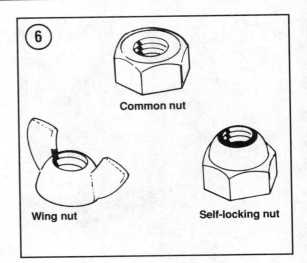

Washers

There are 2 basic types of washers: flat washers and lockwashers. Flat washers are simple discs with a hole to fit a screw or bolt. Lockwashers are designed to prevent a fastener from working loose due to vibration, expansion and contraction. **Figure 7** shows several types of washers. Washers are also used in the following functions:

a. As spacers.

b. To prevent galling or damage of the equipment by the fastener.

c. To help distribute fastener load during torquing.

d. As seals.

Note that flat washers are often used between a lockwasher and a fastener to provide a smooth bearing surface. This allows the fastener to be turned easily with a tool.

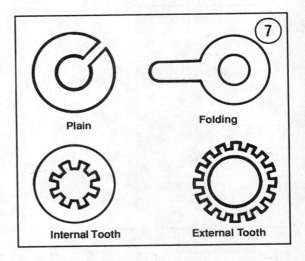

Cotter Pins

Cotter pins (**Figure 8**) are used to secure special kinds of fasteners. The threaded stud must have a hole in it; the nut or nut lockpiece has castellations around which the cotter pin ends wrap. Cotter pins should not be reused after removal.

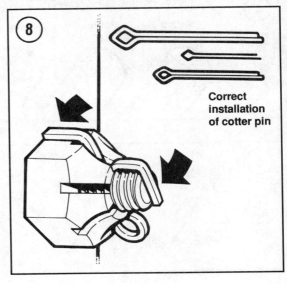

Snap Rings

Snap rings can be internal or external design. They are used to retain items on shafts (external type) or within tubes (internal type). In some applications, snap rings of varying thicknesses are used to control the end play of parts assemblies. These are often called selective snap rings. Snap rings should be replaced during installation as removal weakens and deforms them.

Two basic styles of snap rings are available: machined and stamped snap rings. Machined snap rings (**Figure 9**) can be installed in either direction (shaft or housing) because both faces are machined, thus creating two sharp edges. Stamped snap rings (**Figure 10**) are manufactured with one sharp edge and one rounded edge. When installing stamped snap rings in a thrust situation (transmission shafts, fork tubes, etc.), the sharp edge must face away from the part producing the thrust. When installing snap rings, observe the following:

a. Compress or expand snap rings only enough to install them.

b. After the snap ring is installed, make sure it is completely seated in its groove.

LUBRICANTS

Periodic lubrication assures long life for any type of equipment. The *type* of lubricant used is just as important as the lubrication service itself, although

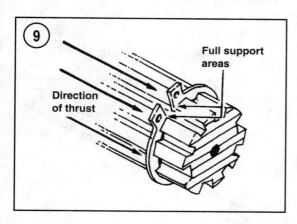

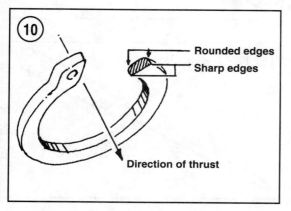

in an emergency the wrong type of lubricant is better than none at all. The following paragraphs describe the types of lubricants most often used on motorcycle equipment. Be sure to follow the manufacturer's recommendations for lubricant types.

Generally, all liquid lubricants are called "oil." They may be mineral-based (including petroleum bases), natural-based (vegetable and animal bases), synthetic-based or emulsions (mixtures). "Grease" is an oil to which a thickening base has been added so that the end product is semi-solid. Grease is often classified by the type of thickener added; lithium soap is commonly used.

Engine Oil

Oil for motorcycle and automotive engines is classified by the American Petroleum Institute (API) and the Society of Automotive Engineers (SAE) in several categories. Oil containers display these classifications on the top or label.

API oil classification is indicated by letters; oils for gasoline engines are identified by an "S." The engines covered in this manual require SE or SF graded oil.

Viscosity is an indication of the oil's thickness. The SAE uses numbers to indicate viscosity; thin oils have lower numbers while thick oils have higher numbers. A "W" after the number indicates that the viscosity testing was done at low temperature to simulate cold-weather operation. Engine oils fall into the 5W-30 and 20W-50 range.

Multi-grade oils (for example 10W-40) are less viscous (thinner) at low temperatures and more viscous (thicker) at high temperatures. This allows the oil to perform efficiently across a wide range of engine operating conditions. The lower the number, the better the engine will start in cold climates. Higher numbers are usually recommended for engine running in hot weather conditions.

Grease

Greases are graded by the National Lubricating Grease Institute (NLGI). Greases are graded by number according to the consistency of the grease; these range from No. 000 to No. 6, with No. 6 being the most solid. A typical multipurpose grease is NLGI No. 2. For specific applications, equipment manufacturers may require grease with an additive such as molybdenum disulfide (MOS2).

PARTS REPLACEMENT

Kawasaki makes frequent changes during a model year; some minor, some relatively major. When you order parts from the dealer or other parts distributor, always order by engine and frame number. Write the numbers down and carry them with you. Compare new parts to old before purchasing them. If they are not alike, have the parts manager explain the difference to you.

BASIC HAND TOOLS

Many of the procedures in this manual can be carried out with simple hand tools and test equipment familiar to the average home mechanic. Keep your tools clean and in a tool box. Keep them organized with the sockets and related drives together, the open-end and combination wrenches together, etc. After using a tool, wipe off dirt and grease with a clean cloth and return the tool to its correct place.

Top-quality tools are essential; they are also more economical in the long run. If you are now starting to build your tool collection, stay away from the "advertised specials" featured at some parts houses, discount stores and chain drug stores. These are usually a poor grade tool that can be sold cheaply. They are usually made of inferior material, and are thick, heavy and clumsy. Their rough finish makes them difficult to clean and they usually don't last very long. If it is ever your misfortune to use such tools you will probably find out that the wrenches do not fit the heads of bolts and nuts correctly and damage fasteners.

Quality tools are made of alloy steel and are heat treated for greater strength. They are lighter and better balanced than cheap ones. Their surface is smooth making them a pleasure to work with and easy to clean. The initial cost of good-quality tools may be more, but they are cheaper in the long run. Don't try to buy everything in all sizes in the beginning; do it a little at a time until you have the necessary tools. To sum up tool buying, "...the bitterness of poor quality lingers long after the sweetness of low price has faded."

The following tools are required to perform virtually any repair job. Each tool is described and the recommended size given for starting a tool collection. Additional tools and some duplicates may be added as you become familiar with the vehicle. Kawasaki motorcycles are built with metric fasteners—so if you are starting your collection now, buy metric sizes.

Screwdrivers

The screwdriver is a very basic tool, but if used improperly it will do more damage than good. The slot on a screw has a definite dimension and shape. A screwdriver must be selected to conform with that shape. Use a small screwdriver for small screws and a large one for large screws or the screw head will be damaged.

Two basic types of screwdrivers are required: common (flat-blade) screwdrivers (**Figure 11**) and Phillips screwdrivers (**Figure 12**).

Screwdrivers are available in sets which often include an assortment of common and Phillips blades. If you buy them individually, buy at least the following:

   a. Common screwdriver—5/16 × 6 in. blade.

   b. Common screwdriver—3/8 × 12 in. blade.

   c. Phillips screwdriver-size 2 tip, 6 in. blade.

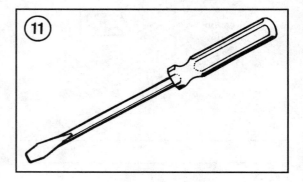

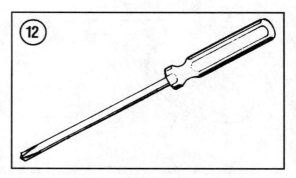

Use screwdrivers only for driving screws. Never use a screwdriver for prying or chiseling metal. Do not try to remove a Phillips or Allen head screw with a common screwdriver (unless the screw has a combination head that will accept either type); you can damage the head so that the proper tool will be unable to remove it.

Keep screwdrivers in the proper condition and they will last longer and perform better. Always keep the tip of a common screwdriver in good condition. **Figure 13** shows how to grind the tip to the proper shape if it becomes damaged. Note the symmetrical sides of the tip.

Pliers

Pliers come in a wide range of types and sizes. Pliers are useful for cutting, bending and crimping. They should never be used to cut hardened objects or turn bolts or nuts. **Figure 14** shows several pliers useful in motorcycle repairs.

Each type of pliers has a specialized function. Gas pliers are general purpose pliers and are used mainly for holding things and for bending. Locking pliers, such as Vise-grips, are used either as pliers or to hold objects very tightly like a vise. Needlenose pliers are used to hold or bend small objects. Channel-lock pliers can be adjusted to hold various sizes of objects; the jaws remain parallel to grip around objects such as pipe or tubing. There are many more types of pliers.

Box-end and Open-end Wrenches

Box-end and open-end wrenches are available in sets or separately in a variety of sizes. The size number stamped near the end refers to the distance between 2 parallel flats on the hex head bolt or nut.

Box-end wrenches are usually superior to open-end wrenches (**Figure 15**). Open-end wrenches grip the nut on only 2 flats. Unless a wrench fits well, it may slip and round off the points on the nut. The

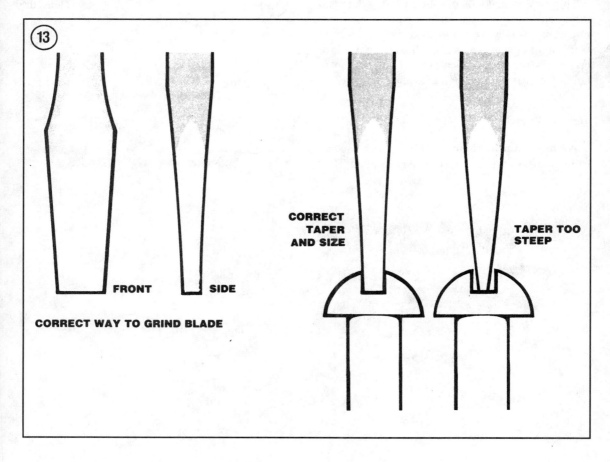

FRONT SIDE

CORRECT WAY TO GRIND BLADE

CORRECT TAPER AND SIZE

TAPER TOO STEEP

box-end wrench grips on all 6 flats. Both 6-point and 12-point openings on box wrenches are available. The 6-point gives superior holding power; the 12-point allows a shorter swing.

Combination wrenches which are open on one side and boxed on the other are also available. Both ends are the same size. See **Figure 16**.

Adjustable Wrenches

An adjustable wrench can be adjusted to fit a variety of nuts or bolt heads (**Figure 17**). However, it can loosen and slip, causing damage to the nut and perhaps to your knuckles. Use an adjustable wrench only when other wrenches are not available.

Adjustable wrenches come in sizes ranging from 4-18 in. overall. A 6 or 8 in. wrench is recommended as an all-purpose wrench.

Socket Wrenches

This type is undoubtedly the fastest, safest and most convenient to use. Sockets which attach to a ratchet handle (**Figure 18**) are available with 6-point or 12-point openings and 1/4, 3/8, 1/2 and 3/4 inch drives. The drive size indicates the size of the square hole which mates with the ratchet handle.

Torque Wrench

A torque wrench (**Figure 19**) is used with a socket to measure how tightly a nut or bolt is installed. They come in a wide price range and with either 3/8 or 1/2 square drive which mates with the socket. Purchase one that measures 0-140 N•m (0-100 ft.-lb).

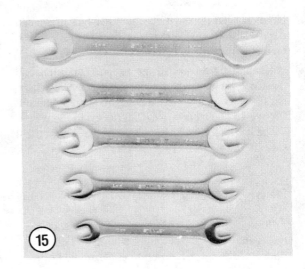

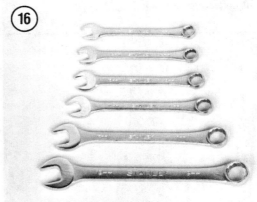

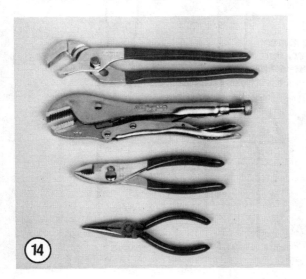

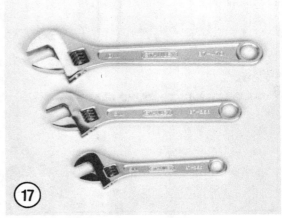

Impact Driver

This tool makes removal of tight fasteners easy and eliminates damage to bolts and screw slots.

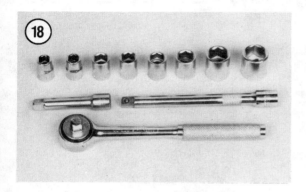

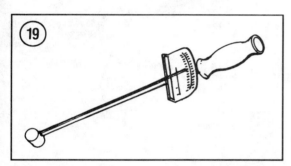

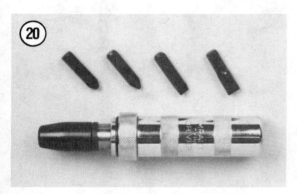

Impact drivers and interchangeable bits (**Figure 20**) are available at most large hardware and motorcycle dealers. However, make sure the socket is designed for impact use. Do not use regular hand type sockets as they may shatter.

Hammers

The correct hammer is necessary for repairs. Use only a hammer with a face (or head) of rubber or plastic or the soft-faced type that is filled with buckshot. These are sometimes necessary in engine teardowns. *Never* use a metal-faced hammer as severe damage will result in most cases. You can always produce the same amount of force with a soft-faced hammer.

Feeler Gauge

This tool has both flat and wire measuring gauges and is used to measure spark plug gap. See **Figure 21**. Wire gauges are used to measure spark plug gap; flat gauges are used for all other measurements.

Vernier Caliper

This tool is invaluable when reading inside, outside and depth measurements to close precision. The vernier caliper can be purchased from large dealers or mail order houses. See **Figure 22**.

Special Tools

A few special tools may be required for major service. These are described in the appropriate chapters and are available either from Kawasaki dealers or other manufacturers as indicated.

TEST EQUIPMENT

Voltmeter, Ammeter and Ohmmeter

A good voltmeter is required for testing ignition and other electrical systems. Voltmeters are available with analog meter scales or digital readouts. An instrument covering 0-20 volts is satisfactory. It should also have a 0-2 volt scale for testing points or individual contacts where voltage drops are much smaller. Accuracy should be 1/2 volt.

An ohmmeter measures electrical resistance. This instrument is useful in checking continuity (for open and short circuits) and testing lights. A self-powered 12-volt test light can often be used in its place.

The ammeter measures electrical current. These are useful for checking battery starting and charging currents.

Some manufacturers combine the 3 instruments into one unit called a multimeter or VOM. See **Figure 23**.

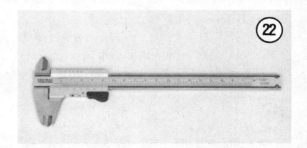

Compression Gauge

An engine with low compression cannot be properly tuned and will not develop full power. A compression gauge measures the amount of pressure present in the engine's combustion chambers during the compression stroke. This indicates general engine condition.

The easiest type to use has screw-in adaptors that fit into the spark plug holes (**Figure 24**). Press-in rubber-tipped types (**Figure 25**) are also available.

Dial Indicator

Dial indicators (**Figure 26**) are precision tools used to check dimension variations on machined parts such as transmission shafts and axles and to check crankshaft and axle shaft end play. Dial indicators are available with various dial types for different measuring requirements.

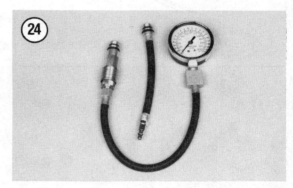

Strobe Timing Light

This instrument is necessary for checking ignition timing. By flashing a light at the precise instant the spark plug fires, the position of the timing mark can be seen. The flashing light makes a moving mark appear to stand still opposite a stationary mark.

Suitable lights range from inexpensive neon bulb types to powerful xenon strobe lights. See **Figure 27**. A light with an inductive pickup is recommended to eliminate any possible damage to ignition wiring.

Portable Tachometer

A portable tachometer is necessary for tuning. See **Figure 28**. Ignition timing and carburetor adjustments must be performed at the specified idle speed.

The best instrument for this purpose is one with a low range of 0-1,000 or 0-2,000 rpm and a high range of 0-4,000 rpm. Extended range (0-6,000 or 0-8,000 rpm) instruments lack accuracy at lower speeds. The instrument should be capable of detecting changes of 25 rpm on the low range.

Expendable Supplies

Certain expendable supplies are also required. These include grease, oil, gasket cement, shop rags and cleaning solvent. Ask your dealer for the special locking compounds, silicone lubricants and lube products which make vehicle maintenance simpler and easier. Cleaning solvent is available at some service stations.

MECHANIC'S TIPS

Removing Frozen Nuts and Screws

When a fastener rusts and cannot be removed, several methods may be used to loosen it. First, apply penetrating oil such as Liquid Wrench or WD-40 (available at hardware or auto supply stores). Apply it liberally and let it penetrate for 10-15 minutes. Rap the fastener several times with a small hammer; do not hit it hard enough to cause damage. Reapply the penetrating oil if necessary.

For frozen screws, apply penetrating oil as described, then insert a screwdriver in the slot and rap the top of the screwdriver with a hammer. This loosens the rust so the screw can be removed in the normal way. If the screw head is too chewed up to use this method, grip the head with locking pliers and twist the screw out.

Avoid applying heat unless specifically instructed as it may melt, warp or remove the temper from parts.

Remedying Stripped Threads

Occasionally, threads are stripped through carelessness or impact damage. Often the threads can be cleaned up by running a tap (for internal threads on nuts) or die (for external threads on bolts) through the threads. See **Figure 29**. To clean or repair spark plug threads, a spark plug tap can be used (**Figure 30**).

Removing Broken Screws or Bolts

When the head breaks off a screw or bolt, several methods are available for removing the remaining portion.

If a large portion of the remainder projects out, try gripping it with locking pliers. If the projecting portion is too small, file it to fit a wrench or cut a slot in it to fit a screwdriver. See **Figure 31**.

If the head breaks off flush, use a screw extractor. To do this, centerpunch the exact center of the re-

maining portion of the screw or bolt. Drill a small hole in the screw and tap the extractor into the hole. Back the screw out with a wrench on the extractor. See **Figure 32**.

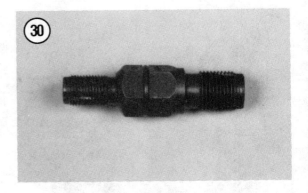

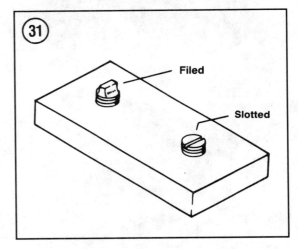

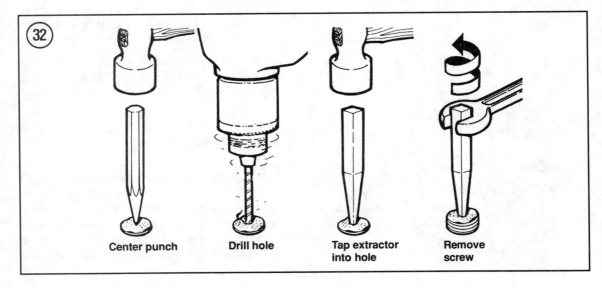

Center punch   Drill hole   Tap extractor into hole   Remove screw

Table 1 ENGINE AND CHASSIS NUMBERS

Model	Year	Frame Serial No.	Engine Serial No.
EX500 A1	1987	JKAEXA1-HA00000-010500	EX500AE000001-008000
EX500 A2	1988	JKAEXA10JA010501-on	EX500AE008001-on
EX500 A3	1989	JKAEXVA1-KA020501-on	EX500AE018001-on
EX500 A4	1990	JKAEXVA1-LA33001-on	EX600AE018001-on
EX500 A5	1991	JKAEXCA1-MA048001-on	EX500AE018001-on
EX500 A6	1992	JKAEXVA1-NA060001-on	EX500AE018001-on
EX500 A7	1993	JKAEXVA1-PA075001-on	EX500AE018001-on

See Supplement for EX500D1-on.

Table 2 CONVERSION FORMULAS

Multiply:	By:	To get the equivalent of:
Length		
Inches	25.4	Millimeter
Inches	2.54	Centimeter
Miles	1.609	Kilometer
Feet	0.3048	Meter
Millimeter	0.03937	Inches
Centimeter	0.3937	Inches
Kilometer	0.6214	Mile
Meter	3.281	Mile
Fluid volume		
U.S. quarts	0.9463	Liters
U.S. gallons	3.785	Liters
U.S. ounces	29.573529	Milliliters
Imperial gallons	4.54609	Liters
Imperial quarts	1.1365	Liters
Liters	0.2641721	U.S. gallons
Liters	1.0566882	U.S. quarts
Liters	33.814023	U.S. ounces
Liters	0.22	Imperial gallons
Liters	0.8799	Imperial quarts
Milliliters	0.033814	U.S. ounces
Milliliters	1.0	Cubic centimeters
Milliliters	0.001	Liters
Torque		
Foot-pounds	1.3558	Newton-meters
Foot-pounds	0.138255	Meters-kilograms
Inch-pounds	0.11299	Newton-meters
Newton-meters	0.7375622	Foot-pounds
Newton-meters	8.8507	Inch-pounds
Meters-kilograms	7.2330139	Foot-pounds

Table 3 GENERAL TIGHTING TORQUES*

Nut	Bolt	ft.-lb.	N•m
10 mm	6 mm	4.5	6
12 mm	8 mm	11	15
14 mm	10 mm	22	30
17 mm	12 mm	40	54
19 mm	14 mm	51	69
22 mm	16 mm	94	127

*This table lists general torque for standard fasteners with standard ISO pitch threads. Use these
specifications only if specific values are not provided for a given fastener.

CHAPTER TWO

TROUBLESHOOTING

Every motorcycle engine requires an uninterrupted supply of fuel and air, proper ignition and adequate compression. If any of these are lacking, the engine will not run.

Diagnosing mechanical problems is relatively simple if you use orderly procedures and keep a few basic principles in mind.

The troubleshooting procedures in this chapter analyze typical symptoms and show logical methods of isolating causes. These are not the only methods. There may be several ways to solve a problem, but only a systematic approach can guarantee success.

Never assume anything. Do not overlook the obvious. If you are riding along and the bike suddenly quits, check the easiest, most accessible problem spots first. Is there gasoline in the tank? Has a spark plug wire fallen off?

If nothing obvious turns up in a quick check, look a little further. Learning to recognize and describe symptoms will make repairs easier for you or a mechanic at the shop. Describe problems accurately and fully. Saying "it won't run" isn't the same thing as saying "it quit at high speed and won't start," or, "it sat in my garage for 3 months and then wouldn't start."

Gather as many symptoms as possible to aid in diagnosis. Note whether the engine lost power gradually or all at once. Remember that the more complicated a machine is the easier it is to troubleshoot because symptoms point to specific problems.

After the symptoms are defined, areas which could cause problems are tested and analyzed. Guessing at the cause of a problem may provide the solution, but it can easily lead to frustration, wasted time and a series of expensive, unnecessary parts replacements.

You do not need fancy equipment or complicated test gear to determine whether repairs can be attempted at home. A few simple checks could save a large repair bill and lost time while the bike sits in a dealer's service department. On the other hand, be realistic and don't attempt repairs beyond your abilities. Service departments tend to charge heavily for putting together a disassembled engine that may have been abused. Some won't even take on such a job—so use common sense and don't get in over your head.

OPERATING REQUIREMENTS

An engine has 3 basic needs to run properly: correct fuel/air mixture, compression and a spark at the correct time. If one or more are missing, the engine will not run. Four-stroke engine operating principles are illustrated in **Figure 1**. The electrical

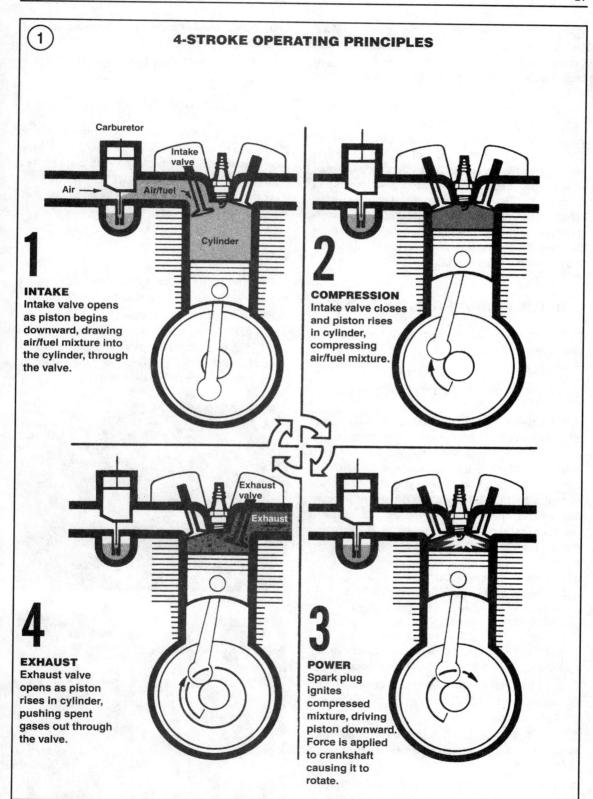

4-STROKE OPERATING PRINCIPLES

1

INTAKE
Intake valve opens
as piston begins
downward, drawing
air/fuel mixture into
the cylinder, through
the valve.

2

COMPRESSION
Intake valve closes
and piston rises
in cylinder,
compressing
air/fuel mixture.

4

EXHAUST
Exhaust valve
opens as piston
rises in cylinder,
pushing spent
gases out through
the valve.

3

POWER
Spark plug
ignites
compressed
mixture, driving
piston downward.
Force is applied
to crankshaft
causing it to
rotate.

system is the weakest link of the 3 basics. More problems result from electrical breakdowns than from any other source. Keep that in mind before you begin tampering with carburetor adjustments and the like.

If the machine has been sitting for any length of time and refuses to start, check and clean the spark plugs and then look to the gasoline delivery system. This includes the fuel tank, fuel shutoff valve and fuel line to the carburetor. Gasoline deposits may have formed and gummed up the carburetor jets and air passages. Gasoline tends to lose its potency after standing for long periods. Condensation may contaminate the fuel with water. Drain the old fuel from the fuel tank, fuel lines and carburetors and try starting with a fresh tankful.

TROUBLESHOOTING INSTRUMENTS

Chapter One lists the instruments needed and instruction on their use.

EMERGENCY TROUBLESHOOTING

When the bike is difficult to start, or won't start at all, it doesn't help to wear down the battery using the electric starter. Check for obvious problems even before getting out your tools. Go down the following list step by step. Do each one; you may be embarrassed to find the kill switch off, but that is better than wearing down the battery. If the bike still will not start, refer to the appropriate troubleshooting procedures which follow in this chapter.

> *WARNING*
> *During Step 1, do not use an open flame to check in the tank. A serious explosion is certain to result.*

1. Is there fuel in the tank? Open the filler cap and rock the bike. Listen for fuel sloshing around.

2. Is the fuel supply valve in the ON position? Turn the valve to the RESERVE position to be sure you get the last remaining gas.

3. Make sure the kill switch (**Figure 2**) is not stuck in the OFF position or that the wire is not broken and shorting out.

4. Are the spark plug wires on tight? Push both spark plug wires on (**Figure 3**) and slightly rotate them to

clean the electrical connection between the plug and the spark plug wire connector.

5. Is the choke in the right position?

ENGINE STARTING

An engine that refuses to start or is difficult to start is very frustrating. More often than not, the problem is very minor and can be found with a simple and logical troubleshooting approach.

The following items will help isolate engine starting problems.

Engine Fails to Start

Perform the following spark test to determine if the ignition system is operating properly.

1. Remove one of the spark plugs.

2. Connect the spark plug wire and connector to the spark plug and touch the spark plug base to a good ground like the engine cylinder head. Position the spark plug so you can see the electrodes.

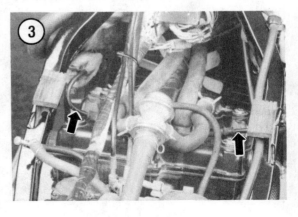

2

WARNING
During the next step, do not hold the spark plug, spark plug wire or connector with fingers. The high voltage generated by the ignition system could produce serious or fatal shocks. Use a pair of insulated pliers to hold the spark plug or wire.

3. Crank the engine over with the starter. A fat blue spark should be evident across the spark plug electrodes.
4. If the spark is good, check for one or more of the following possible malfunctions:
   a. Obstructed fuel line or fuel filter.
   b. Leaking head gasket.
   c. Low compression.
5. If the spark is not good, check for one or more of the following:
   a. Loose electrical connections.
   b. Dirty electrical connections.
   c. Loose or broken ignition coil ground wire.
   d. Broken or shorted high tension lead to the spark plug (**Figure 3**).
   e. Discharged battery.
   f. Disconnected or damaged battery connection.
   g. Neutral, starter lockout or side stand switch trouble.

Engine is Difficult to Start

Check for one or more of the following possible malfunctions:
   a. Fouled spark plug(s).
   b. Improperly adjusted choke.
   c. Intake manifold air leak.
   d. Contaminated fuel system.
   e. Improperly adjusted carburetor.
   f. Weak ignition unit.
   g. Weak ignition coils.
   h. Poor compression.
   i. Engine and transmission oil too heavy.

Engine Will Not Crank

Check for one or more of the following possible malfunctions:
   a. Blown fuse.
   b. Discharged battery.
   c. Defective starter motor.
   d. Seized piston(s).

   e. Seized crankshaft bearings.
   f. Broken connecting rod.

ENGINE PERFORMANCE

In the following checklist, it is assumed that the engine runs, but is not operating at peak performance. This will serve as a starting point from which to isolate a performance malfunction.

The possible causes for each malfunction are listed in a logical sequence and in order of probability.

Engine Will Not Idle

   a. Carburetor incorrectly adjusted.
   b. Fouled or improperly gapped spark plug(s).
   c. Leaking head gasket.
   d. Obstructed fuel line or fuel shutoff valve.
   e. Obstructed fuel filter.
   f. Ignition timing incorrect due to defective ignition component(s).
   g. Valve clearance incorrect.

Engine Misses at High Speed

   a. Fouled or improperly gapped spark plugs.
   b. Improper carburetor main jet selection.
   c. Ignition timing incorrect due to defective ignition component(s).
   d. Weak ignition coil(s).
   e. Obstructed fuel line or fuel shutoff valve.
   f. Obstructed fuel filter.
   g. Clogged carburetor jets.

Engine Overheating

   a. Incorrect carburetor adjustment or jet selection.
   b. Ignition timing incorrect due to improper adjustment or defective ignition component(s).
   c. Improper spark plug heat range.
   d. Damaged or blocked cooling fins.
   e. Oil level low.
   f. Oil not circulating properly.
   g. Valves leaking.
   h. Heavy engine carbon deposits.

**Engine Overheating
(Water-cooling problems)**

    a. Clogged radiator.

    b. Damaged thermostat.

    c. Worn or damaged radiator cap.

    d. Water pump worn or damaged.

    e. Fan relay damaged.

    f. Thermostatic fan switch damaged.

    g. Damaged fan blade(s)

**Excessive Exhaust Smoke and Engine Runs
Roughly**

    a. Clogged air filter element.

    b. Carburetor adjustment incorrect—mixture too rich.

    c. Choke not operating properly.

    d. Water or other contaminants in fuel.

    e. Clogged fuel line.

    f. Ignition coil defective.

    g. Spark plugs fouled.

    h. IC igniter or pickup coil defective.

    i. Loose or defective ignition circuit wire.

    j. Short circuit from damaged wire insulation.

    k. Loose battery cable connection.

    l. Valve timing incorrect.

    m. Intake manifold or air cleaner air leak.

Engine Loses Power at Normal Riding Speed

    a. Carburetor incorrectly adjusted.

    b. Engine overheating.

    c. Ignition timing incorrect due to defective ignition component(s).

    d. Incorrectly gapped spark plugs.

    e. Obstructed muffler.

    f. Dragging brakes(s).

Engine Lacks Acceleration

    a. Carburetor mixture too lean.

    b. Clogged fuel line.

    c. Ignition timing incorrect due to defective ignition component(s).

    d. Dragging brakes(s).

ENGINE NOISES

Often the first evidence of an internal engine problem is a strange noise. That knocking, clicking or tapping sound which you never heard before may be warning you of impending trouble.

While engine noises can indicate problems, they are difficult to interpret correctly; inexperienced mechanics can be seriously misled by them.

Professional mechanics often use a special stethoscope (which looks like a doctor's stethoscope) for isolating engine noises. You can do nearly as well with a "sounding stick" which can be an ordinary piece of dowling, a length of broom handle or a section of small hose. By placing one end in contact with the area to which you want to listen and the other end near your ear, you can hear sounds emanating from that area. The first time you do this, you may be horrified at the strange sounds coming from even a normal engine. If possible, have an experienced friend or mechanic help you sort out the noises. Consider the following when troubleshooting engine noises:

1. *Knocking or pinging during acceleration*— caused by using a lower octane fuel than recommended. May also be caused by poor fuel. Pinging can also be caused by a spark plug of the wrong heat range. Refer to *Correct Spark Plug Heat Range* in Chapter Three.

2. *Slapping or rattling noises at low speed or during acceleration*—may be caused by piston slap, i.e., excessive piston-cylinder wall clearance.

3. *Knocking or rapping while decelerating*—usually caused by excessive rod bearing clearance.

4. *Persistent knocking and vibration*—usually caused by worn main bearing(s).

5. *Rapid on-off squeal*—compression leak around cylinder head gasket or spark plug(s).

6. *Valve train noise*—check for the following:

    a. Valves adjusted incorrectly.

    b. Loose valve adjuster.

    c. Valve sticking in guide.

    d. Low oil pressure.

    e. Damaged rocker arm or shaft. Rocker arm may be binding on shaft.

ENGINE LUBRICATION

An improperly operating engine lubrication system will quickly lead to engine seizure. The engine oil level should be checked weekly and the tank refilled, as described in Chapter Three. Oil pump service is described in Chapter Four.

Oil Consumption High or Engine Smokes Excessively

   a. Worn valve guides.
   b. Worn or damaged piston rings.

Excessive Engine Oil Leaks

   a. Clogged air cleaner breather hose.
   b. Loose engine parts.
   c. Damaged gasket sealing surfaces.

CLUTCH

The three basic clutch troubles are:
   a. Clutch noise.
   b. Clutch slipping.
   c. Improper clutch disengagement or dragging.

All clutch troubles, except adjustments, require partial clutch disassembly to identify and cure the problem. The troubleshooting chart in **Figure 4** lists clutch troubles and checks to make. Refer to Chapter Five for clutch service procedures.

TRANSMISSION

The basic transmission troubles are:
   a. Excessive gear noise.
   b. Difficult shifting.
   c. Gears pop out of mesh.
   d. Incorrect shift lever operation.

Transmission symptoms are sometimes hard to distinguish from clutch symptoms. The troubleshooting chart in **Figure 5** lists transmission troubles and checks to make. Refer to Chapter Six for transmission service procedures. Be sure that the clutch is not causing the trouble before working on the transmission.

CHARGING SYSTEM

Charging system testing procedures are described in Chapter Eight.

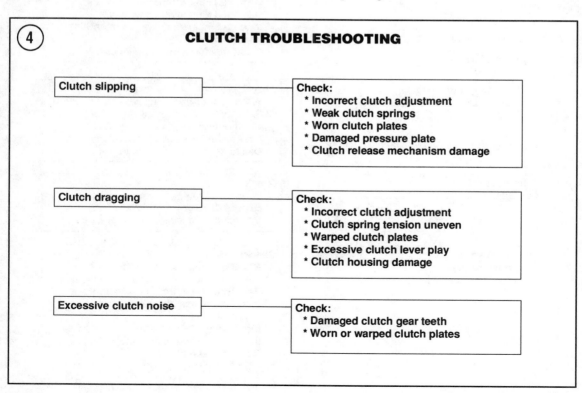

④ **CLUTCH TROUBLESHOOTING**

Clutch slipping

Check:
* Incorrect clutch adjustment
* Weak clutch springs
* Worn clutch plates
* Damaged pressure plate
* Clutch release mechanism damage

Clutch dragging

Check:
* Incorrect clutch adjustment
* Clutch spring tension uneven
* Warped clutch plates
* Excessive clutch lever play
* Clutch housing damage

Excessive clutch noise

Check:
* Damaged clutch gear teeth
* Worn or warped clutch plates

STARTING SYSTEM

The basic starter-related troubles are:

a. The starter does not crank.

b. The starter cranks, but the engine does not start.

Testing

Starting system problems are relatively easy to find. In most cases, the trouble is a loose or dirty electrical connection. Use the troubleshooting chart in **Figure 6** with the following tests.

Starter does not crank

1. Turn on the headlight and push the starter button. Check for one of the following conditions.

2. *Starter does not crank and headlight does not come on:* The battery is dead or there is a loose battery connection. Check the battery charge as described in Chapter Three. If the battery is okay, check the starter connections at the battery, solenoid and at the starter switch. Clean and tighten all connections.

3. *Headlight comes on, but goes out when the starter button is pushed:* There may be a bad connection at the battery. Wiggle the battery terminals and recheck. If the starter starts cranking, you've found the

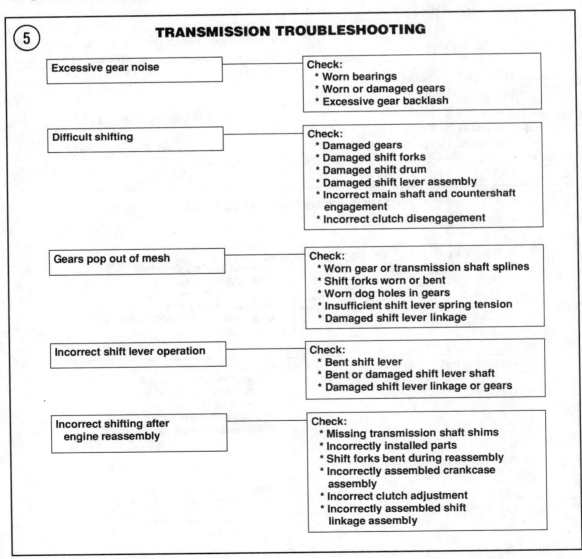

⑤ **TRANSMISSION TROUBLESHOOTING**

Excessive gear noise	Check: * Worn bearings * Worn or damaged gears * Excessive gear backlash
Difficult shifting	Check: * Damaged gears * Damaged shift forks * Damaged shift drum * Damaged shift lever assembly * Incorrect main shaft and countershaft engagement * Incorrect clutch disengagement
Gears pop out of mesh	Check: * Worn gear or transmission shaft splines * Shift forks worn or bent * Worn dog holes in gears * Insufficient shift lever spring tension * Damaged shift lever linkage
Incorrect shift lever operation	Check: * Bent shift lever * Bent or damaged shift lever shaft * Damaged shift lever linkage or gears
Incorrect shifting after engine reassembly	Check: * Missing transmission shaft shims * Incorrectly installed parts * Shift forks bent during reassembly * Incorrectly assembled crankcase assembly * Incorrect clutch adjustment * Incorrectly assembled shift linkage assembly

problem. Remove and clean the battery terminal clamps. Clean the battery posts also. Reinstall the terminal clamps and tighten securely.

4. *Headlight comes on, but dims slightly when the starter button is pushed:* The problem is probably in the starter. Remove and test the starter as described in Chapter Eight.

5. *Headlight comes on, but dims severely when the starter button is pushed:* Either the battery is nearly dead or the starter or engine is partially seized. Check the battery as described in Chapter Three. Check the starter as described in Chapter Eight before checking for partial engine seizure.

6. *Headlight comes on and stays bright when the starter button is pushed:* The problem is in the starter button, side stand switch, starter button-to-solenoid wiring or in the starter itself. Check the starter switch, kill switch, side stand switch, starter relay and the starter circuit relay. Check each switch by bypassing it with a jumper wire. Check the starter as described in Chapter Eight.

Starter spins but engine does not crank

If the starter spins at normal or high speed but the engine fails to crank, the problem is in the starter drive mechanism.

NOTE
Depending upon battery condition, the battery will eventually run down as the starter button is continually pressed. Remember that if the starter cranks normally, but the engine fails to start, the starter is working properly. It's time to start checking other engine systems. Don't wear the battery down.

ELECTRICAL PROBLEMS

If bulbs burn out frequently, the cause may be excessive vibration, loose connections that permit sudden current surges or the installation of the wrong type of bulb.

Most light and ignition problems are caused by loose or corroded ground connections. Check these before replacing a bulb or electrical component.

IGNITION SYSTEM

The ignition system is of the breakerless inductive discharge type. See Chapter Eight. Most problems involving failure to start, poor driveability or rough running are caused by trouble in the ignition system.
Note the following symptoms:
  a. Engine misses.
  b. Stumbles on acceleration (misfiring).
  c. Loss of power at high speed (misfiring).

⑥ STARTER TROUBLESHOOTING

Symptom	Probable Cause	Remedy
Starter does not work	Low battery	Recharge battery
	Worn brushes	Replace brushes
	Defective relay	Repair or replace
	Defective switch	Repair or replace
	Defective wiring or connection	Repair wire or clean connection
	Internal short circuit	Repair or replace defective component
Starter action is weak	Low battery	Recharge battery
	Pitted relay contacts	Clean or replace
	Worn brushes	Replace brushes
	Defective connection	Clean and tighten
	Short circuit in commutator	Replace armature
Starter runs continuously	Stuck relay	Replace relay
Starter turns; does not turn engine	Defective starter clutch	Replace starter clutch

d. Hard starting (or failure to start).

e. Rough idle.

Most of the symptoms can also be caused by a carburetor that is worn or improperly adjusted. Considering the law of averages, however, the odds are far better that the source of the problem will be found in the ignition system rather than the fuel system.

ELECTRONIC IGNITION TROUBLESHOOTING

The following basic tests are designed to pinpoint and isolate problems quickly in the primary circuit of the breakerless inductive discharge ignition system.

Spark Test

Perform the following test to determine if the ignition system is operating properly.

1. Remove one of the spark plugs.

2. Connect the spark plug wire and connector to the spark plug and touch the spark plug base to a good ground like the engine cylinder head. Position the spark plug so you can see the electrodes.

> *WARNING*
> *During the next step, do not hold the spark plug, spark plug wire or connector. The high voltage generated by the ignition system could produce serious or fatal shocks. If necessary, use a pair of insulated pliers to hold the spark plug or wire.*

3. Crank the engine over with the starter. A fat blue spark should be evident across the spark plug electrodes.

4A. If a spark is obtained in Step 3, the problem is not in the ignition or coil. Check the fuel system and spark plugs.

4B. If no spark is obtained, proceed with the following tests.

Testing

Test procedures for troubleshooting the ignition system arc found in the diagnostic chart in **Figure 7**. A multimeter, as described in Chapter One, is required to perform the test procedures.

Before beginning actual troubleshooting, read the entire test procedure (**Figure 7**). When required, the diagnostic chart will refer you to a certain chapter for test procedures.

Preignition

Preignition is the premature burning of fuel and is caused by hot spots in the combustion chamber. The fuel actually ignites before it is supposed to. Glowing deposits in the combustion chamber, inadequate cooling or an overheated spark plug can all cause preignition. This is first noticed in the form of a power loss but will eventually result in extended damage to the internal parts of the engine because of higher combustion chamber temperatures.

Detonation

Commonly called "spark knock" or "fuel knock," detonation is the violent explosion of fuel in the combustion chamber prior to the proper time of combustion. Severe damage can result. Use of low octane gasoline is a common cause of detonation.

Even when high octane gasoline is used, detonation can still occur if the engine is improperly timed. Other causes are over-advanced ignition timing, lean fuel mixture at or near full throttle, inadequate engine cooling, or the excessive accumulation of deposits on piston and combustion chamber.

EXCESSIVE VIBRATION

Usually this is caused by loose engine mounting hardware. If not, it can be difficult to find without disassembling the engine. High speed vibration may be due to a bent axle shaft or loose or faulty suspension components. Vibration can also be caused by the following conditions:

a. Broken Frame.

b. Severely worn primary chain.

c. Worn drive chain.

d. Primary chain links tight due to improper lubrication.

e. Improperly balanced wheels.

f. Defective or damaged wheels.

g. Defective or damaged tires.

h. Internal engine wear or damage.

⑦

IGNITION SYSTEM DIAGNOSIS

2

TEST 1: Isolate the problem to the ignition system by following the troubleshooting procedures in this chapter.

Ignition spark present.	TEST 2: Perform the ignition spark test as described in this chapter.	No spark or weak spark.
The ignition system is providing spark. If all other systems are good the engine should run.		Check for poor contact at the spark plug cap and all ignition connectors. Repair any that are damaged and recheck for spark. If a no spark condition exists, perform Test 3. If the spark is weak, perform Test 4.

Switch condition normal.	TEST 3: Check the following switches as described in Chapter Eight (1) neutral; (2) ignition; (3) engine stop switch.	Switch condition abnormal.
Perform TEST 4.		Replace and retest.

Readings correct.	TEST 4: Measure the ignition coil primary and secondary resistance as described in Chapter Eight.	Readings incorrect.
Perform TEST 5.		Replace the ignition coil and retest.

Readings correct.	TEST 5: Measure the pickup coil resistance as described in Chapter Eight.	Readings incorrect.
		Replace the pickup coil and test.

If the ignition system is still inoperative, carefully recheck all components, including wiring and connections. If all components are good, consider the IC Igniter unit defective by process of elimation.

FRONT SUSPENSION AND STEERING

Poor handling may be caused by improper tire pressure, a damaged or bent frame or front steering components, worn wheel bearings or dragging brakes. Possible causes of suspension and steering malfunctions are listed below.

Irregular or Wobbly Steering

a. Loose wheel axle nuts.
b. Loose or worn steering head bearings.
c. Excessive wheel hub bearing play.
d. Damaged cast wheel.
e. Unbalanced wheel assembly.
f. Worn hub bearings.
g. Incorrect wheel alignment.
h. Bent or damaged steering stem or frame (at steering neck).
i. Tire incorrectly seated on rim.
j. Excessive front end loading from non-standard equipment.

Stiff Steering

a. Low front tire air pressure.
b. Bent or damaged steering stem or frame (at steering neck).
c. Loose or worn steering head bearings.
d. Steering stem nut too tight.

Stiff or Heavy Fork Operation

a. Incorrect fork springs.
b. Incorrect fork oil viscosity.
c. Excessive amount of fork oil.
d. Bent fork tubes.

Poor Fork Operation

a. Worn or damaged fork tubes.
b. Fork oil level low due to leaking fork seals.
c. Bent or damaged fork tubes.
d. Contaminated fork oil.
e. Incorrect fork springs.
f. Heavy front end loading from non-standard equipment.

Poor Rear Shock Absorber Operation

a. Weak or worn spring.
b. Damper unit leaking.
c. Shock shaft worn or bent.
d. Incorrect rear shock spring.
e. Rear shock adjusted incorrectly.
f. Heavy rear end loading from non-standard equipment.
g. Incorrect loading.

BRAKE PROBLEMS

Sticking disc brakes may be caused by a stuck piston(s) in a caliper assembly or warped pad shim(s). See **Figure 8** for disc brake troubles and checks to make.

A sticking drum brake may be caused by worn or weak return springs, dry pivot and cam bushings or improper adjustment. Grabbing brakes may be caused by greasy linings which must be replaced. Brake grab may also be due to an out-of-round drum. Glazed linings will cause loss of stopping power. See **Figure 9** for drum brake troubles and checks to make.

CARBURETOR TROUBLESHOOTING

Basic carburetor troubleshooting procedures are found in **Figure 10**.

Figures 8-10 are on the following pages.

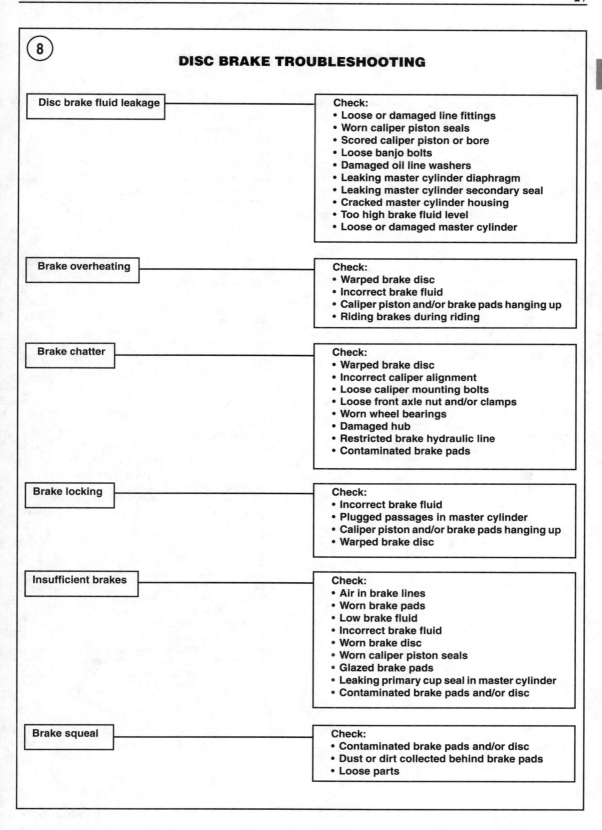

(8)

DISC BRAKE TROUBLESHOOTING

2

Disc brake fluid leakage

Check:
- Loose or damaged line fittings
- Worn caliper piston seals
- Scored caliper piston or bore
- Loose banjo bolts
- Damaged oil line washers
- Leaking master cylinder diaphragm
- Leaking master cylinder secondary seal
- Cracked master cylinder housing
- Too high brake fluid level
- Loose or damaged master cylinder

Brake overheating

Check:
- Warped brake disc
- Incorrect brake fluid
- Caliper piston and/or brake pads hanging up
- Riding brakes during riding

Brake chatter

Check:
- Warped brake disc
- Incorrect caliper alignment
- Loose caliper mounting bolts
- Loose front axle nut and/or clamps
- Worn wheel bearings
- Damaged hub
- Restricted brake hydraulic line
- Contaminated brake pads

Brake locking

Check:
- Incorrect brake fluid
- Plugged passages in master cylinder
- Caliper piston and/or brake pads hanging up
- Warped brake disc

Insufficient brakes

Check:
- Air in brake lines
- Worn brake pads
- Low brake fluid
- Incorrect brake fluid
- Worn brake disc
- Worn caliper piston seals
- Glazed brake pads
- Leaking primary cup seal in master cylinder
- Contaminated brake pads and/or disc

Brake squeal

Check:
- Contaminated brake pads and/or disc
- Dust or dirt collected behind brake pads
- Loose parts

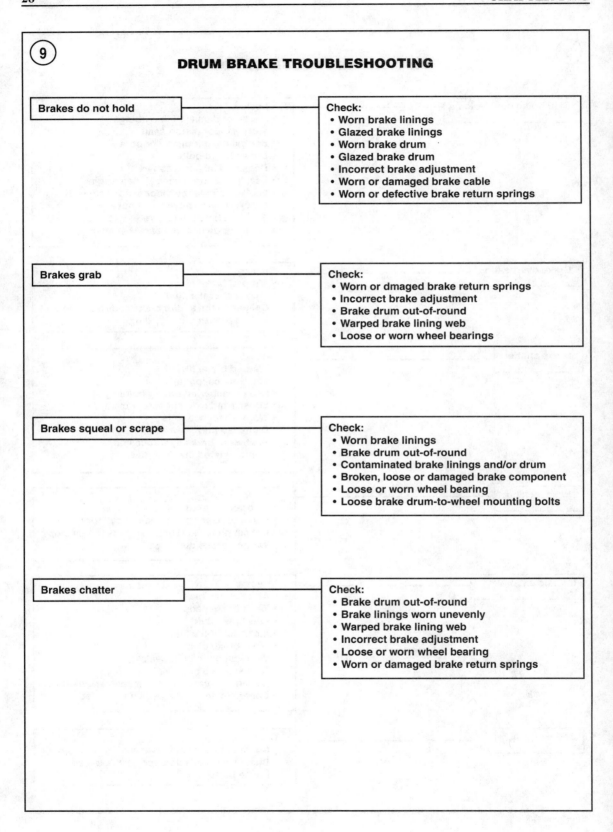

⑨

DRUM BRAKE TROUBLESHOOTING

Brakes do not hold

Check:
- Worn brake linings
- Glazed brake linings
- Worn brake drum
- Glazed brake drum
- Incorrect brake adjustment
- Worn or damaged brake cable
- Worn or defective brake return springs

Brakes grab

Check:
- Worn or dmaged brake return springs
- Incorrect brake adjustment
- Brake drum out-of-round
- Warped brake lining web
- Loose or worn wheel bearings

Brakes squeal or scrape

Check:
- Worn brake linings
- Brake drum out-of-round
- Contaminated brake linings and/or drum
- Broken, loose or damaged brake component
- Loose or worn wheel bearing
- Loose brake drum-to-wheel mounting bolts

Brakes chatter

Check:
- Brake drum out-of-round
- Brake linings worn unevenly
- Warped brake lining web
- Incorrect brake adjustment
- Loose or worn wheel bearing
- Worn or damaged brake return springs

⑩	CARBURETOR TROUBLESHOOTING		
CONDITION	**SYMPTOM**	**CONDITION**	**SYMPTOM**

Rich mixture	Rough idle
	Black exhaust smoke
	Hard starting, especially
	  when hot
	Gas-fouled spark plugs
	Black deposits in exhaust
	  pipe
	Poor gas mileage
	Engine performs worse as
	  it warms up
		Lean mixture	Backfiring
			Rough idle
			Overheating
			Hesitation upon
			  acceleration
			Engine speed varies
			  at fixed throttle
			Loss of power
			White color on spark
			  insulator
			Poor accelerator

2

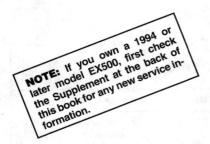
NOTE: If you own a 1994 or later model EX500, first check the Supplement at the back of this book for any new service information.

CHAPTER THREE

PERIODIC LUBRICATION, MAINTENANCE AND TUNE -UP

Your bike can be cared for in two ways: preventive and corrective maintenance. Because a motorcycle is subjected to tremendous heat, stress and vibration – even in normal use – preventive maintenance prevents costly and unexpected corrective maintenance. When neglected, any bike becomes unreliable and actually dangerous to ride. When properly maintained, your Kawasaki is one of the most reliable bikes available and will give many miles and years of dependable and safe riding.

By maintaining a routine service schedule as described in this chapter, costly mechanical problems and unexpected breakdowns can be prevented. The procedures presented in this chapter can be easily performed by anyone with average mechanical skills. **Table 1** is the suggested maintenance schedule. **Tables 1-8** are located at the end of this chapter.

ROUTINE CHECKS

The following simple checks should he carried out at each fuel stop.

Engine Oil Level

Refer to *Periodic Lubrication* in this chapter.

Coolant Level

Check the coolant level when the engine is cool.

Remove the fuel tank mounting bolts and screws and move the tank backwards.

Check the level in the coolant reserve tank. The level should be between the FULL and LOW marks (**Figure 1**). If necessary, add coolant to the reserve tank (not to the radiator) so the level is to the FULL mark (**Figure 1**).

General Inspection

1. Examine the engine for signs of oil or fuel leakage.

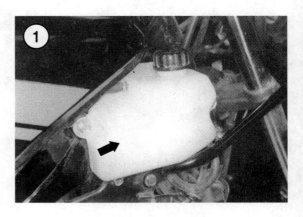

2. Check the tires for imbedded stones. Pry them out with a suitable tool from your tool kit.

3. Make sure all lights work.

NOTE
At least check the brake light. It can burn out anytime. Motorists cannot stop as quickly as you and need all the warning you can give.

Tire Pressure

Tire pressure must be checked with the tires cold. Correct tire pressure depends on the load you are carrying. See **Table 2**.

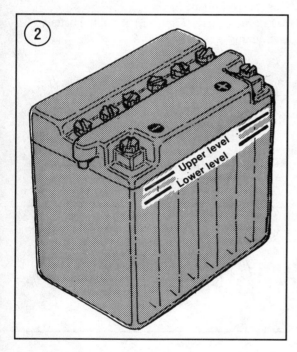

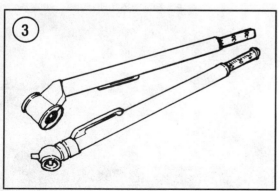

Battery

Remove the left-hand side cover and check the battery electrolyte level. The level must be between the upper and lower level marks on the case (**Figure 2**).

For complete details, see *Battery Removal/Installation and Electrolyte Level Check* in this chapter.

Lights and Horn

With the engine running, check the following.

1. Pull the front brake lever and check that the brake light comes on.

2. Push the rear brake pedal and check that the brake light comes on soon after you have begun depressing the pedal.

3. With the engine running, check to see that the headlight and taillight are on.

4. Move the dimmer switch up and down between the high and low positions, and check to see that both headlight elements are working.

5. Push the turn signal switch to the left position and the right position and check that all 4 turn signal lights are working.

6. Push the horn button and note that the horn blows loudly.

7. If the horn or any light failed to work properly, refer to Chapter Eight.

MAINTENANCE INTERVALS

The services and intervals shown in **Table 1** are recommended by the factory. Strict adherence to these recommendations will insure long life from your Kawasaki. If the bike is run in an area of high humidity, the lubrication services must be done more frequently to prevent possible rust damage.

For convenience when maintaining your motorcycle, most of the services shown in **Table 1** are described in this chapter. Those procedures which require more than minor disassembly or adjustment are covered elsewhere in the appropriate chapter.

TIRES

Tire pressure should be checked and adjusted to accommodate rider and luggage weight. A simple, accurate gauge (**Figure 3**) can be purchased for a few dollars and should be carried in your motorcycle tool kit. The appropriate tire pressures are shown in **Table 2**.

> *NOTE*
> *After checking and adjusting the air pressure, make sure to reinstall the air valve cap. The cap prevents small pebbles and/or dirt from collecting in the valve stem; these could allow air leakage or result in incorrect tire pressure readings.*

Tire Inspection

Check tire tread for excessive wear, deep cuts, imbedded objects such as stones, nails, etc. If you find a nail in a tire, mark its location with a light crayon before pulling it out. This will help locate the hole for repair. Refer to Chapter Ten for tire changing and repair information.

Check local traffic regulations concerning minimum tread depth. Measure with a tread depth gauge (**Figure 4**) or small ruler. Kawasaki recommends replacement when the front tread depth is 1 mm (0.04 in.) or less. For the rear tire, the recommended limit is 2 mm (0.08 in.).

Rim Inspection

Frequently inspect the wheel rims. If a rim has been damaged, it might have been knocked out of alignment. Improper wheel alignment can cause severe vibration and result in an unsafe riding condition. If the rim portion of an alloy wheel is damaged, the wheel must be replaced as it cannot be repaired.

BATTERY

> *CAUTION*
> *If it becomes necessary to remove the battery vent tube when performing any of the following procedures, make sure to route the tube correctly during installation to prevent acid from spilling on parts.*

Removal/Installation and Electrolyte Level Check

The battery is the heart of the electrical system. It should be checked and serviced as indicated (**Table**

1). Most electrical system troubles can be attributed to neglect of this vital component.

In order to service the electrolyte level correctly, it is necessary to remove the battery from the frame. The electrolyte level should be maintained between the two marks on the battery case (**Figure 2**). If the electrolyte level is low, it's a good idea to remove the battery completely so that it can be thoroughly cleaned, serviced and checked.

1. Remove the left-hand side cover and remove the seat.
2. Disconnect the negative battery cable from the battery.
3. Disconnect the positive battery cable.
4. Disconnect the battery vent tube.
5. Remove the junction box.
6. Lift the battery (**Figure 5**) out of the battery box and remove it.

> *WARNING*
> *Protect your eyes, skin and clothing. If electrolyte gets into your eyes, flush your eyes thoroughly with clean water and get prompt medical attention.*

> *CAUTION*
> *Be careful not to spill battery electrolyte on painted or polished surfaces. The*

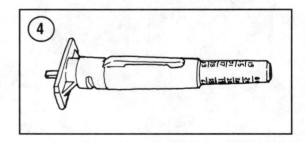

liquid is highly corrosive and will damage the finish. If it is spilled, wash it off immediately with soapy water and thoroughly rinse with clean water.

7. Remove the caps from the battery cells and add distilled water. Never add electrolyte (acid) to correct the level. Fill only to the upper battery level mark (**Figure 2**). Reinstall the battery caps and gently shake the battery for several minutes to mix the existing electrolyte with the new water. Remove the battery caps.

8. After the level has been corrected and the battery allowed to stand for a few minutes, check the specific gravity of the electrolyte in each cell with a hydrometer (**Figure 6**). Follow the manufacturer's instructions for reading the instrument. See *Battery Testing* in this chapter.

9. After the battery has been refilled, recharged or replaced, install it by reversing these removal steps.

Testing

Hydrometer testing is the best way to check battery condition. Use a hydrometer with numbered graduations from 1.100 to 1.300 rather than one with just color-coded bands. To use the hydrometer, squeeze the rubber ball, insert the tip into the cell and release the ball. Draw enough electrolyte to float the weighted float inside the hydrometer. Note the number in line with the electrolyte surface; this is the specific gravity for this cell. Return the electrolyte to the cell from which it came.

The specific gravity of the electrolyte in each battery cell is an excellent indication of that cell's condition (**Table 3**). A fully charged cell will read 1.260-1.280 while a cell in good condition reads from 1.230-1.250. Anything below 1.125 is practically dead.

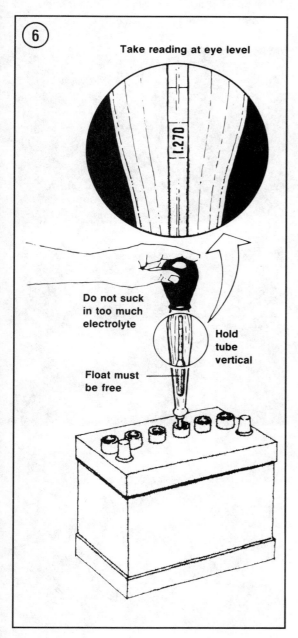

Take reading at eye level

1.270

Do not suck in too much electrolyte

Hold tube vertical

Float must be free

NOTE
Specific gravity varies with temperature. For each 10° that electrolyte temperature exceeds 80° F, add 0.004 to reading indicated on hydrometer. Subtract 0.004 for each 10° below 80° F.

If the cells test in the poor range, the battery requires recharging. The hydrometer is useful for checking the progress of the charging operation. **Table 3** shows approximate state of charge.

Charging

CAUTION
Always remove the battery from the motorcycle before connecting charging equipment.

WARNING
During charging highly explosive hydrogen gas is released from the battery.

The battery should be charged only in a well-ventilated area, and open flames and cigarettes should be kept away. Never check the charge of the battery by arcing across the terminals; the resulting spark can ignite the hydrogen gas.

1. Connect the positive (+) charger lead to the positive battery terminal and negative (–) charger lead to the negative battery terminal.

2. Remove all vent caps from the battery, set the charger at 12 volts, and switch it on. If the output of the charger is variable, it is best to select a low setting—1 1/2 to 2 amps.

CAUTION
The electrolyte level must be maintained at the upper level during the charging cycle; check and refill as necessary.

3. After battery has been charged for about 8 hours, turn the charger off, disconnect the leads and check the specific gravity. It should be within the limits specified in **Table 3**. If it is, and remains stable for one hour, the battery is charged.

4. To ensure good electrical contact, cables must be clean and tight on the battery's terminals. If the cables terminals are badly corroded, even after performing the above cleaning procedures, the cables should be disconnected, removed from the bike and cleaned separately with a wire brush and a baking soda solution. After cleaning, apply a very thin coating of petroleum jelly (Vaseline) to the battery terminals before reattaching the cables. After connecting the cables, apply a light coating to the connections also—this will delay future corrosion.

New Battery Installation

When replacing the old battery with a new one, be sure to charge it completely (specific gravity, 1.260-1.280) before installing it in the bike. Failure to do so, or using the battery with a low electrolyte level will permanently damage the battery.

PERIODIC LUBRICATION

Engine Oil Level Check

Engine oil level is checked through the inspection window located at the bottom of the clutch cover on the right-hand side (**Figure 7**).

1. Place the bike on the centerstand. Start the engine and let it reach normal operating temperature.
2. Stop the engine and allow the oil to settle.
3. The oil level should be between the maximum and minimum window marks (**Figure 7**). If necessary,

remove the oil fill cap (**Figure 8**) and add the recommended oil (**Table 4**) to raise the oil to the proper level. Do not overfill. Install the oil fill cap.

Engine Oil and Filter Change

The factory-recommended oil and filter change interval is specified in **Table 1**. This assumes that the motorcycle is operated in moderate climates. The time interval is more important than the mileage interval because combustion acids, formed by gasoline and water vapor, will contaminate the oil

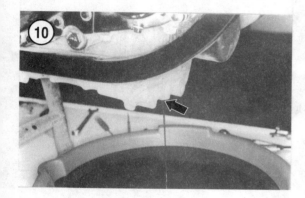

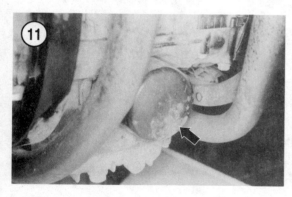

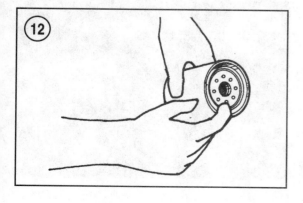

even if the motorcycle is not run for several months. If a motorcycle is operated under dusty conditions, the oil will get dirty more quickly and should be changed more frequently than recommended.

Use only a detergent oil with an API classification of SE or SF. The classification is stamped on top of the can (**Figure 9**) or on the container label. Try always to use the same brand of oil. Use of oil additives is not recommended. Refer to **Table 4** for recommended weights of oil.

There are a number of ways to discard the used oil safely. The easiest way is to pour it from the drain pan into a gallon plastic bleach, juice or milk container for disposal.

> *NOTE*
> *Never dispose of motor oil in the trash, on the ground or down a storm drain. Many service stations and oil retailers accept use oil for recycling. Do not combine other fluids with motor oil for recycling. To locate a recycler, contact the American Petroleum Institute (API) at www.recycleoil.org.*

1. Place the motorcycle on the centerstand.

2. Start the engine and run it until it is at normal operating temperature, then turn it off.

3. Place a drip pan under the crankcase and remove the drain plug. See **Figure 10**.

4. The EX500 uses an automotive type spin-on filter. Service the oil filter as follows:

   a. Remove the filter (**Figure 11**) with a filter wrench.

   b. Discard the oil filter.

   c. Wipe the crankcase gasket surface with a clean, lint-free cloth.

   d. Coat the neoprene gasket on the new filter with clean oil (**Figure 12**).

   e. Screw the new filter onto the crankcase *by hand* until the filter gasket just touches the base. Stop when you feel the slightest resistance in turning the filter. Then tighten the filter *by hand* 2/3 more turn.

> *CAUTION*
> *Do not overtighten and do not use a filter wrench or the filter may leak.*

5. Reinstall the oil drain plug and tighten it securely.

6. Remove the oil filler cap (**Figure 8**) and fill the crankcase with the correct weight (**Table 4**) and quantity of oil (**Table 5**).

7. Screw in the oil fill plug securely.

8. After completing Step 7, start the engine and allow it to idle. Check for leaks.

9. Turn the engine off and check for correct oil level (**Figure 7**); adjust if necessary.

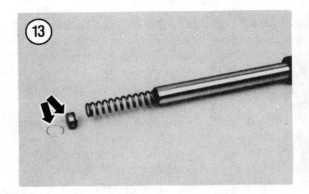

Front Fork Oil Change

1. Place the bike on the centerstand. Support the front end so that the front tire is clear of the ground.

2. Remove the front fork (see Chapter Ten).

3. The fork cap and the spring are held in position by a circlip (**Figure 13**). To remove the circlip, have an assistant depress the fork cap (**Figure 14**) using a suitable size drift or socket. Then pry the circlip (**Figure 15**) out of its groove in the fork with a small screwdriver. When the circlip is removed, release tension from the fork cap and remove it together with the fork spring (**Figure 16**).

4. Place a drip pan under the fork and remove the drain screw (**Figure 17**). Allow the oil to drain for at least 5 minutes.

5. Pump the fork up and down to expel all oil from the fork tube.

6. Install the drain screw (**Figure 17**).

7. Fill the fork tube with slightly less than the specified quantity of oil. See **Table 6**.

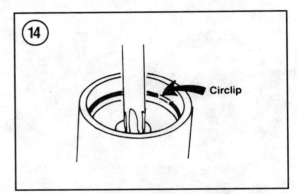

Circlip

> *NOTE*
> *In order to measure the correct amount of fluid, use a baby bottle. These bottles have measurements in fluid ounces (oz.) and cubic centimeters (cc) imprinted on the side.*

> *NOTE*
> *The amount of oil poured in is not as accurate a measurement as the actual level of the oil. You may have to add more oil later in this procedure.*

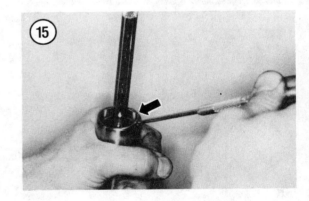

8. After filling the fork tube, slowly pump the fork up and down to distribute the oil throughout the fork damper.

9. Refer to **Table 6**. With the fork tube in a vertical position, measure the distance from the top of the fork tube to the surface of the oil (**Figure 18**).

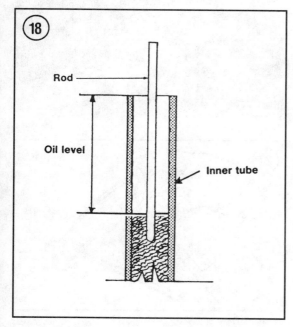

Rod

Oil level

Inner tube

10. Add oil, if required, to bring the level up to specifications (**Table 6**). Do not overfill the fork tube.

> *CAUTION*
> *An excessive amount of oil can cause a hydraulic locking of the forks during compression, destroying the oil seals.*

11. Install the fork spring and fork cap. Have an assistant compress the fork cap and install a *new* circlip. Make sure the circlip seats fully in the groove in the fork tube before releasing the fork cap. See **Figure 14**.

12. Repeat Steps 3-11 for the opposite side.

13. Install all components that were removed.

14. Tighten the upper triple clamp bolts to 20 N•m (14.5 ft.-lb).

15. Road test the bike and check for oil and air leaks.

Control Cables

The control cables should be lubricated at the intervals specified in **Table 1**. At this time, they should also be inspected for fraying, and the cable sheath should be checked for chafing. The cables are relatively inexpensive and should be replaced when found to be faulty.

They can be lubricated with a cable lubricant and a cable lubricator.

> *NOTE*
> *The main cause of cable breakage or cable stiffness is improper lubrication. Maintaining the cables as described in this section will assure long service life.*

1. Disconnect the clutch (A, **Figure 19**) and choke (B, **Figure 19**) cables from the left-hand side handlebar. Disconnect the throttle cables from the throttle grip (**Figure 20**).

> *NOTE*
> *On the throttle cable, it is necessary to remove the screws that clamp the housing together to gain access to the cable ends.*

2. Attach a lubricator (**Figure 21**) to the cable following the manufacturer's instructions.

NOTE
Cable lubricators can be purchased at most motorcycle dealers.

3. Insert the nozzle of the lubricant can into the lubricator, press the button on the can and hold it down until the lubricant begins to flow out of the other end of the cable.

NOTE
Place a shop cloth at the end of the cable(s) to catch all excess lubricant that will flow out.

NOTE
If lubricant does not flow out the end of the cable, check the entire cable for fraying, bending or other damage.

4. Remove the lubricator, reconnect and adjust the cable(s) as described in this chapter.

Swing Arm Bearings

The rear swing arm needle bearings should be cleaned in solvent and lubricated with a molybdenum disulfide grease at the intervals specified in **Table 1**.

Refer to *Rear Swing Arm Removal/Installation* in Chapter Eleven for complete details.

Uni-Trak Linkage Lubrication

The Uni-Trak tie-rod and connecting rod bushings should be cleaned in solvent and lubricated with molybdenum disulfide grease at the intervals specified in **Table 1**. The Uni-Trak linkage must be removed to service the bushings. Refer to *Tie-Rod Removal/Installation* and *Rocker Arm Removal/Installation* in Chapter Eleven.

Brake Cam Lubrication

The brake cam (**Figure 22**) on rear drum brakes should be lubricated according to the maintenance schedule given in **Table 1**. Refer to Chapter Twelve.

Speedometer Cable Lubrication

Lubricate the speedometer cables every year or whenever needle operation is erratic.

1. Remove the cable from the instrument cluster (**Figure 23**). The fairing bracket has been removed for clarity.
2. Pull the cable from the sheath.
3. If the grease is contaminated, thoroughly clean off all old grease.
4. Thoroughly coat the cable with a good grade of multi-purpose grease and reinstall into the sheath.
5. Make sure the cable is correctly seated into the drive unit.

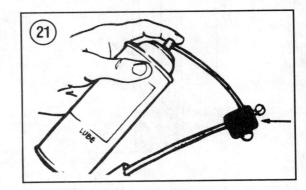

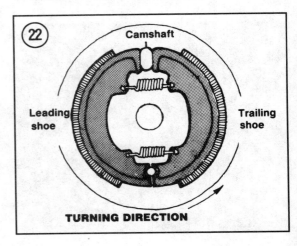

NOTE
If the cable does not seat into the drive unit, it will be necessary to disconnect the cable at its lower connection.

PERIODIC MAINTENANCE

Drive Chain

The factory-installed drive chain on all EX500 models has O-rings installed between the chain plates. Lubrication for the chain pins is permanently sealed by the O-rings (**Figure 24**). However, the chain rollers require external oiling. For the O-ring chain to work properly, it requires proper cleaning and lubrication practices. Do not clean the O-ring chain with a high-pressure water hose, such as those found in coin-operated car washes. The high pressure can damage the chain's O-rings and cause premature chain failure.

A properly maintained drive chain will provide maximum service life and reliability. The drive chain should be lubricated before each ride and during the day as required.

Periodic Lubrication

1. Place the motorcycle on the centerstand.
2. Shift the transmission to NEUTRAL.
3. Oil the bottom run of the chain with a commercial chain lubricant specified for use on O-ring drive chains.
4. Rotate the wheel until all of the chain is lubricated.
5. Moisten a shop cloth in solvent or with soap and water and wipe off any chain lubrication residue from the rear tire and rim.

NOTE
*If the drive chain is obviously dirty, remove and clean it as described under **Drive Chain Cleaning** in Chapter Eleven before lubricating it as described in this procedure.*

Drive Chain Inspection/Adjustment

NOTE
As the drive chain stretches and wears from use, the chain will become tighter at one point. The chain must be checked and adjusted at this point.

1. Place the motorcycle on its centerstand.
2. Turn the rear wheel and check the chain for its tightest point. Mark this spot and turn the wheel so

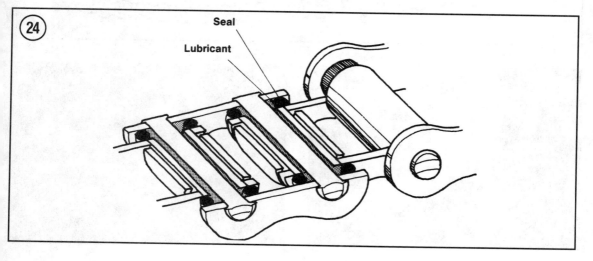

Seal

Lubricant

that the mark is located on the chain's lower run, midway between both drive sprockets. Check and adjust the drive chain as follows.

3. With thumb and forefinger, lift up and press down the chain at that point, measuring the distance the chain moves vertically.

4. The drive chain should have approximately 35-40 mm (1 3/8-1 9/16 in.) of vertical travel at midpoint (**Figure 25**). If necessary, adjust the chain as follows:

5. Remove the cotter pin from the rear torque link nut and the axle nut.

6. Loosen the rear torque link nut (A, **Figure 26**) and the axle nut (B, **Figure 26**).

7. Loosen the axle adjuster locknut (C, **Figure 26**) on both sides of the wheel.

8. Turn each adjuster bolt clockwise to take up slack in the chain. To loosen the chain, turn each adjuster bolt counterclockwise. Be sure to turn each adjuster stud (**Figure 27**) equally to maintain rear wheel alignment. Adjust the chain until the correct amount of free play is obtained (Step 4). See **Figure 25**.

9. Check rear wheel alignment by sighting along the chain as it runs over the rear sprocket. It should not appear to bend sideways. See **Figure 28**.

10. Partially tighten the axle nut, spin the wheel and stop it forcefully with the brake pedal, then tighten the axle nut. This centers the brake shoes in the drum and prevents a "spongy" feeling brake.

11. Tighten the chain adjuster locknuts (C, **Figure 26**) and the rear torque link nut (A, **Figure 26**).

12. Recheck chain play.

13. Tighten the axle nut to 110 N•m (80 ft.-lb.).

14. Install new cotter pins through the rear torque link nut and the axle nut. Bend cotter pin ends to secure.

15. Adjust the rear brake as described in this chapter.

Disc Brake Inspection

The hydraulic brake fluid in the disc brake master cylinder should be checked every month. The disc brake pads should be checked at the intervals specified in **Table 1**. Replacement is described in Chapter Twelve.

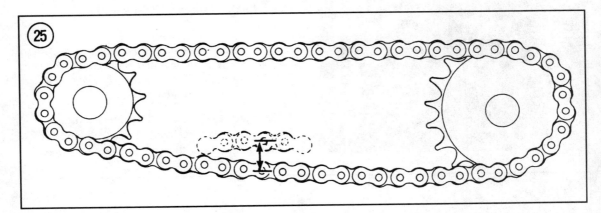

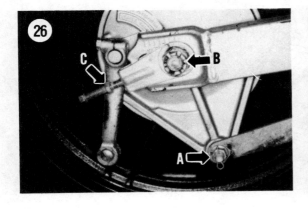

Disc Brake Fluid Level Inspection

The translucent reservoir or transparent window should be checked and the fluid level should be between the upper and lower level lines (**Figure 29**).

Adding Brake Fluid

1. Clean the outside of the reservoir cap thoroughly with a dry rag and remove the reservoir cap. Remove the washer and diaphragm under the cap.

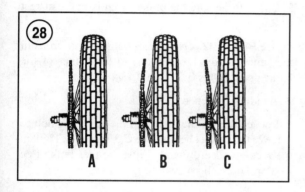

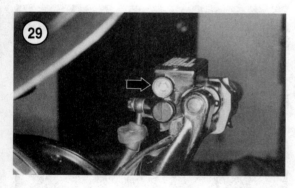

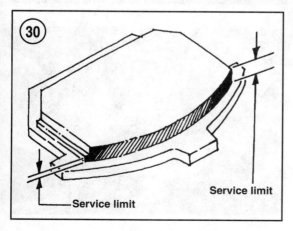

2. The fluid level in the reservoir should be up to the upper level line. Add fresh brake fluid as required.

> *WARNING*
> *Use only brake fluid clearly marked DOT 3 and specified for disc brakes. Others may vaporize and cause brake failure.*

> *CAUTION*
> *Be careful not to spill brake fluid on painted or plated surfaces as it will destroy the surface. Wash immediately with soapy water and thoroughly rinse it off*

3. Reinstall all parts. Make sure the cap is tightly secured.

> *NOTE*
> *If the brake fluid was so low as to allow air in the hydraulic system, the brakes will have to be bled. Refer to **Bleeding The System** in Chapter Twelve.*

Disc Brake Lines and Seals

Check brake lines between the master cylinder and the brake caliper. If there is any leakage, tighten the connections and bleed the brakes as described in Chapter Twelve. If this does not stop the leak or if a line is obviously damaged, cracked or chafed, replace the line and seals and bleed the brake. See *Brake Hose Replacement* in Chapter Twelve.

Disc Brake Pad Inspection

Inspect the disc brake pads for wear according to the maintenance schedule.
1. Apply the front brake.
2. Shine a light between the caliper and the disc (from in front of the fork leg) and inspect the brake pads.
3. If either pad lining thickness is 1/32 in. (1 mm) or less, replace both pads as a set. See **Figure 30**.
4. Replace brake pads as described in Chapter Twelve.

Disc Brake Fluid Change

Every time you remove the reservoir cap a small amount of dirt and moisture enters the brake fluid.

The same thing happens if a leak occurs or when any part of the hydraulic system is loosened or disconnected. Dirt can clog the system and cause unnecessary wear. Water in the fluid vaporizes at high temperatures, impairing the hydraulic action and reducing brake performance.

To change brake fluid, follow the *Bleeding the Brake System* procedure in Chapter Twelve. Continue adding new fluid to the master cylinder and bleeding at the caliper until the fluid leaving the caliper is clean and free of contaminants and air bubbles.

> *WARNING*
> *Use brake fluid clearly marked DOT 3 only. Others may vaporize and cause brake failure.*

Front Disc Brake Lever Adjustment

Periodic adjustment of the front disc brake is not required because disc pad wear is automatically compensated. If there is excessive play in the front brake lever, check the lever pivot hole and bolt for excessive wear. Replace worn parts.

Rear Brake

Brake drum and lining wear will increase brake pedal play and decrease braking effectiveness. Proper brake adjustment consists of the following inspections and adjustments:

    a. Brake shoe adjustment.
    b. Brake pedal height adjustment.
    c. Brake pedal travel adjustment.
    d. Rear brake light switch adjustment.

> *WARNING*
> *Do not ride the bike until you are sure the rear brake is adjusted and operating correctly.*

Rear Brake Shoe Inspection

Before adjusting the rear brake or at the specified maintenance intervals (**Table 1**), inspect the rear brake shoes as follows:
1. Apply the rear brake fully.
2. Check the brake lining wear indicator on the backing plate (**Figure 31**). When the wear indicator pointer moves out of the USABLE RANGE, disas-

semble the brake and inspect the linings. See Chapter Twelve.

3. The brake cam lever should form an angle of 80-90° with the brake rod (**Figure 31**). If the angle exceeds 100°, disassemble the brake and inspect the linings and cam (Chapter Twelve).

Rear Brake Pedal Height Adjustment

1. Place the motorcycle on the centerstand.

2. Check to be sure the brake pedal is in the at-rest position.

3. See **Figure 32**. The correct height position from the center of the footpeg (A) to the center of the brake pedal (B) is 0-20 mm (0-3/4 in.).

4. To adjust, proceed to Step 5.

5. Loosen the locknut and turn the adjusting bolt to achieve the correct height. See C, **Figure 32**. Tighten the locknut securely and adjust the rear brake free play and brake light switch.

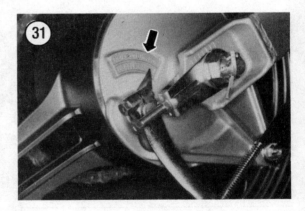

Rear Brake Pedal Free Play

Adjust the brake pedal to the correct height as described earlier. Then turn the adjustment nut on the end of the brake rod (**Figure 33**) until the brake pedal has 0-20 mm (3/4 in.) free play. Free play is the distance the pedal travels from the at-rest position to the applied position when the pedal is depressed lightly.

Rotate the rear wheel and check for brake drag. Also operate the pedal several times to make sure it

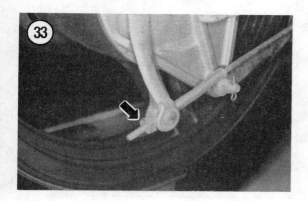

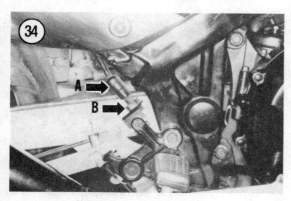

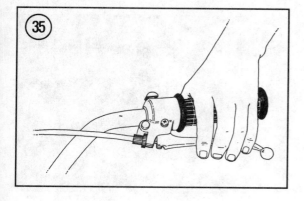

returns to the at-rest position immediately after release.

Rear Brake Light Switch Adjustment

1. Turn the ignition switch to the ON position.
2. Depress the brake pedal. The brake light should come on just as the rear brake begins to work.
3. To make the light come on earlier, hold the switch body (A, **Figure 34**) and turn the adjusting locknut (B, **Figure 34**) to move the switch body *rearward*. To delay the light, move the switch body *forward*. Tighten the locknuts.

Clutch Lever Adjustment

Pull the clutch lever until resistance is felt. Then measure the distance from the adjuster locknut and the clutch lever (**Figure 35**). This is clutch cable free play. The clutch cable should have about 2-3 mm (3/32-1/8 in.) free play. Minor adjustment can be made at the hand lever. Loosen the locknut, turn the adjuster as required and tighten the locknut.

NOTE
If sufficient free play cannot be obtained at the hand lever, additional adjustment can be made at the clutch mechanism adjuster.

Clutch Mechanism Adjustment

1. Loosen the clutch cable adjuster nuts (**Figure 36**) at the crankcase as far as they will go.
2. At the clutch lever, loosen the locknut and turn the adjuster until 5-6 mm (3/16-1/4 in.) of threads are showing between the locknut and the adjuster body (**Figure 37**).
3. At the crankcase, pull the clutch cable forward and tighten the adjuster nuts (**Figure 36**).
4. At the clutch, turn the adjuster as required to get about 2-3 mm (3/32-1/8 in.) of cable play at the clutch lever.
5. Tighten all locknuts.

Throttle Cable Play

Always check the throttle cables before you make any carburetor adjustments. Too much free play causes delayed throttle response; too little free play will cause unstable idling.

Check the throttle cable from grip to carburetors. Make sure they are not kinked or chafed. Replace them if necessary.

Make sure that the throttle grip rotates smoothly from fully closed to full open. Check at center, full left, and full right position of steering.

Check free play at the throttle grip flange. Kawasaki specifies about 2-3 mm (3/32-1/8 in.). If adjustment is required, proceed as follows.

> *WARNING*
> *If idle speed increases when the handle-bar is turned to right or left, check throttle cable routing. Do not ride the motorcycle in this unsafe condition.*

Throttle Cable Adjustment

The EX500 is equipped with two throttle cables: an accelerator cable for opening the throttle valves, and a decelerator cable for closing the valves.

1. Loosen the accelerator cable (outer) (**Figure 38**) locknut at the handlebar and turn the adjuster until the correct amount of free play at the throttle grip is obtained. Tighten the locknut.

2. If the correct throttle grip free play cannot be obtained by performing Step 1, proceed with Step 3.

3. Remove the fuel tank as described in Chapter Seven.

4. Loosen both cable locknuts at the carburetors (A, **Figure 39**) to obtain as much slack in the throttle grip as possible.

5. Close the throttle grip and lengthen the decelerator cable adjusting nut (B, **Figure 39**) until its inner cable becomes tight. Tighten the locknut.

6. Lengthen the accelerator adjusting nut (C, **Figure 39**) until the correct free play is obtained at the throttle grip. Tighten the locknut.

7. Operate the throttle grip a few times. Then check that the throttle linkage rests against the idle adjusting screw when the throttle grip is closed.

8. The throttle grip should now be adjusted correctly. If not, the throttle cables may be stretched and should be replaced.

9. Reinstall the fuel tank after completing the adjustment.

10. Park the motorcycle on its centerstand. Sit on the seat and start the engine. Then lean back so that the

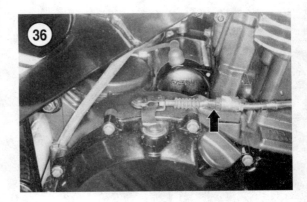

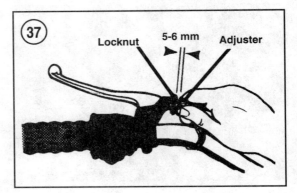

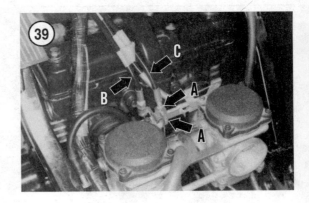

front wheel clears the ground. Turn the handlebars from right to left to check for abnormal idle speed variances due to improper cable routing.

> *WARNING*
> *If idle speed increases when the handlebar is turned to right or left, check throttle cable routing. Do not ride the motorcycle in this unsafe condition.*

Choke Cable Adjustment

1. Check for correct choke cable free play at the choke lever as follows:

   a. Pull the choke lever until the cable begins to move the choke plunger at the carburetor. See **Figure 40**. The distance the choke lever traveled is choke cable play.

   b. The correct amount of choke lever play is 2-3 mm (3/32-1/8 in.).

   c. If the choke lever play is incorrect, proceed to Step 2.

2. Remove the fuel tank as described in Chapter Seven.

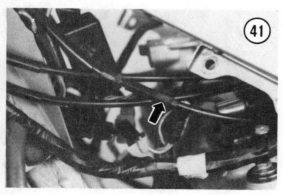

3. Locate the choke cable midline adjuster (**Figure 41**) and loosen the locknut. Turn the adjuster until the correct amount of choke lever play is obtained in Step 1. Tighten the locknut and recheck the adjustment.

4. Reinstall the fuel tank.

Fuel Shutoff Valve/Filter

At the intervals specified in **Table 1**, remove and drain the fuel tank. Remove the fuel shutoff valve and clean it of all dirt and debris. Replace worn or damaged O-rings and gaskets.

Fuel and Vacuum Line Inspection

Inspect all fuel and vacuum lines for cracks or deterioration; replace if necessary. Make sure the hose clamps are in place and holding securely.

Exhaust System

Check for exhaust leakage at all fittings. Do not forget the crossover pipe connections. Tighten all bolts and nuts; replace any gaskets as necessary. Refer to *Exhaust System* in Chapter Seven.

Air Filter Removal/Installation

A clogged air filter can decrease the efficiency and life of the engine. Never run the bike without the air filter installed; even minute particles of dust can cause severe internal engine wear.

The service intervals specified in **Table 1** should be followed with general use. However, the air cleaner should be serviced more often if the bike is ridden in dusty areas.

1. Remove the fuel tank as described in Chapter Seven.

2. Remove the fuel tank bracket bolts and remove the bracket (**Figure 42**).

3. Remove the air filter cover screws and remove the cover (**Figure 43**).

4. Remove the air filter element (**Figure 44**).

5. Install by reversing these steps.

6. Route the wiring harness as shown in **Figure 42** when installing the fuel tank bracket.

Air Filter Cleaning/Inspection

WARNING
Wear suitable protective clothing and
eye protection when working with sol-
vent.

1. Clean the element in a high flash-point solvent.

2. Dry the element by shaking or blow dry with compressed air from the inside of the element as shown in **Figure 45**A.

3. Inspect the element for tears or other damage that would allow unfiltered air to pass into the engine. Check the sponge gasket on the element for tears. Replace the element if necessary.

4. Apply SE class SAE 30 oil to the outside of the element by soaking a clean, lint-free cloth with oil and patting the filter surface as shown in **Figure 45**B.

Wheel Bearings

The wheel bearings should be cleaned and re-packed at the service intervals specified in **Table 1**. Refer to Chapter Ten and Chapter Eleven for complete service procedures.

Steering Play

The steering head should be checked for looseness at the intervals specified in **Table 1**.

1. Prop up the motorcycle so that the front tire clears the ground.

2. Remove the front fairing. See Chapter Thirteen.

3. Center the front wheel. Push lightly against the left handlebar grip to start the wheel turning to the right, then let go. The wheel should continue turning under its own momentum until the forks hit their stop.

4. Center the wheel, and push lightly against the right handlebar grip.

5. The steering adjustment is not too tight if the front wheel will turn all the way to the stop with a light push in either direction.

6. Center the front wheel and kneel in front of it. Grasp the bottom of the 2 front fork slider legs. Try to pull the forks toward you, and then try to push them toward the engine. If no play is felt, the steering adjustment is not too loose.

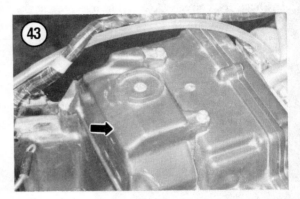

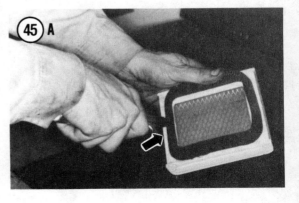

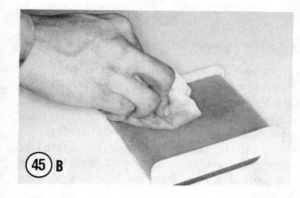

45 B

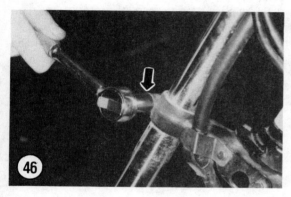

46

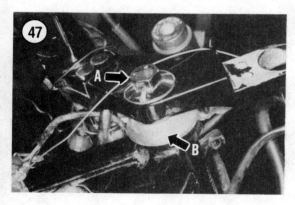

47

A

B

7. If the steering adjustment is too tight or too loose, readjust it as described in this chapter.

Adjustment

1. Prop up the motorcycle so that the front tire clears the ground.
2. Remove the front fairing. See Chapter Thirteen.
3. Remove the fuel tank.
4. Loosen the lower front fork bridge bolts (**Figure 46**).
5. Loosen the steering stem nut (A, **Figure 47**).
6. Loosen or tighten the steering stem locknut (B, **Figure 47**) less than 1/8 turn at a time.
7. Tighten the steering stem nut to 47 N•m (35 ft-lb.).
8. Tighten the lower front fork clamp bolts to 29 N•m (22 ft-lb.).
9. Recheck the steering as described under *Inspection* in this chapter.
10. Perform Steps 4-9 until the adjustment is correct.
11. Install the fuel tank and front fairing.

Steering Head Bearings

The steering head bearings should be lubricated at the intervals specified in **Table 1**. See *Steering Head* in Chapter Ten.

Rear Suspension/Uni-Trak Spring Preload Adjustment

By changing the spring preload, the rear shock absorber can be adjusted to various riding and loading conditions. See *Uni-Trak Preload Adjustment* in Chapter Eleven.

Cooling System Inspection

At the intervals indicated in **Table 1**, the following items should be checked. If you do not have the test equipment, the tests can be performed by a Kawasaki dealer, radiator shop or service station.

> *WARNING*
> *Do not remove the radiator cap when the engine is hot.*

1. Have the radiator cap pressure tested (**Figure 48**). The specified radiator cap relief pressure is 11-15 psi (0.75-1.05 kg/cm^2). The cap must be able to sustain

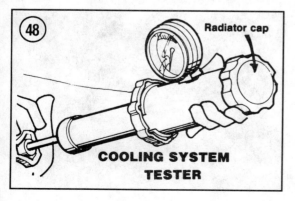

48

Radiator cap

COOLING SYSTEM TESTER

this pressure for 6 seconds. Replace the radiator cap if it does not hold pressure or if the relief pressure is too high or too low.

> *CAUTION*
> *If test pressure exceeds the specifications, the radiator may be damaged.*

2. Leave the radiator cap off and have the entire cooling system pressure tested (**Figure 49**). The entire cooling system should be pressurized up to, but not exceeding, 15 psi (1.5 kg/cm^2). The system must be able to sustain this pressure for 6 seconds. Replace or repair any components that fail this test.
3. Check all cooling system hoses for damage or deterioration. Replace any hose that is questionable. Make sure all hose clamps are tight.
4. Carefully clean any road dirt, bugs, mud, etc. from the radiator core. Use a whisk broom, compressed air or low-pressure water aimed at the backside of the radiator core. If the radiator has been hit by a small rock or other item, *carefully* straighten out the fins with a screwdriver or fin comb.

Coolant Change

The cooling system should be completely drained and refilled at the intervals indicated in **Table 1**.

> *CAUTION*
> *Use only a high quality ethylene glycol antifreeze specifically labeled for use with aluminum engines. Do not use an alcohol-based antifreeze.*

In areas where freezing temperatures occur, add a higher percentage of antifreeze to protect the system in temperatures far below those likely to occur. **Table 7** lists the recommended amount of antifreeze. The following procedure must be performed when the engine is cool.

> *CAUTION*
> *Be careful not to spill antifreeze on painted surfaces as it will destroy the surface. Wash immediately with soapy water and rinse thoroughly with clean water.*

1. Place the bike on centerstand.
2. Remove the fuel tank.
3. Remove the coolant reservoir cover.

> *WARNING*
> *Do not remove the radiator cap when the engine is hot.*

4. Remove the radiator cap (A, **Figure 50**).
5. Place a drain pan under the water pump. Remove the drain screw (**Figure 51**) and sealing washer from the water pump cover and allow the coolant to drain into the pan. Do not install the drain screw yet.
6. Take the bike off the centerstand and tip the bike from side to side to drain any residual coolant from the cooling system. Place the bike back onto the centerstand.
7. Install the drain screw with the sealing washer into the water pump cover.
8. Remove the reservoir tank (B, **Figure 50**) and drain it of all coolant. Reinstall the reservoir tank.
9. Refill the radiator. Add the coolant through the radiator filler neck (A, **Figure 50**), not the reservoir tank. Use the recommended mixture of antifreeze and purified water (**Table 7**). Do not install the radiator cap at this time.
10. Start the engine and let it run at idle speed until the engine reaches normal operating temperature. Make sure there are no air bubbles in the coolant and

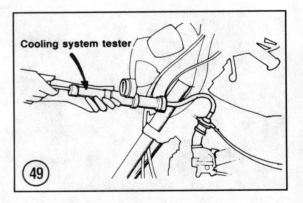

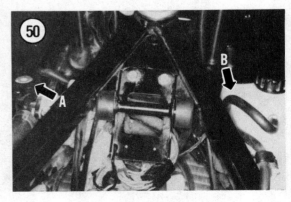

that the coolant level stabilizes at the correct level. Add coolant as necessary.

11. Install the radiator cap (A, **Figure 50**).

12. Add coolant to the reservoir tank to correct the level.

13. Install the radiator and coolant reservoir covers.

14. Install the fuel tank.

15. Test ride the bike and readjust the coolant level in the reserve tank if necessary.

Front Suspension Check

1. Apply the front brake and pump the forks up and down as vigorously as possible. Check for smooth operation and check for any oil leaks.

2. Make sure the upper and lower fork bridge bolts are tight.

3. Check that the front axle pinch bolt is tight.

4. Check that the front axle nut is tight.

> *WARNING*
> *If any of the previously mentioned bolts and nuts are loose, refer to Chapter Ten for correct procedures and torque specifications.*

Rear Suspension Check (Uni-Trak)

1. Place the bike on the centerstand.

2. Push hard on the rear wheel sideways to check for side play in the rear swing arm bushings or bearings.

3. Check the tightness of the upper and lower spring mounting nuts and bolts.

4. Make sure the rear axle nut is tight and the cotter pin is still in place.

> *WARNING*
> *If any of the previously mentioned nuts or bolts are loose, refer to Chapter Eleven for correct procedures and torque specifications.*

Nuts, Bolts and Other Fasteners

Constant vibration can loosen many fasteners on a motorcycle. Check the tightness of all fasteners, especially those on:

a. Engine mounting hardware.
b. Engine crankcase covers.
c. Handlebar and front forks.
d. Gearshift lever.
e. Sprocket bolts and nuts.
f. Brake pedal and lever.
g. Exhaust system.
h. Lighting equipment.

TUNE-UP

A complete tune-up restores performance and power that is lost due to normal wear and deterioration of engine parts. Because engine wear occurs over a combined period of time and mileage, the engine tune-up should be performed at the intervals specified in **Table 1**. More frequent tune-ups may be required if the bike is ridden primarily in stop-and-go traffic.

Table 8 summarizes tune-up specifications.

Before starting a tune-up procedure, make sure to have all the necessary new parts on hand.

Because different systems in an engine interact, the procedures should be done in the following order:

a. Clean or replace air filter element.
b. Adjust valve clearance.
c. Check engine compression.
d. Check or replace spark plugs.
e. Synchronize carburetors and set idle speed.

Tools

To perform a tune-up on your Kawasaki, you will need the following tools:

a. Spark plug wrench.
b. Socket wrench and assorted sockets.
c. Flat feeler gauge.

d. Compression gauge.
e. Spark plug wire feeler gauge and gapper tool.
f. Carburetor synchronization tool—to measure manifold vacuum.

Air Filter Element

The air filter element should be cleaned or replaced before doing other tune-up procedures. Refer to *Air Filter Cleaning/Inspection* in this chapter.

Valve Clearance

1. Place the motorcycle on the centerstand.
2. Remove the cylinder head cover. Refer to *Cylinder Head Cover Removal/Installation* in Chapter Four.
3. Remove the 2 alternator cover caps (A, **Figure 52**).
4. Position the right piston at top dead center (TDC) on its compression stroke. To do this, turn the crankshaft to the right (clockwise) with the bolt on the end of the crankshaft (B, **Figure 52**) and at the same time watch the right-hand side cylinder intake and exhaust valves. After valves have opened and closed (moved down then up) continue to turn the crankshaft until the "C" mark on the rotor aligns with the notch in the edge of the upper hole in the alternator cover (C, **Figure 52**). When the right piston is at TDC, the camshaft lobes will be facing away from the rocker arms and both camshaft sprockets will be positioned as shown in **Figure 53**.
5. Insert a feeler gauge between the right cylinder's intake and exhaust valve stem and rocker arm. The correct clearance is listed in **Table 8**. The clearance is measured correctly when there is a slight drag on the feeler gauge when it is inserted and withdrawn.

If the clearance is within tolerance, go on to Step 7. If adjustment is required, continue with Step 6.

6. Adjust by loosening the adjuster locknut (**Figure 54**) and turning the adjuster as required to get the proper clearance. Hold the adjuster steady and tighten the locknut securely. Check that the locknut is tightened to 25 N•m (18 ft.-lb.).

7. Turn the crankshaft one full turn clockwise, so that the "T" mark for the left cylinder lines up with the index pointer and both camshaft sprockets are

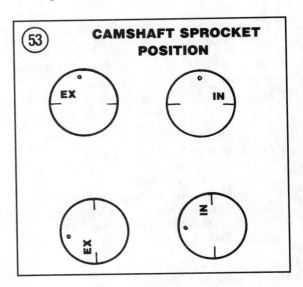

(53) **CAMSHAFT SPROCKET POSITION**

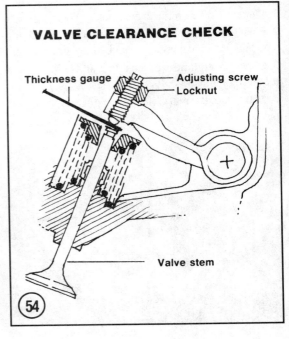

VALVE CLEARANCE CHECK

Thickness gauge — Adjusting screw
— Locknut

Valve stem

(54)

(52)

aligned as shown in **Figure 53**. Repeat Steps 5 and 6 for the left cylinder (**Figure 55**).

8. Install the cylinder head cover. Refer to *Cylinder Head Cover Removal/Installation* in Chapter Four.

Compression Test

At every tune-up, check cylinder compression. Record the results and compare them at the next check. A running record will show trends in deterioration so that corrective action can be taken before complete failure can occur.

The results, when properly interpreted, can indicate general cylinder, piston ring and valve condition.

> *NOTE*
> *The valves must be properly adjusted to interpret the results of this test correctly.*

1. Warm the engine to normal operating temperature. Ensure that the choke valve and throttle valve are completely open. Shut the engine off.

2. Remove the spark plugs. Insert spark plugs into spark leads and properly ground on a clean engine location.

> *NOTE*
> *A screw-in type compression tester will be required for this procedure.*

3. Connect a compression tester (**Figure 56**) to one cylinder following manufacturer's instructions.

4. Have an assistant crank the engine over until there is no further rise in pressure.

5. Remove the tester and record the reading.

6. Repeat Steps 3-5 for the other cylinder.

7. Standard compression pressure is specified in **Table 8**. Pressure should fall within specified limits. A high or low reading indicates worn or broken rings, leaking or sticky valves, a blown head gasket, carbon buildup or a combination of all.

If a low reading is obtained on one of the cylinders, it indicates valve or ring trouble. To determine which, pour about a teaspoon of engine oil through the spark plug hole onto the top of the piston. Turn the engine over once to distribute the oil, then take another compression test and record the reading. If the compression increases significantly, the valves are good but the rings are defective on that cylinder. If compression does not increase, the valves require servicing.

> *NOTE*
> *If the compression is low, the engine cannot be tuned to maximum performance. The worn parts must be replaced and the engine rebuilt.*

Correct Spark Plug Heat Range

Spark plugs are available in various heat ranges that are hotter or colder than the spark plugs originally installed at the factory.

Select plugs in a heat range designed for the loads and temperature conditions under which the engine will operate. Using an incorrect heat range can cause piston seizure, scored cylinder walls or damaged piston crowns.

In general, use a hotter plug for low speeds, low loads and low temperatures. Use a colder plug for high speeds, high engine loads and high temperatures.

NOTE
In areas where seasonal temperature variations are great, Kawasaki recommends a "two-plug system"—a cold plug for hard summer riding and a hot plug for slower winter operation. This may prevent spark plug and engine problems.

The reach (length) of a plug is also important. A longer than normal plug could interfere with the valves and pistons, causing permanent and severe damage (**Figure 57**). The standard heat range spark plugs are listed in **Table 8**.

Spark Plug Removal/Cleaning

1. Grasp the spark plug leads as near to the plug as possible and pull them off the plugs.

2. Blow away any dirt that has accumulated in the spark plug wells.

CAUTION
Foreign matter could fall into the cylinders when the plugs are removed, causing serious engine damage.

3. Remove the spark plugs with a spark plug wrench.

NOTE
If plugs are difficult to remove, apply penetrating oil, like WD-40 or Liquid Wrench, around base of plugs and let soak in (about 10-20 minutes).

4. Inspect spark plugs carefully. Look for plugs with broken center porcelain, excessively eroded electrodes and excessive carbon or oil fouling. Replace such plugs.

NOTE
Spark plug cleaning with the use of a sand-blast type device is generally not recommended. While this type of cleaning is thorough, the plug must be perfectly free of all abrasive cleaning material when done. If not, it is possible for the cleaning material to fall into the engine during operation and cause damage.

Gapping and Installing the Plugs

New plugs should be carefully gapped to ensure a reliable, consistent spark. You must use a special spark plug gapping tool with a wire gauge.

1. Remove the new plugs from the box. Do *not* screw in the small pieces that are loose in each box (**Figure 58**); they are not used.

2. Insert a round gauge between the center and the side electrode of each plug (**Figure 59**). The correct gap is found in **Table 8**. If the gap is correct, you will feel a slight drag as you pull the gauge through. If there is no drag, or the gauge won't pass through, bend the side electrode *with the gapping tool* (**Figure 60**) to set the proper gap (**Table 8**).

3. Put a small drop of oil on the threads of each spark plug.

4. Screw each spark plug in by hand until it seats. Very little effort is required. If force is necessary, you

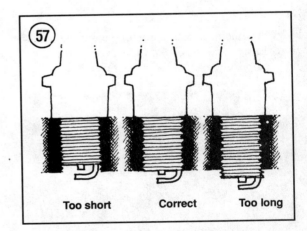

Too short   Correct   Too long

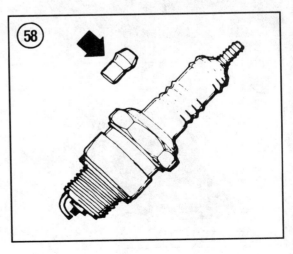

have the plug cross-threaded; unscrew it and try again.

NOTE
If a spark plug is difficult to install, the cylinder head threads may be dirty or slightly damaged. To clean the threads, apply grease to the threads of a spark plug tap and screw it carefully into the cylinder head. Turn the tap slowly until it is completely installed. If the tap cannot be installed, the threads are severely damaged.

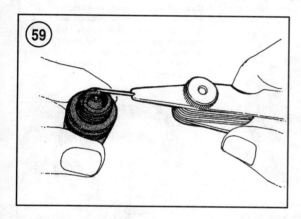

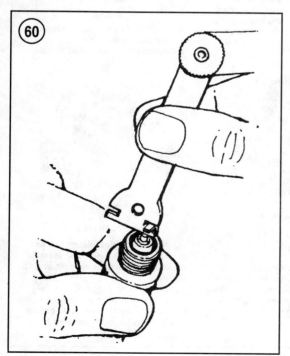

5. Tighten the spark plugs to a torque of 13 N·m (115 in.-lb.). If you don't have a torque wrench, an additional 1/4 to 1/2 turn is sufficient after the gasket has made contact with the head. If you are reinstalling old, regapped plugs and are reusing the old gasket, tighten only an additional 1/4 turn.

CAUTION
Do not overtighten. Besides making the plug difficult to remove, the excessive torque will squash the gasket and destroy its sealing ability.

6. Install each spark plug wire. Make sure it goes to the correct spark plug.

Reading Spark Plugs

Much information about engine and spark plug performance can be determined by careful examination of the spark plugs. This information is more valid after performing the following steps.

1. Ride bike a short distance at full throttle in any gear.

2. Turn off kill switch before closing throttle, and simultaneously, pull in clutch and coast to a stop. Do not downshift transmission in stopping.

3. Remove spark plugs and examine them. Compare them to **Figure 61**.

If the insulator tip is white or burned, the plug is too hot and should be replaced with a colder one.

A too-cold plug will have sooty deposits ranging in color from dark brown to black. Replace with a hotter plug and check for too-rich carburetion or evidence of oil blow-by at the piston rings.

If either plug is found unsatisfactory, replace them both.

ELECTRONIC IGNITION

The ignition system on the EX500 is completely electronic; no mechanical advance unit is used. The ignition timing is fixed and no adjustment is provided. If the engine is running poorly and the trouble has been traced to the ignition system, refer to Chapter Two for troubleshooting procedures.

SPARK PLUG CONDITION

(61)

NORMAL

- Identified by light tan or gray deposits on the firing tip.
- Can be cleaned.

GAP BRIDGED

- Identified by deposit buildup closing gap between electrodes.
- Caused by oil or carbon fouling. If deposits are not excessive, the plug can be cleaned.

OIL FOULED

- Identified by wet black deposits on the insulator shell bore and electrodes.
- Caused by excessive oil entering combustion chamber through worn rings and pistons, excessive clearance between valve guides and stems, or worn or loose bearings. Can be cleaned. If engine is not repaired, use a hotter plug.

CARBON FOULED

- Identified by black, dry fluffy carbon deposits on insulator tips, exposed shell surfaces and electrodes.
- Caused by too cold a plug, weak ignition, dirty air cleaner, too rich a fuel mixture, or excessive idling. Can be cleaned.

LEAD FOULED

- Identified by dark gray, black, yellow, or tan deposits or a fused glazed coating on the insulator tip.
- Caused by highly leaded gasoline. Can be cleaned.

WORN

- Identified by severely eroded or worn electrodes.
- Caused by normal wear. Should be replaced.

FUSED SPOT DEPOSIT

- Identified by melted or spotty deposits resembling bubbles or blisters.
- Caused by sudden acceleration. Can be cleaned.

OVERHEATING

- Identified by a white or light gray insulator with small black or gray brown spots and with bluish-burnt appearance of electrodes.
- Caused by engine overheating, wrong type of fuel, loose spark plugs, too hot a plug, or incorrect ignition timing. Replace the plug.

PREIGNITION

- Identified by melted electrodes and possibly blistered insulator. Metallic deposits on insulator indicate engine damage.
- Caused by wrong type of fuel, incorrect ignition timing or advance, too hot a plug, burned valves, or engine overheating. Replace the plug.

CARBURETOR

Idle Speed

Proper idle speed setting is necessary to prevent stalling and to provide adequate engine compression braking. It cannot be set accurately with the bike's tachometer. A portable tachometer is strongly recommended for this procedure.

1. Attach a portable tachometer, following the manufacturer's instructions.
2. Start the engine and warm it to normal operating temperature.
3. Turn the idle speed adjusting screw (**Figure 62**) to set the idle speed as specified in **Table 8**. If you do not have a portable tachometer, set the idle at the lowest speed at which the engine will idle smoothly.

NOTE
Figure 62 shows the idle speed adjusting screw from a rear view with the air box removed for clarity.

4. Accelerate the engine a couple of times to see if it settles down to the set speed. Readjust, if necessary.
5. Disconnect the portable tachometer.

Idle Mixture

The idle mixture screw is set and sealed at the factory and requires no adjustment.

Carburetor Synchronization

Synchronizing the carburetors ensures that one cylinder doesn't try to run faster than the other, resulting in cut power and lower gas mileage. You can check for a rough balance by listening to the exhaust noise at idle and feeling pressure at the mufflers, but the only accurate way to synchronize the carburetors is to use a set of vacuum gauges that measure the intake vacuum of both cylinders at the same time.

1. Start the engine and warm it to normal operating temperature.
2. Stop the engine and remove the rubber covers and vacuum plug screws.
3. Attach the vacuum gauges, following the manufacturer's instructions. Start the engine and check that the difference between the cylinders is less than 2.7 in. (2 cm) Hg. Identical readings are desirable.
4. If the difference is greater, loosen the locknut and turn the synchronizing screw located between the carburetors (**Figure 63**) as required to equalize the vacuum in both cylinders.

NOTE
Figure 63 shows the synchronizing screw with the carburetor removed for clarity.

5. Tighten the locknut. You may have to remove the fuel tank to reach the synchronizing screw. If you can synchronize the carburetors before the float bowls run dry, fine; if not, you'll have to supply fuel from a temporary hookup.

WARNING
When supplying fuel by temporary means, make sure the fuel tank is secure and that all fuel lines are tight—no leaks.

6. Reset the idle speed, stop the engine and disconnect the vacuum gauges. Install the vacuum plug screws and rubber covers. When installing vacuum plug screws, make sure the sealing gaskets are in good condition; replace them if necessary.

Table 1 MAINTENANCE SCHEDULE

Weekly/gas stop	• Check tire pressure cold; adjust to suit load and speed • Check brakes for a solid feel • Check brake lever play; adjust if necessary • Check brake pedal play; adjust if necessary • Check throttle grip for smooth opening and return • Check clutch lever play; adjust if necessary • Check for smooth but not loose steering • Check axles, suspension, controls and linkage nuts, bolts and fasteners; tighten if necessary • Check engine oil level; add oil if necessary • Check lights and horn operation, expecially brake light • Check for any abnormal engine noise and leaks • Check coolant level • Check kill switch operation • Lubricate drive chain
Monthly/500 miles (800 km)	• Check battery electrolyte level (more frequently in hot weather); add distilled water if necessary • Check disc brake fluid level; add if necessary • Check drive chain tension; adjust if necessary
6 months/3,000 miles (5,000 km)	All above checks and the following: • Check carburetor synchronization; adjust if necessary • Check carburetor idle speed; adjust if necesary • Check spark plugs, set gap; replace if necessary • Check air suction valve • Check evaporative emission control system * • Check brake pad wear • Check brake light switch operation; adjust if necessary • Check rear brake pedal free play; adjust if necessary • Adjust clutch • Check steering play; adjust if necessary • Check drive chain wear • Change engine oil and filter • Check tire wear • Lubricate all pivot points • Check and tighten all nuts, bolts and fasteners • Clean air filter element
Yearly/6,000 miles (10,000 km)	• Check for throttle free play; adjust if necessary • Check valve clearance, adjust if necessary • Lubricate swing arm pivot shaft • Lubricate Uni-trak linkage • Check radiator hoses • Check fuel system hoses, clamps and all fittings
2 years/12,000 miles (20,000 km)	• Change front fork oil • Change brake fluid • Change coolant • Lubricate steering stem bearings • Replace master cylinder cups and seals • Replace caliper piston seal and dust seal • Lubricate wheel bearings • Lubricate speedometer gear
Every 4 years	• Replace fuel hoses

* California models.

Table 2 TIRES AND TIRE PRESSURE

Tire Size	Pressure @ load 0-215 lb. (0-97.5 kg)	Over 215 lb. (Over 97.5 kg)
Front-100/90-16 54H Tubeless	28 psi (196 kPa)	32 psi (221 kPa)
Rear-120/90-16 63H Tubeless	32 psi (221 kPa)	36 psi (245 kPa)

Table 3 STATE OF CHARGE

Specific gravity	State of charge
1.110-1.130	Discharged
1.140-1.160	Almost discharged
1.170-1.190	One-quarter charged
1.200-1.220	One-half charged
1.230-1.250	Three-quarters charged
1.260-1.280	Fully charged

Table 4 RECOMMENDED LUBRICANTS AND FUEL

Engine oil	Rated SE or SF; 10W-40, 10W-50 or 20W-50
Front fork oil	SAE 10W20
Brake fluid	DOT 3
Fuel	87 pump octane (RON + MON)/2 91 research octane (RON)
Battery	Distilled water
Cooling system	Permanent type antifreeze compounded for aluminum engines and radiator

Table 5 ENGINE OIL CAPACITY

	Liter	U.S. Quart
Without filter change	2.8	2.9
With filter change	3.4	3.59

Table 6 FRONT FORK OIL CAPACITY

	Dry capacity	Oil change capacity	Oil level	
	mL	mL	inch	mm
All models	287 ±2.5	245	5.1	131

Fork oil level is checked with forks springs removed and forks fully compressed.

Table 7 COOLING SYSTEM SPECIFICATIONS

Capacity	1.8L (1.90 qt.)
Coolant type	Antifreeze suited for aluminum engines
Coolant ratio	50% purified water/50% coolant
Radiator cap	11-15 psi (0.75-1.05 kg/cm^2)
Thermostat	
Opening temperature	176.9-182.3° F
	(80.5-83.5°C)
Valve opening lift	Not less than 8 mm (5/16 in.)
	203°F (95°C)

Table 8 TUNE-UP SPECIFICATIONS

Spark plugs (standard heat range)	
Type	NGK DR8ES or ND X27ESR-U
Gap	0.6-0.7 mm (0.024-0.028 in.)
Valve clearance (cold)	
Intake	0.13-0.18 mm (0.005-0.007 in.)
Exhaust	0.18-0.23 mm (0.007-0.009 in.)
Idle speed	1150-1250 rpm
Idle mixture	—
Compression	
Standard	128-196 psi (9.0-13.8 kg/cm^2)

ENGINE

The engine is a liquid-cooled double overhead cam eight-valve parallel twin. Valves are operated by two chain-driven overhead camshafts. The crankshaft and pistons are so arranged that cylinders fire alternately; while either piston is at firing position on its compression stroke, the other piston is on the exhaust stroke.

This chapter provides complete service and overhaul procedures, including information for disassembly, removal, inspection, service and reassembly of the engine.

Before starting any work, read the service hints in Chapter One. You will do a better job with this information fresh in your mind.

Table 1 and **Table 2** at the end of the chapter list complete engine specifications and tightening torques.

SERVICING ENGINE IN FRAME

Many components can be serviced while the engine is mounted in the frame:

a. Cylinder head.
b. Cylinders and pistons.
c. Gearshift mechanism.
d. Clutch (partial disassembly).
e. Carburetors.
f. Starter motor and gears.
g. Alternator and electrical systems.

ENGINE

Removal/Installation

1. Place the motorcycle on its centerstand. Remove fairing(s), left- and right-hand side covers, and accessories such as crash bars.
2. Remove the seat, junction box and disconnect the negative battery terminal (**Figure 1**).
3. Remove the fuel tank as described in Chapter Seven and fuel tank bracket.
4. Drain the engine oil as described in Chapter Three.
5. Drain the cooling system as described in Chapter Three.
6. Remove the following as described in Chapter Nine:

a. Radiator and fan; refer to *Radiator and Fan Removal/Installation*.

b. Thermostat housing; refer to *Thermostat Removal/Installation*.

7. Remove the coolant reservoir tank from the right-hand side.

8. Disconnect the spark plug wires. Then, if needed, disconnect the ignition coil electrical connectors and remove the coils (**Figure 2**).

9. Remove the exhaust system as described in Chapter Seven.

10. Remove the carburetors as described in Chapter Seven.

11. Remove the air filter housing as described in Chapter Seven.

12. Loosen the clutch cable at the hand grip (**Figure 3**). Then disconnect the clutch cable at the crankcase (**Figure 4**).

13. Disconnect the crankcase breather hose.

14. Remove the gearshift lever (**Figure 5**).

15. Remove the engine primary sprocket cover (**Figure 6**).

16. Disconnect the following wiring connectors:

a. Starter motor (**Figure 7**).

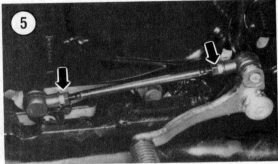

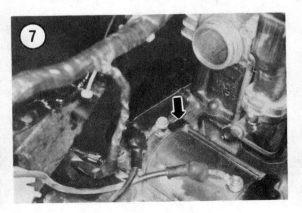

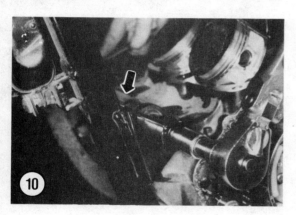

b. Neutral switch (**Figure 8**).

c. Oil pressure switch (**Figure 9**).

17. Remove the following as described in this chapter:

a. Cylinder head.

b. Cylinder.

c. Pistons.

d. Alternator.

e. Starter.

18. Remove the clutch plates as described in Chapter Five.

19. Remove the external shift mechanism. See Chapter Six.

20. Remove the drive chain. See Chapter Eleven.

21. Examine the engine to make sure everything has been disconnected and positioned out of the way.

22. Place wooden blocks under the crankcase to support the engine once the mounting bolts are removed.

23. Loosen, but do not remove, all front (**Figure 10**) and rear (**Figure 11**) engine mount nuts.

24. Remove the front engine mount through-bolts, nuts and rubber spacers (**Figure 10**).

NOTE
Due to the box frame design, the right portion of the frame must be removed before the engine can be removed even if the cylinder and cylinder head are removed.

25. Remove bolts located on right frame section and remove it (**Figure 12**).

26. Withdraw the upper and lower engine mount through-bolts (**Figure 11**).

27. Lift the crankcase (**Figure 13**) to the right to remove it.

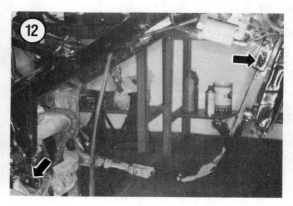

28. While the engine is removed for service, check all of the frame engine mounts for cracks or other damage. If any cracks are detected, take the chassis assembly to a Kawasaki dealer for further examination.

29. Install by reversing the removal steps while noting the following.

30. After the engine is positioned correctly, install the engine mount brackets, bolts and nuts.

31. Tighten the engine mount nuts and bolts to the specifications in **Table 2**.

32. Fill the crankcase with the recommended type and quantity of engine oil. Refer to Chapter Three.

33. Refill the cooling system. Refer to Chapter Three.

34. Adjust the following as described in Chapter Three:

  a. Clutch.

  b. Drive chain.

  c. Rear brake.

  d. Throttle cable.

35. Start the engine and check for leaks.

CYLINDER HEAD AND CAMSHAFTS

This section describes removal, inspection and installation procedures for the cylinder head and camshaft components. Valves and valve components are described in a separate section.

Cylinder Head Cover Removal/Installation

1. Place the motorcycle on the centerstand.

2. Drain the engine coolant as described in Chapter Three.

3. Remove the seat and fuel tank as described in Chapter Seven.

4. Disconnect the ignition coil wiring and remove the ignition coils (**Figure 2**).

5. *U.S. models:* Remove the air suction valves and hoses (**Figure 14**).

6. Remove the 2 cylinder head water pipes (**Figure 15**).

7. Remove the cylinder head cover bolts and remove the cover (**Figure 16**).

8. Installation is the reverse of these steps. Note the following.

9. Replace the cylinder head cover gasket (**Figure 17**), if necessary.

10. Install the 2 cylinder head cover dowel pins (**Figure 18**).

11. Apply a non-hardening gasket sealer (such as RTV) to the mating areas indicated in **Figure 19**. Apply sealer to both left- and right-hand sides of the cylinder head.

12. Tighten the cylinder head cover bolts to the specifications in **Table 2**.

Camshaft Removal

1. Remove the cylinder head cover as described in this chapter.

2. Loosen the valve adjuster locknuts and loosen the adjusters (A, **Figure 20**).

3. Remove the cam chain tensioner as described in this chapter.

4. Remove the cylinder head oil pipes (B, **Figure 20**).

> *CAUTION*
> *The oil pipes can be easily damaged. Place them in a box until reassembly.*

5. Remove the upper chain guide (**Figure 21**).

> *NOTE*
> *Each camshaft cap is marked with an arrow (pointing forward) and with a letter representing position. See **Figure 22** and **Figure 23**. If the camshaft cap markings on your bike differ from those in **Figure 23** or there are no marks, label them for direction and position before performing Step 6.*

6. Remove the camshaft cap bolts and remove the caps (**Figure 24**).

7. Secure the camshaft chain with wire. Then remove both camshafts with their sprockets (**Figure 25**).

Cylinder Head Removal

1. Remove the 2 cylinder head oil line banjo bolts (**Figure 26**) and copper washers.
2. Remove the front (**Figure 27**) and rear (**Figure 28**) 6 mm cylinder head bolts.
3. Remove the 10 mm cylinder head bolts (**Figure 29**).

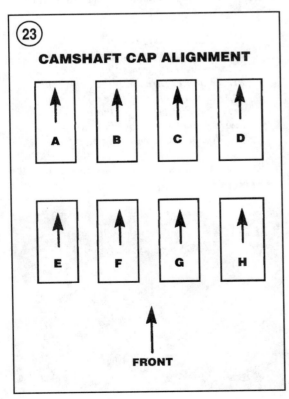

CAMSHAFT CAP ALIGNMENT

A B C D

E F G H

FRONT

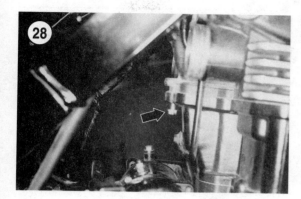

4. Loosen the cylinder head (**Figure 30**) by tapping around the perimeter with a rubber or plastic mallet.

CAUTION
Remember, the cooling fins are fragile and may be damaged if tapped on too hard. Never use a metal hammer.

5. Remove the cylinder head (**Figure 30**) by pulling straight up and off the cylinder. Feed the camshaft chain through the cylinder head and resecure. Place a clean shop rag into the cam chain opening in the cylinder to prevent the entry of foreign matter.

NOTE
After removing the cylinder head, check the top and bottom mating surfaces for any indication of leakage. Also check the head and base gaskets for signs of leakage. A blown gasket could indicate possible cylinder head warpage or other damage.

6. Remove the cylinder head gasket (A, **Figure 31**) and the two dowel pins (B, **Figure 31**). Discard the gasket.

Camshaft Inspection

1. Check cam lobes (A, **Figure 32**) for wear. The lobes should not be scored and the edges should be square. Slight damage may be removed with a silicon carbide oilstone. Use No. 100-120 grit initially, then polish with a No. 280-320 grit.

2. Even though the cam lobe surfaces appear to be satisfactory, with no visible signs of wear, they must be measured with a micrometer as shown in **Figure 33**. Replace the shaft(s) if worn beyond the service

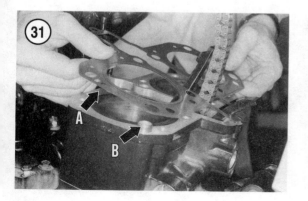

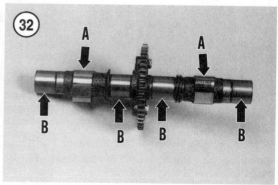

limits (measurements less than those given in **Table 1**).

3. Check the camshaft bearing journals (B, **Figure 32**) for wear and scoring.

4. Even though the camshaft bearing journal surface appears satisfactory, with no visible signs of wear, the camshaft bearing journals must be measured with a micrometer. Replace the shaft(s) if worn beyond the service limits (measurements less than those given in **Table 1**).

5. Place the camshaft on a set of V-blocks and check its runout with a dial indicator. Replace the camshaft if runout exceeds specifications in **Table 1**. Repeat for the opposite camshaft.

6. Inspect the camshaft sprockets (**Figure 34**) for wear; replace if necessary.

7. Check the camshaft bearing journals in the cylinder head (**Figure 35**) and camshaft caps (**Figure 36**) for wear and scoring. They should not be scored or excessively worn. If necessary, replace the cylinder head and camshaft caps as a matched pair.

Camshaft Bearing Clearance Measurement

This procedure requires the use of a Plastigage set. The camshaft must be installed into the head. Before installation, wipe all oil residue from each cam bearing journal and bearing surface in the head and all camshaft caps.

1. Install the camshafts into the cylinder head.

2. Install all locating dowels into their camshaft caps.

3. Wipe all oil from the cam bearing journals before using the Plastigage material.

4. Place a strip of Plastigage material on top of each cam bearing journal (**Figure 37**), parallel to the cam.

5. Place the camshaft cap into position.

6. Install all camshaft cap bolts. Install finger-tight at first, then tighten in a crisscross pattern (**Figure 38**) to the final torque specification listed in **Table 2**.

> *CAUTION*
> *Do not rotate the camshaft with the Plastigage material in place.*

7. Gradually remove the camshaft cap bolts in a crisscross pattern. Remove the camshaft caps carefully.

8. Measure the width of the flattened Plastigage according to manufacturer's instructions (**Figure 39**).

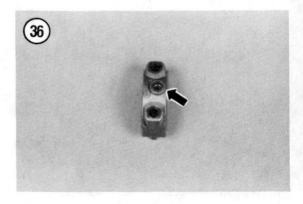

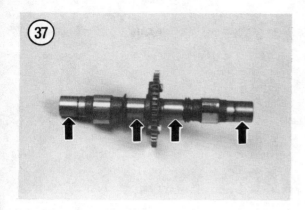

9. If the clearance exceeds the wear limits in **Table 1**, measure the camshaft bearing journals with a micrometer and compare to the limits in **Table 1**. If the camshaft bearing journal is less than dimension specified, replace the cam. If the cam is within specifications, the cylinder head and camshaft caps must be replaced as a matched set.

> *CAUTION*
> *Remove all particles of Plastigage from all camshaft bearing journals and the camshaft holder. Be sure to clean the camshaft holder groove. This material must not be left in the engine as it can plug up an oil control orifice and cause severe engine damage.*

Cylinder Head Inspection

1. Remove all traces of gasket from cylinder head and cylinder mating surfaces. Do not scratch the gasket surface.

2. Without removing valves, remove all carbon deposits from the combustion chambers (**Figure 40**) with a wire brush or wooden scraper. Take care not to damage the head, valves or spark plug threads.

> *CAUTION*
> *If the combustion chambers are cleaned while the valves are removed, make sure to keep the scraper or wire brush away from the valve seats to prevent damaging the seat surfaces. A damaged or even slightly scratched valve seat will cause poor valve seating.*

3. Examine the spark plug threads in the cylinder head for damage. If damage is minor or if the threads are dirty or clogged with carbon, use a spark plug

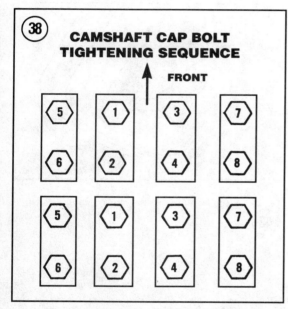

CAMSHAFT CAP BOLT TIGHTENING SEQUENCE

FRONT

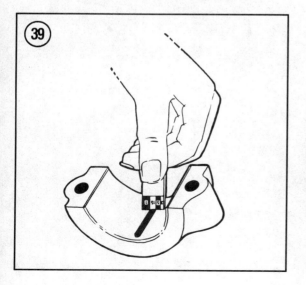

thread tap to clean the threads following the manu-facturer's instructions. If thread damage is severe, refer further service to a Kawasaki dealer or machine shop.

4. After all carbon is removed from combustion chambers, and valve ports and the spark plug thread holes are repaired, clean the entire head in solvent and blow dry with compressed air.

5. Clean away all carbon on the piston crowns. Do not remove the carbon ridge at the top of the cylinder bore (**Figure 41**).

6. Check for cracks in the combustion chamber and exhaust ports. A cracked head must be replaced.

7. After the head has been thoroughly cleaned, place a straightedge across the gasket surface at several points (**Figure 42**). Measure warp by inserting a feeler gauge between the straightedge and cylinder head at each location. Maximum allowable warpage is listed in **Table 1**. If warpage exceeds this limit, the cylinder head must be replaced.

8. Check the valves and valve guides as described under *Valves and Valve Components* in this chapter.

Oil Pipes Cleaning/Inspection

1. Examine the cylinder head pipes (**Figure 43**) and main oil pipes (**Figure 44**) for damage. Check the brazed joints for cracking or other apparent damage. Check the cylinder oil pipe O-rings (**Figure 45**) for wear. If the O-ring surfaces are not perfectly smooth, replace them.

2. Flush the oil pipes with solvent and allow to dry.

Cylinder Head Installation

1. If removed, install the rear chain guide (**Figure 46**).

2. Clean the cylinder head (**Figure 47**) and cylinder mating surfaces of all gasket residue.

NOTE
*The cylinder head gasket is marked with the word UP on one side. This side must face up (**Figure 48**).*

3. Install a new cylinder head gasket (A, **Figure 31**) and the 2 dowel pins (B, **Figure 31**).

4. Install the cylinder head (**Figure 30**).

5. Install the bolts securing the cylinder head. Tighten the 10 mm bolts in 2-3 stages in a crisscross

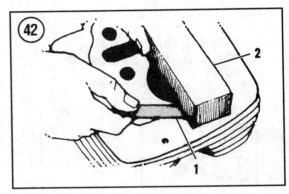

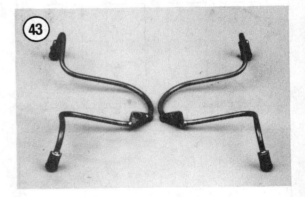

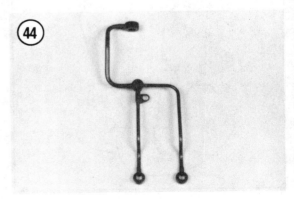

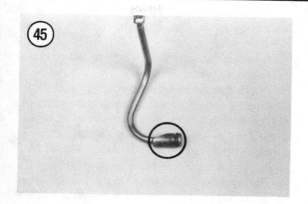

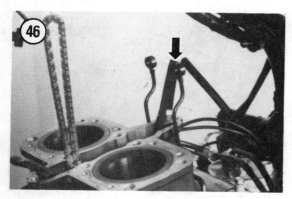

pattern (**Figure 49**) to the torque specifications listed in **Table 2**.

6. Tighten the front (**Figure 27**) and rear (**Figure 28**) cylinder head 6 mm bolts to the torque specifications listed in **Table 2**.

7. Install the main oil pipe and banjo bolts, using new copper washers. Tighten the banjo bolts to the specifications listed in **Table 2**.

Camshaft Installation

1. The intake and exhaust sprockets are identical. If the sprockets were removed from the camshafts, install them as follows:

    a. Install the sprockets onto their camshafts so that the sides marked with an IN and EX face to the left.

    b. There are 4 holes drilled into each sprocket. On the intake camshaft, use the sprocket bolt holes marked IN. On the exhaust camshaft, use the sprocket bolt holes marked EX.

    c. Tighten the sprocket bolts to the specifications in **Table 2**.

2. Coat all camshaft lobes and bearing journals with molybdenum disulfide grease or assembly oil.

3. Also coat the bearing surfaces in the cylinder head and camshaft bearing caps.

4. Lift up on the cam chain and slide the 2 camshafts through and seat them in the cylinder head. Engage the cam chain with the cam sprockets. Remove the wire from the cam chain.

5. Remove the 2 caps on the alternator cover (**Figure 50**).

6. Using a socket on the crankshaft bolt (A, **Figure 51**), turn the crankshaft clockwise until the "C" TDC

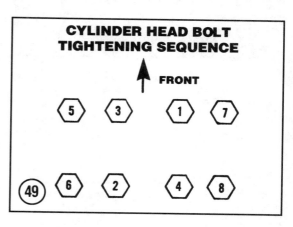

CYLINDER HEAD BOLT TIGHTENING SEQUENCE

↑ FRONT

⬡5 ⬡3 ⬡1 ⬡7

⬡6 ⬡2 ⬡4 ⬡8

mark for the No. 2 (right side) cylinder is aligned with the notch in the upper hole (B, **Figure 51**).

7. Lift the cam chain off the sprocket. Without turning the crankshaft, align the EX line on the exhaust cam sprocket and IN on the intake cam sprocket with the upper cylinder head surface as shown in **Figure 52**.

8. Refer to **Figure 52**. Locate the punch mark on the intake sprocket. Beginning with this mark, count off 24 cam chain pins toward the exhaust sprocket. The 24th pin must align with the punch mark on the exhaust sprocket. If it does not, recheck your pin

count and reposition the intake or exhaust camshaft as required.

9. Check that the cam chain is properly seated in the front and rear cam chain guides.

10. Check that the camshaft cap dowel pins are in place and loosely install the camshaft caps in their original positions. The arrow on each cap must face to the front of the bike and the alphabet lettering must be installed in the order shown in **Figure 53**.

11. Install the upper cam chain guide (**Figure 54**).

12. Tighten the camshaft cap bolts marked No. 1 and 2 (**Figure 55**) for the exhaust and intake cams. This

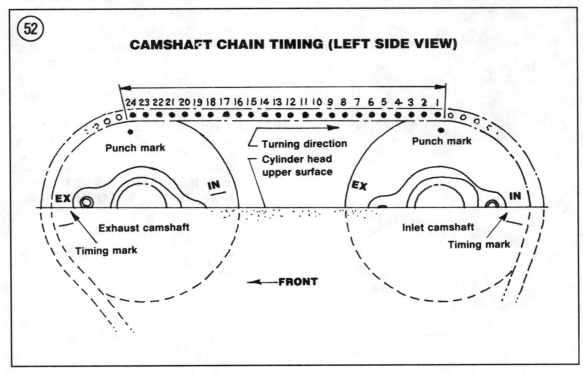

CAMSHAFT CHAIN TIMING (LEFT SIDE VIEW)

24 23 22 21 20 19 18 17 16 15 14 13 12 11 10 9 8 7 6 5 4 3 2 1

Punch mark

Turning direction

Cylinder head upper surface

Punch mark

EX

IN

EX

IN

Exhaust camshaft

Timing mark

Inlet camshaft

Timing mark

◄—FRONT

CAMSHAFT CAP ALIGNMENT

A   B   C   D

E   F   G   H

↑
FRONT

53

will seat the camshafts in position. Then tighten all bolts in a crisscross pattern to the torque specification in **Table 2**.

13. Slowly turn the crankshaft clockwise 2 full turns, using the bolt (A, **Figure 51**) on the left end of the crankshaft. Check that all cam sprocket timing marks again align as shown in **Figure 52** when the "C" TDC mark on the rotor is aligned with the notch in the alternator cover upper hole (B, **Figure 51**). If all marks align as indicated, cam timing is correct. If not, readjust as necessary.

CAUTION
*If there is any binding while turning the crankshaft, **stop**. Recheck the camshaft timing marks. Improper timing can cause valve and piston damage.*

14. Position the oil pipes into the cylinder head. Then push both ends of one pipe into the head at the same time. Repeat for the opposite side. Install the oil pipe mounting bolts and tighten securely. See **Figure 56**.

15. Install the cam chain tensioner as described in this chapter.

16. Install the cylinder head cover as described in this chapter.

ROCKER ARM ASSEMBLIES

The rocker arms are identical (same Kawasaki part No.) but they will develop different wear patterns during use. It is recommended that all parts be marked during removal so that they can be assembled in their original positions.

54

55 **CAMSHAFT CAP BOLT TIGHTENING SEQUENCE**

↑
FRONT

5   1   3   7

6   2   4   8

5   1   3   7

6   2   4   8

56

Removal/Inspection/Installation

NOTE
The rocker arms can be removed with the cylinder head installed on the engine. The following procedure is shown with the cylinder removed for clarity.

1. *Cylinder head installed on engine:* Remove the camshafts as described in this chapter.

2. With an Allen wrench, loosen one of the rocker arm shafts (**Figure 57**) and remove it. See **Figure 58**.

3. Remove the rocker arm and spring (**Figure 59**).

4. Repeat Steps 2 and 3 for the remaining rocker arms.

5. Wash all parts in cleaning solvent and thoroughly dry.

6. Inspect the rocker arm pad (**Figure 60**) where it rides on the cam lobe and where the adjuster (**Figure 61**) rides on the valve stem. If the pad is scratched or unevenly worn, inspect the cam lobe for scoring, chipping or flat spots. Replace the rocker arm if defective.

NOTE
*If the rocker arm pad (**Figure 60**) is worn, also check the mating cam lobe for wear or damage. See **Figure 62**.*

7. Measure the inside diameter of the rocker arm bore (A, **Figure 63**) with an inside micrometer and check against dimension in **Table 1**. Replace if worn to the service limit or greater.

8. Inspect the rocker arm shaft for wear or scoring. Measure the outside diameter (B, **Figure 63**) with a micrometer and check against dimension in **Table 1**. Replace if worn to the service limit or greater.

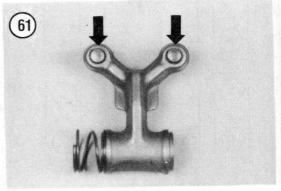

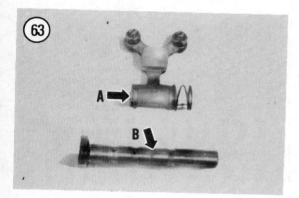

9. Coat the rocker arm shaft and rocker arm bore with assembly oil.

10. Assemble the springs (**Figure 64**) onto each rocker arm so that the spring will face against the camshaft chain after installation.

11. Install the rocker arm and spring (**Figure 59**).

12. Install the rocker arm shaft (**Figure 58**) and tighten it to the torque specifications in **Table 2**.

CAM CHAIN TENSIONER

The automatic tensioner is continuously self-adjusting. The tensioner pushrod is free to move inward, but can't move out. Whenever the cam chain tensioner bolts are loosened, the tensioner assembly must be completely removed and reset as described in this section.

Removal/Installation

1. Loosen the front cam chain tensioner cap bolt (A, **Figure 65**).

2. Remove the 2 tensioner mounting bolts (B, **Figure 65**) and the tensioner assembly.

3. Remove the tensioner cap bolt (**Figure 66**).

CAUTION
When performing Step 4, do not turn the tensioner counterclockwise as this could cause the rod to disconnect.

4. Hold the tensioner in your hand as shown in **Figure 67** and insert a small screwdriver into the end of the tensioner body. Turn the rod *clockwise* while pushing it in until it protrudes approximately 10 mm through the rear of the tensioner body.

5. While holding the rod in position (**Figure 68**) install the tensioner onto the cylinder. Then remove

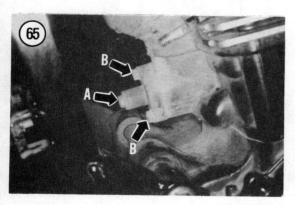

the screwdriver and install and tighten the mounting bolts to the specifications in **Table 2**.

NOTE
If the tensioner rod slips before installing the mounting bolts, remove the tensioner and repeat this procedure.

6. Install the tensioner cap bolt.

VALVES AND VALVE COMPONENTS

Refer to **Figure 69** for this procedure.
1. Remove the cylinder head as described in this chapter.
2. Install a valve spring compressor squarely over the valve retainer with the other end of the tool placed against valve head (**Figure 70**).
3. Tighten valve spring compressor until the split valve keepers separate. Lift out split keepers with needlenose pliers (**Figure 71**).
4. Gradually loosen valve spring compressor and remove from head. Lift off the upper valve seat.

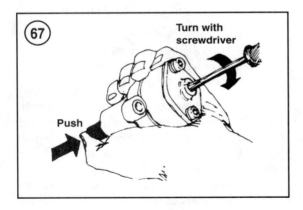

67

Turn with
screwdriver

Push

68

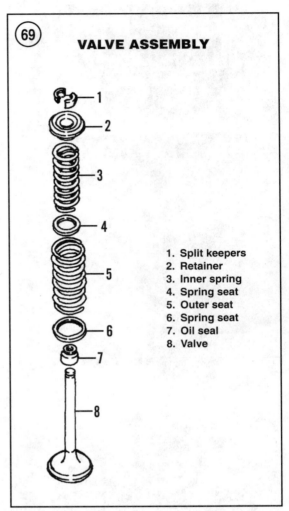

69

VALVE ASSEMBLY

1. Split keepers
2. Retainer
3. Inner spring
4. Spring seat
5. Outer seat
6. Spring seat
7. Oil seal
8. Valve

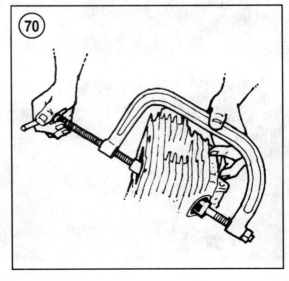

70

4

CAUTION
*Remove any burrs from the valve stem grooves before removing the valve (**Figure 72**). Otherwise the valve guides will be damaged.*

5. Remove the inner and outer springs and valve.

6. Remove the oil seal.

7. Remove the lower spring seat.

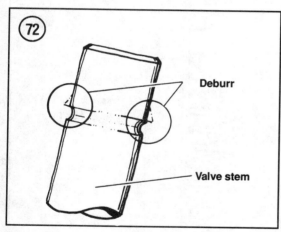

Deburr

Valve stem

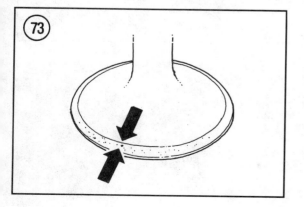

CAUTION
All component parts of each valve assembly must be kept together. Do not mix with like components from other valves or excessive wear may result.

8. Repeat Steps 2-7 and remove remaining valve(s).

Inspection

1. Clean valves with a wire brush and solvent.

2. Inspect the contact surface of each valve for burning (**Figure 73**). Minor roughness and pitting can be removed by lapping the valve as described in this chapter. Excessive unevenness to the contact surface is an indication that the valve is not serviceable. The contact surface of the valve may be ground on a valve grinding machine, but it is best to replace a burned or damaged valve with a new one.

3. Inspect the valve stem for wear and roughness and measure the runout of the valve stem as shown in **Figure 74**. The runout should not exceed the wear limit specifications (**Table 1**).

4. Measure valve stems for wear using a micrometer (**Figure 75**). Compare with specifications in **Table 1**.

5. Remove all carbon and varnish from the valve guides with a stiff spiral wire brush.

NOTE
Step 6 and Step 7 require special measuring equipment. If you do not have the required measuring devices, proceed to Step 8.

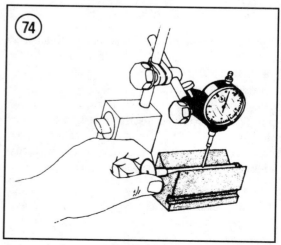

6. Measure each valve guide at tip, center and bottom with a small hole gauge. Compare measurements with specifications in **Table 1**.

7. Replace the valves (Step 4) or valve guides (Step 6) if they exceed the wear limits in **Table 1**.

8. Insert each valve in its guide. Hold the valve just slightly off its seat and rock it sideways. If it rocks more than slightly, the guide is probably worn and should be replaced. As a final check, take the head to a dealer and have the valve guides measured.

9. Measure the valve spring length with a vernier caliper (**Figure 76**). All should be of length specified in **Table 1** with no bends or other distortion. Replace defective springs.

10. Measure the tilt of all valve springs as shown in **Figure 77**. Replace if tilt exceeds 1.5 mm (0.059 in.).

11. Check the valve spring retainer and valve keepers. If they are in good condition, they may be reused.

12. Inspect valve seats (**Figure 78**). If worn or burned, they must be reconditioned. This should be performed by your dealer or local machine shop. Seats and valves in near-perfect condition can be reconditioned by lapping with fine carborundum paste. Lapping, however, is always inferior to precision grinding.

Installation

1. Coat the valve stems with molybdenum disulfide paste and insert into cylinder head.

2. Install the bottom spring seat and a new seal.

NOTE
Oil seals should be replaced whenever
a valve is removed or replaced.

3. Install valve springs with the narrow pitch end (end with coils closest together) facing the cylinder head (**Figure 79**).

4. Install the upper valve seat.

5. Push down on the upper valve seat with the valve spring compressor and install valve keepers. After releasing tension from compressor, examine valve keepers and make sure they are seated correctly (**Figure 80**).

NOTE
Tap the valve spring with a rubber ham-
mer to ensure that valve keepers are in
place and seated correctly.

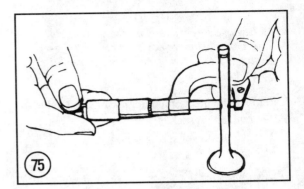

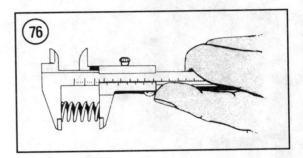

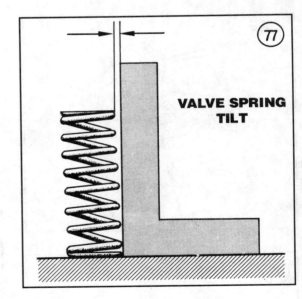

VALVE SPRING
TILT

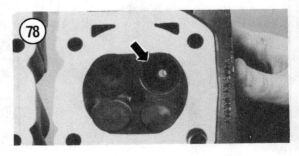

6. Repeat Steps 1-5 for remaining valve(s).

Valve Guide Replacement

When guides are worn so that there is excessive stem-to-guide clearance or valve tipping, they must be replaced. Replace all, even if only one is worn. This job should only be done by a Kawasaki dealer or qualified specialist as special tools are required.

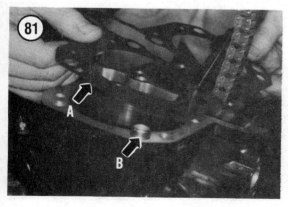

Valve Seat Reconditioning

This job is best left to your dealer or local machine shop. They have the special equipment and knowledge for this exacting job. You can still save considerable money by removing the cylinder head and taking just the head to the shop.

Valve Lapping

Valve lapping is a simple operation which can restore the valve seal without machining if the amount of wear or distortion is not too great.

1. Smear a light coating of fine grade valve lapping compound on seating surface of valve.

2. Insert the valve into the head.

3. Wet the suction cup of the lapping stick and stick it onto the head of the valve. Lap the valve to the seat by spinning the lapping stick in both directions. Every 5 to 10 seconds, rotate the valve 180° in the valve seat. Lap only enough to achieve a precise seating ring around valve head.

4. Closely examine valve seat in cylinder head. It should be smooth and even with a smooth, polished seating "ring."

5. Thoroughly clean the valves and cylinder head in solvent to remove all grinding compound. Any compound left on the valves or the cylinder head will end up in the engine and will cause excessive wear and damage.

6. After the lapping has been completed and the valve assemblies have been reinstalled into the head, the valve seal should be tested. Check the seal of each valve by pouring solvent into each of the intake and exhaust ports. There should be no leakage past the seat. If leakage occurs, the combustion chamber will appear wet. If fluid leaks past any of the seats, disassemble that valve assembly and repeat the lapping procedure until there is not leakage.

CYLINDER

Removal

1. Remove the cylinder head as described in this chapter.

2. Remove the head gasket (A, **Figure 81**) and dowel pins (B, **Figure 81**).

3. Remove the rear chain guide (**Figure 82**).

4. Loosen the cylinder by tapping around the perimeter with a rubber or plastic mallet.

5. Pull the cylinder (**Figure 83**) straight up and off the piston and cylinder studs.

> *NOTE*
> *Be sure to keep the cam chain wired up to prevent it from falling into the lower crankcase.*

6. Stuff clean shop rags into the crankcase opening to prevent objects from falling into the crankcase.

7. Remove the dowel pins (A, **Figure 84**) and base gasket (B, **Figure 84**).

Inspection

1. Wash the cylinder bore in solvent to remove any oil and carbon particles. The bore must be cleaned thoroughly before attempting any measurement as incorrect readings may be obtained.

2. Measure the cylinder bores with a cylinder gauge (**Figure 85**) or inside micrometer at the points shown in **Figure 86**.

3. Measure in 2 axes—in line with the piston pin and 90° to the pin. If the taper or out-of-round is greater than specifications (**Table 1**), the cylinders must be rebored to the next oversize and new pistons and rings installed. Rebore both cylinders even though only one may be worn.

> *NOTE*
> *The new pistons should be obtained first before the cylinders are bored so that the pistons can be measured; each cylinder must be bored to match one piston only. Piston-to-cylinder clearance is specified in Table 1.*

4. If the cylinder(s) are not worn past the service limits, check the bore carefully for scratches or gouges. The bore still may require boring and reconditioning.

5. If the cylinders require reboring, remove all dowel pins from the cylinder before leaving it with the dealer or machine shop.

> *CAUTION*
> *After having the cylinders rebored, wash them thoroughly in hot soapy water. This is the best way to clean the cylinder of all fine grit material left from the bore job. After washing the cylinder,*

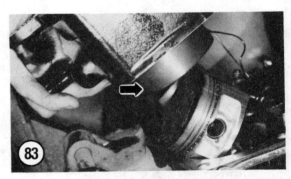

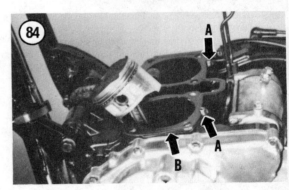

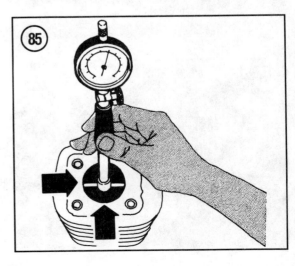

run a clean white cloth through the cylinder; it should show no traces of dirt or other debris. If the rag is dirty, the cylinder is not clean and must be rewashed. After the cylinder is thoroughly cleaned, dry and then lubricate the cylinder walls with clean engine oil to protect the cylinder liners from rust.

Installation

1. If the base gasket is stuck to the bottom of the cylinder it should be removed and the cylinder surface cleaned thoroughly.

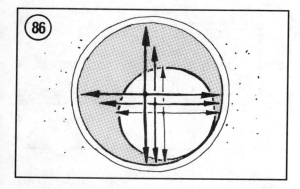

2. Check that the bottom cylinder surface (**Figure 87**) is clean of all old gasket material.

3. Install the 2 dowel pins onto the crankcase (A, **Figure 84**).

4. Install a new cylinder base gasket (B, **Figure 84**) to the crankcase. Make sure all holes align.

5. Install a piston holding fixture under the pistons.

6. Lubricate cylinders and pistons liberally with engine oil before installation.

7. Carefully align the cylinder with the pistons (**Figure 88**).

> *NOTE*
> *Once the cylinder is installed, run the chain and wire up through the cylinder.*

8. Compress each ring as it enters the cylinder with your fingers or by using aircraft type hose clamps of appropriate diameter.

> *CAUTION*
> *Don't tighten the clamp any more than necessary to compress the rings. If the rings can't slip through easily, the clamp may gouge the rings.*

9. Remove the piston holding fixture and push the cylinder all the way down.

10. Install the cylinder head and camshafts as described in this chapter.

PISTONS AND PISTON RINGS

Piston Removal/Installation

1. Remove the cylinder head and cylinder as described in this chapter.

2. Stuff the crankcase with clean shop rags to prevent objects from falling into the crankcase.

3. Lightly mark the piston crown with a L (left) or R (right) so they will be installed into the correct cylinder.

4. Remove the piston rings as described in this chapter.

5. Before removing the piston, hold the rod tightly and rock the piston. Any rocking motion (do not confuse with the normal sliding motion) indicates wear on the piston pin, rod bushing, pin bore or, more likely, a combination of all three. Mark the piston and pin so that they will be reassembled into the same set.

6. Remove the circlips from the piston pin bore (**Figure 89**).

7. Remove the piston pin. If the pin is tight, use a homemade tool as shown in **Figure 90**.

8. Inspect the piston as described in this chapter.

9. Coat the connecting rod bushing, piston pin and piston with assembly oil.

10. Place the piston over the connecting rod. If you are installing old parts, make sure the piston is installed on the correct rod as marked during removal. The arrow on each piston crown must face to the front of the engine.

11. Insert the piston pin and push it until it starts into the connecting rod bushing. If the pin does not slide easily, use the homemade tool (**Figure 90**), but eliminate the piece of pipe. Push the pin in until it is centered in the piston.

12. Install *new* circlips in the piston pin bore.

13. Install rings as described in this chapter.

14. Repeat Steps 1-13 for the opposite piston.

Piston Inspection

1. Carefully clean the carbon from the piston crown (**Figure 91**) with a soft scraper. Do not remove or damage the carbon ridge around the circumference of the piston above the top ring. If the pistons, rings and cylinders are found to be dimensionally correct and can be reused, removal of the carbon ring from the top of the piston or carbon ridges from the cylinders will promote excessive oil consumption.

CAUTION
Do not wire brush piston skirts.

2. Examine each ring groove for burrs, dented edges and wide wear. Pay particular attention to the top compression ring groove, as it usually wears more than the others.

3. Check the oil control holes in the piston (**Figure 92**) for carbon or oil sludge buildup. Clean the holes with a small diameter drill bit.

4. Check the piston skirts (**Figure 93**) for cracks or other damage.

5. Measure piston-to-cylinder clearance as described under *Piston Clearance* in this chapter.

6. If damage or wear indicate piston replacement, select a new piston as described under *Piston Clearance* in this chapter.

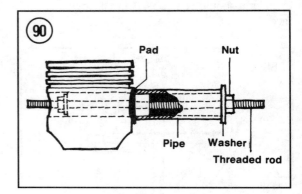

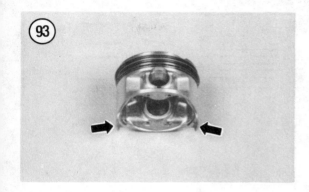

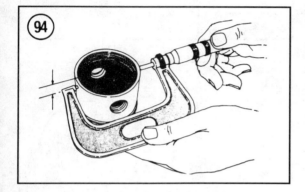

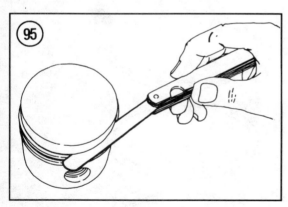

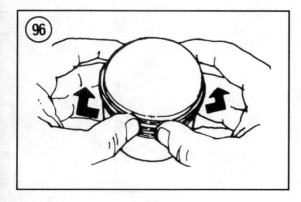

Piston Clearance

1. Make sure the piston and cylinder walls are clean and dry.

2. Measure the inside diameter of the cylinder at a point 13 mm (1/2 in.) from the upper edge with a bore gauge.

3. Measure the outside diameter of the piston at a point 5 mm (3/16 in.) from the lower edge of the piston at 90° to piston pin axis (**Figure 94**).

4. Subtract the piston diameter from the bore diameter; the difference is piston-to-cylinder clearance. Compare to specification in **Table 1**. If clearance is excessive, the piston should be replaced and cylinder rebored. Purchase the new piston first; measure its diameter and add the specified clearance to determine the proper cylinder bore.

NOTE
If one cylinder requires boring, the other cylinder must be bored also.

Piston Ring Removal/Installation

WARNING
The edges of all piston rings are very sharp. Be careful when handling them to avoid cut fingers.

1. Measure the side clearance of each ring in its groove with a flat feeler gauge (**Figure 95**) and compare with the specifications in **Table 1**. If the clearance is greater than specified, the rings must be replaced. If the clearance is still excessive with the new rings, the piston must be replaced.

2. Remove the old rings with a ring expander tool or by spreading the ring ends with your thumbs and lifting the rings up evenly (**Figure 96**).

3. Using a broken piston ring, remove all carbon from the piston ring grooves.

4. Inspect grooves carefully for burrs, nicks or broken or cracked lands. Replace piston if necessary.

5. Check end gap of each ring. To check ring, insert the ring into the bottom of the cylinder bore and square it with the cylinder wall by tapping it with the piston. The ring should be pushed in about 15 mm (5/8 in.). Insert a feeler gauge as shown in **Figure 97**. Compare gap with **Table 1**. Replace ring if gap is too large. If the gap on the new ring is smaller than specified, hold a small file in a vise, grip the ends of

the ring with your thumb and finger and enlarge the gap.

6. Roll each ring around its piston groove as shown in **Figure 98** to check for binding. Minor binding may be cleaned up with a fine-cut file.

7. Install the piston rings in the order shown in **Figure 99**.

NOTE
Install all rings with the manufacturer's markings facing up.

8. Install the piston rings—first the bottom, then the middle, then the top ring—by carefully spreading the ends with your thumbs and slipping the rings over the top of the piston. Remember that the piston rings must be installed with the marks on them facing up toward the top of the piston or there is the possibility of oil pumping past the rings.

9. Make sure the rings are seated completely in their grooves all the way around the piston and that the end gaps are distributed around the piston as shown in **Figure 100**. It is important that the ring gaps are not aligned with each other when installed to prevent

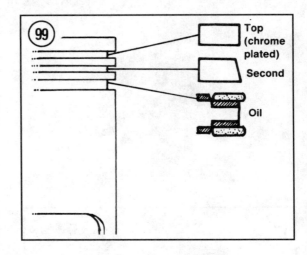

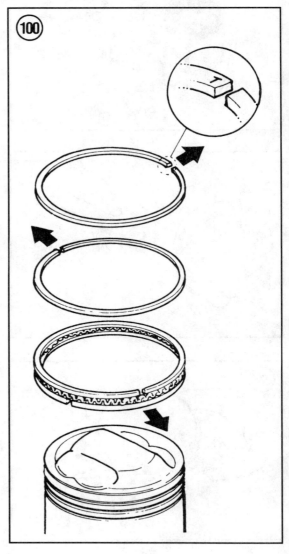

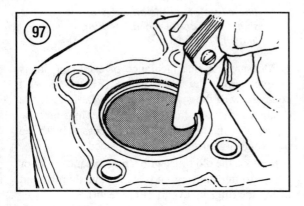

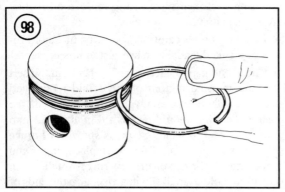

compression pressures from escaping past them
(**Figure 100**).

10. If installing oversize compression rings, check
the number to make sure the correct rings are being
installed. The ring numbers should be the same as
the piston oversize number.

11. If new rings are installed, measure the side
clearance of each ring (**Figure 95**) in its groove and
compare to dimensions in **Table 1**.

OIL PUMP

The engine must be removed and the crankcase
disassembled to remove the oil pump.

Removal/Installation

1. Remove the engine as described in this chapter.
2. Separate the crankcase as described in this chapter.
3. Remove the oil pan.
4. Remove the 3 O-rings (**Figure 101**).
5. Lift the oil pipe (**Figure 102**) out of the crankcase.
6. Remove the bolt (**Figure 103**) and lift the oil pipe
(**Figure 104**) out of the crankcase.
7. Remove the circlip securing the oil pump gear
(**Figure 105**) and remove the gear.
8. Remove the oil pump screws (**Figure 106**) and lift
the oil pump out of the crankcase.
9. Installation is the reverse of these steps. Note the
following.
10. To prime the oil pump, add clean engine oil into
the oil pump opening (**Figure 107**) while turning the
pump shaft.
11. Apply Loctite 242 (blue) to the oil pump screws
before assembly. Tighten the screws securely.
12. Install new O-rings during assembly.

Disassembly/Inspection/Assembly

This procedure describes disassembly and inspection of the oil pump assembly. If any part is worn or damaged, the entire pump assembly must be replaced.

Refer to **Figure 108** for this procedure.

CAUTION
*An impact driver with a Phillips bit will be necessary to loosen the oil pump housing screws (**Figure 109**) in Step 1. Attempting to loosen the screws with a Phillips screwdriver may ruin the screw heads.*

1. Remove the oil pump screws and remove the cover.

2. Remove the outer and inner rotors from the housing.

3. Remove the rotor pin from the pump shaft.

4. Remove the oil pump shaft.

5. Clean all parts in solvent and dry thoroughly with compressed air.

6. Assemble the rotors and check the clearance between the rotors with a flat feeler gauge (**Figure 110**). The clearance should be within the specifications in **Table 1**. If the clearance is greater, replace the rotors as a set.

7. Measure the clearance between the outer rotor and the pump body with a flat feeler gauge (**Figure 111**). If the clearance is greater than the specification in **Table 1**, measure the rotor with a micrometer. If the rotor is less than the service limit in **Table 1**, replace the rotors as a set. If the rotor diameter is within

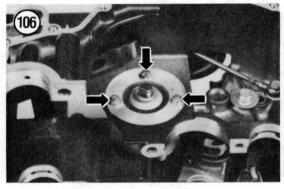

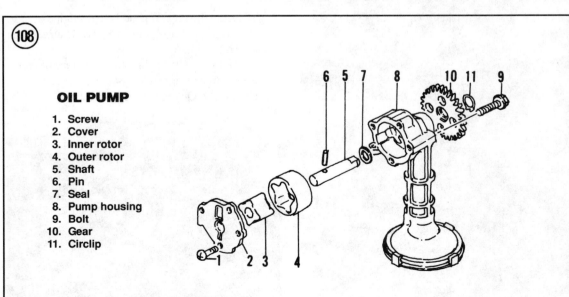

OIL PUMP

1. Screw
2. Cover
3. Inner rotor
4. Outer rotor
5. Shaft
6. Pin
7. Seal
8. Pump housing
9. Bolt
10. Gear
11. Circlip

specification, measure the oil pump body inside diameter with a bore or snap gauge. If the clearance is greater than the service limit, replace the oil pump assembly.

8. Check the rotor end clearance with a straightedge and flat feeler gauge (**Figure 112**). If the clearance is greater than the service limit in **Table 1**, the oil pump must be replaced.

9. Check the strainer screen for tearing or other damage; replace the oil pump assembly if the strainer is damaged.

10. Check the pump shaft for wear or damage.

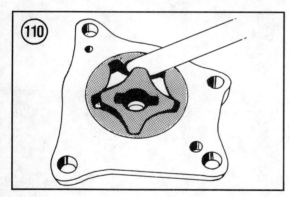

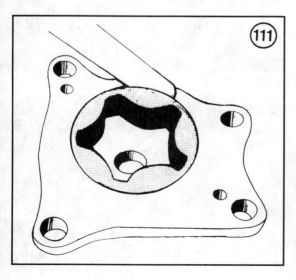

NOTE
Proceed with Step 11 only when the above inspection and measurement steps have been completed and all parts are known to be good.

11. Coat all parts (**Figure 108**) with fresh engine oil before assembly.

12. Reverse Steps 1-4 to reassemble the oil pump.

OIL PRESSURE RELIEF VALVE

Removal/Installation

1. Drain the engine oil as described in Chapter Three.
2. Remove the exhaust pipes.
3. Remove the oil pan (**Figure 113**).
4. Unscrew the relief valve (**Figure 114**) and remove it.
5. Apply Loctite 242 (blue) to the relief valve and install it. Tighten the valve to 15 N•m (11 ft.-lb.).
6. Replace the oil pan gasket if necessary.
7. Install the oil pan and tighten the bolts to 12 N•m (8.5 ft.-lb).
8. Reinstall the exhaust pipes.

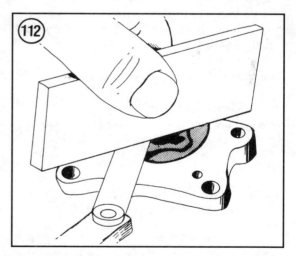

9. Refill the engine oil as described in Chapter Three.

OIL LEVEL SWITCH

Removal/Installation

1. Place the bike on the centerstand.
2. Drain the engine oil as described in Chapter Three.
3. Disconnect the oil level switch electrical connector.
4. Unscrew the oil level switch (**Figure 115**).
5. Installation is the reverse of these steps. Note the following.
6. Make sure the area around the switch mounting position is clean of all dirt and other debris. Tighten the switch securely.
7. Refill the engine oil as described in Chapter Three.

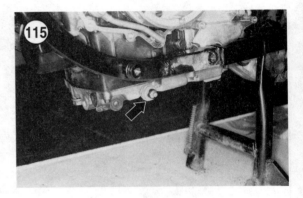

NEUTRAL SWITCH

Removal/Installation

1. Place the bike on the centerstand.
2. Remove the drive chain cover.
3. Disconnect the electrical connector at the neutral switch (**Figure 116**).
4. Remove the neutral switch.
5. Installation is the reverse of these steps. Note the following.
6. Install a new gasket on the switch.
7. Make sure the area around the switch mounting position is clean of all dirt and other debris.
8. Tighten the neutral switch to 15 N·m (11 ft.-lb.).

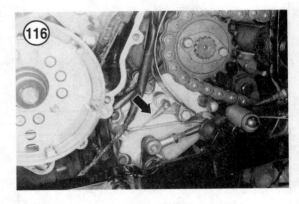

ALTERNATOR, STARTER DRIVE MECHANISM AND STARTER

The alternator and starter are discussed together, because complete removal of one entails removal of the other. Refer to Chapter Eight for alternator and starter service.

Alternator Cover Removal/Installation

1. Raise the seat and disconnect the battery negative lead.
2. Disconnect the alternator electrical connectors.
3. Place an oil pan underneath the alternator cover.

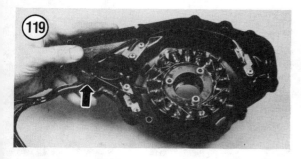

4. Remove the alternator cover bolts and remove the cover (**Figure 117**). Note the path of the wire harness as it must be routed the same during installation.

5. Install by reversing these steps while noting the following.

6. Install a new alternator cover gasket and the 2 dowel pins. See **Figure 118**.

7. Apply silicone sealant, such as RTV, underneath the rubber wiring grommet in the cover (**Figure 119**).

Rotor/Starter Gears Removal

1. Raise the seat and disconnect the battery negative lead.

2. Remove the alternator cover as described in this chapter.

> *CAUTION*
> *The bolt securing the alternator rotor has **left-hand threads**. The bolt must be turned **clockwise** for removal.*

3. Remove the rotor bolt as follows:

   a. To keep the rotor from turning while removing the bolt, use a strap wrench (**Figure 120**) on the outer perimeter of the rotor.

   b. If the drive chain is installed, shift the transmission into gear and hold the rear brake on.

   c. Turning a socket *clockwise,* remove the bolt securing the alternator rotor (**Figure 121**).

4. Screw in a rotor puller (**Figure 122**) until it stops. Use the Kawasaki rotor puller (part No. 57001-254 or 57001-1009), Honda rotor puller (part No. 07933-3330000) or equivalent.

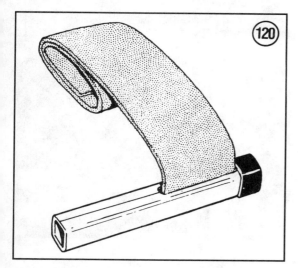

CAUTION
Don't try to remove the rotor without a puller; any attempt to do so will ultimately lead to some form of damage to the engine and/or rotor. Many aftermarket pullers are available from motorcycle dealers or mail order houses. If you can't buy or borrow one, have the dealer remove the rotor.

5. Secure the rotor with the strap wrench used to remove the rotor bolt and turn the rotor puller with a wrench until the rotor is free.

NOTE
If the rotor is difficult to remove, strike the puller with a hammer a few times. This will usually break it loose.

CAUTION
If normal rotor removal attempts fail, do not force the puller as the threads may be stripped out of the rotor causing expensive damage. Take the bike to a dealer and have the rotor removed.

6. Remove the rotor and Woodruff key (**Figure 123**).

7. Remove the chain guide bolts and remove the guide (**Figure 124**).

8. Remove the washer (**Figure 125**).

9. Remove the starter driven gear, chain and the starter drive gear. See **Figure 126**.

Rotor/Starter Gears Inspection

1. Inspect the teeth on the starter driven gear (A, **Figure 127**) and the starter drive gear (B, **Figure 127**). Check for chipped or missing teeth. Replace if necessary.

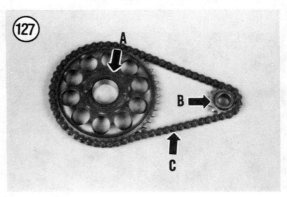

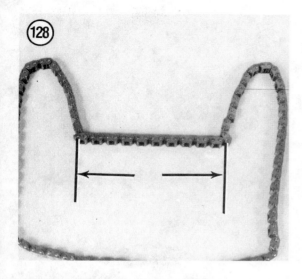

2. Check the drive chain (C, **Figure 127**) for worn or damaged links, pins and side plates. Replace if necessary.

3. Place the drive chain on the workbench and pull it tight. Measure the length of 21 pins (20 links) with a vernier caliper (**Figure 128**). Replace the starter chain if the specified length exceeds 159 mm (6.230 in.).

4. Check the rollers (**Figure 129**) in the starter clutch for uneven or excessive wear; replace as a set if any are bad.

5. To replace the rollers, perform the following:

  a. Remove the rollers (**Figure 129**).

  b. Remove the plungers (**Figure 130**).

  c. Remove the springs (**Figure 131**).

  d. If necessary, secure the rotor with a holding tool and remove the 3 Allen bolts (A, **Figure 132**) and remove the starter clutch housing (B, **Figure 132**).

  e. Check the rollers, plungers and springs for wear, cracks or other damage. Replace if necessary.

  f. If the starter clutch housing was removed, install it by applying Loctite 242 (blue) to the threads of the Allen bolts and torque them to 34 N•m (25 ft.-lb.).

  g. Install the spring, plunger and roller (**Figure 133**) into each receptacle in the starter clutch.

Rotor/Starter Gears Installation

1. Inspect the inside of the rotor (**Figure 134**) for small bolts, washers or other metal "trash" that may have been picked up by the magnets. These small metal bits can cause severe damage to the alternator stator assembly.

2. Using electrical contact cleaner, clean the crankshaft taper and the rotor taper.

3. Assemble the starter driven gear, starter chain and the starter drive gear (**Figure 127**) and install them as shown in **Figure 126**.

4. Install the washer (**Figure 125**) and Woodruff key (**Figure 123**).

5. 1nstall the starter chain guide. Apply Loctite 242 (blue) to the guide bolts before installation. Tighten the bolts securely.

6. With your fingers, rotate the starter driven gear counterclockwise and push the rotor assembly (**Figure 135**) all the way on until it seats.

> *CAUTION*
> *Remember, the bolt securing the alternator rotor has left-hand threads. The bolt must be turned counterclockwise for installation.*

7. Install the alternator rotor bolt.

8. Use the same tool set-up used for removal and tighten the bolt *counterclockwise* to the torque specification listed in **Table 2**.

9. Install the alternator cover as described in this chapter.

10. Connect the battery negative lead and install the seat.

Starter Removal/Installation

1. Remove the alternator cover as described in this chapter.

2. Remove the carburetors (Chapter Seven).

3. Disconnect the electrical cable from terminal on starter motor.

4. Remove the starter mounting bolts.

5. Carefully pry the starter towards the right-hand side and out of the starter sprocket and chain.

6. Install by reversing these steps. Apply oil to the starter O-ring before installation.

7. Adjust the throttle cables as described in Chapter Three.

CRANKCASE

Service to the lower end requires that the crankcase assembly be removed from the motorcycle frame and disassembled (split).

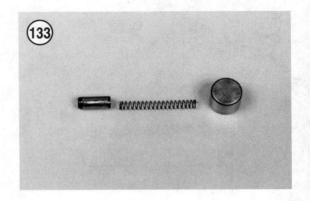

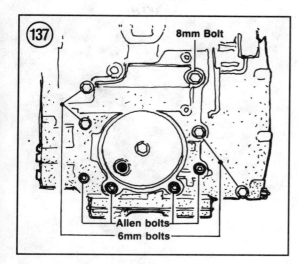

137 8mm Bolt

Allen bolts
6mm bolts

LOWER CASE MOUNTING BOLT TIGHTENING SEQUENCE

138

Disassembly

1. Remove the engine as described in this chapter. Remove all exterior assemblies from the crankcase as described in this chapter and other related chapters.

2. Remove the oil line (**Figure 136**).

3. Remove the upper crankcase bolts (**Figure 137**) in the following order:

    a. 6 mm bolts.

    b. Allen bolts.

    c. 8 mm bolt.

4. Turn the engine so that the bottom end faces up. Remove the following parts:

    a. Oil pan.

    b. Oil pump outer pipe.

    c. Main oil pipe.

5. Loosen the lower crankcase bolts in the following order by reversing the bolt tightening sequence in **Figure 138**:

    a. 6 mm bolts.

    b. 8 mm bolts.

    c. Remove the bolts.

6. Lift the breather pipe (**Figure 139**) out of the upper crankcase and leave it in place.

7. Using a soft-faced mallet, tap around the perimeter of the crankcase and remove the lower crankcase half.

8. After separating the crankcase halves, the transmission and crankshaft and balancer shaft assemblies will stay in the upper crankcase half.

9. Remove the 2 dowel pins. See **Figure 140** and **Figure 141**.

10. Remove the chain guide locking pin (**Figure 142**).

11. Remove the transmission, shift forks and shift drum assemblies as described in Chapter Six.

140

139

12. Remove the crankshaft assembly as described in this chapter.

13. Remove the balancer shaft as described in this chapter.

14. Remove the front cam chain guide (**Figure 143**).

15. Remove the upper (**Figure 144**) and lower (**Figure 145**) primary chain guides.

16. Remove the crankshaft and balancer shaft bearing inserts from the upper and lower crankcase halves. See **Figure 146**. Mark the backsides of the inserts so they can be reinstalled into the same positions.

Inspection

1. Thoroughly clean the inside and outside of both crankcase halves with cleaning solvent. Dry with compressed air. Make sure there is no solvent residue left in the cases as it will contaminate the engine oil.

2. Make sure all oil passages are clean; blow them out with compressed air.

3. Check the crankcases for cracks or other damage. Inspect the mating surfaces of both halves. They must be free of gouges, burrs or any damage that could cause an oil leak.

4. Inspect the crankshaft and balancer shaft bearing inserts as described in this chapter.

Assembly

1. Before installation of all parts, coat all parts with assembly oil or engine oil.

2. Install the crankshaft and balancer shaft bearing inserts in both the upper and lower crankcase halves (**Figure 146**). If reusing old bearings, make sure that they are installed in the same location. Refer to marks made in *Disassembly,* Step 16. Make sure they are locked in place (**Figure 147**).

3. Install the cam chain and primary chain tensioners.

4. Install the crankshaft/clutch housing/primary chain assembly as described in this chapter.

5. Install the balancer shaft as described in this chapter. Make sure the balancer shaft-to-crankshaft timing marks are aligned. See *Balancer Shaft Removal/Installation.*

6. Install the shift drum, shift forks and transmission assemblies as described in Chapter Six.

CAUTION
*When installing the transmission shaft assemblies, make sure the dowel pins (A, **Figure 148**) and both 1/2 circlips (B, **Figure 148**) are in place in the upper crankcase before installing the transmission assemblies. See Chapter Six.*

7. Make sure the case half sealing surfaces are perfectly clean and dry.

8. Install the 2 locating dowel pins. See **Figure 140** and **Figure 141**.

9. Install the front cam chain locking pin (**Figure 142**). Make sure the chain guide is positioned correctly and that the pin does not protrude above the crankcase mating surface.

10. Apply a light coat of gasket sealer to the sealing surfaces of both halves. Cover only flat surfaces, not curved bearing surfaces. Make the coating as thin as possible. Do not apply sealant close to the edge of the bearing inserts (**Figure 149**) as it would restrict oil flow and cause damage.

NOTE
Use Gasgacinch Gasket Sealer, Three Bond or equivalent. A black colored silicone sealant (RTV) works well and blends with the black crankcases.

11. In the upper crankcase, position the shift drum into NEUTRAL. The shift forks should be located in the approximate positions shown in **Figure 150**.

NOTE
*When the transmission is in neutral, the gear positioning lever will be engaged with the shift drum cam detent. See **Figure 151**.*

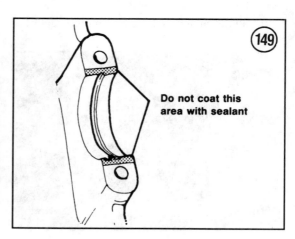

Do not coat this area with sealant

12. Position the lower crankcase onto the upper crankcase. Set the front portion down first and lower the rear while making sure the shift forks engage properly into the transmission assemblies.

13. Lower the crankcase completely.

> *CAUTION*
> *Do not install any crankcase bolts until the sealing surface around the entire crankcase perimeter has seated completely.*

14. Before installing the bolts, slowly spin the transmission shafts and shift the transmission through all 6 gears. This is done to check that the shift forks are properly engaged.

15. Install the breather pipe so that it fits into the passage in the upper crankcase (**Figure 139**).

16. Apply oil to the threads of all lower crankcase bolts and install them.

17. Tighten the 8 mm bolts in two stages in the torque sequence shown in **Figure 138**. Tighten to the following specifications:

    a. Stage 1: 14 N•m. (10 ft.-lb.).

    b. Stage 2: 27 N•m. (20 ft.-lb.).

18. Tighten the 6 mm bolts to 12 N•m (9 ft.-lb.).

19. Turn the crankcase assembly over and install all upper crankcase bolts only finger-tight (**Figure 137**). Tighten the bolts in the following sequence and to the following specifications:

    a. 8 mm bolt: 27 N•m (20 ft.-lb.).

    b. Allen bolts: 12 N•m (9 ft.-lb.).

    c. 6 mm bolts: 12 N•m (9 ft.-lb.).

20. Install the oil pan.

21. Reverse Step 1 and Step 2 and install all engine assemblies that were removed.

22. Install the engine as described in this chapter.

CRANKSHAFT AND CONNECTING RODS

Removal/Installation

1. Split the crankcase as described in this chapter.

2. Remove the transmission countershaft (**Figure 152**).

3. Lift the clutch housing (A, **Figure 153**) and remove the mainshaft (B, **Figure 153**).

4. Remove the washer (**Figure 154**) and spacer (**Figure 155**) from the clutch housing.

5. Remove the clutch housing, primary chain and crankshaft as an assembly. See **Figure 156**.

6. Slip the primary chain off of the clutch housing sprocket and separate the crankshaft/clutch housing assembly. See **Figure 157**.

7. If it is necessary to remove the bearing inserts, refer to *Crankcase Disassembly* in this chapter.

8. Installation is the reverse of these steps. Note the following.

9. When installing the transmission shaft assemblies, make sure the dowel pins (A, **Figure 148**) and both 1/2 circlips (B, **Figure 148**) are in place in the upper crankcase before installing the transmission assemblies.

10. When installing the crankshaft, align the match mark on the crankshaft drive gear with the match mark on the balancer shaft drive gear. See **Figure 158**.

11. If removed, install the primary (A, **Figure 159**) and camshaft (B, **Figure 159**) drive chains over the crankshaft.

Crankshaft Inspection

1. Clean crankshaft thoroughly with solvent. Clean oil holes with rifle cleaning brushes; flush thoroughly and dry with compressed air. Lightly oil all oil journal surfaces immediately to prevent rust.

2. Inspect each journal (**Figure 160**) for scratches, ridges, scoring, nicks, etc.

3. If the surface on all journals is satisfactory, measure the journals with a micrometer and check out-of-roundness, taper and wear on the journals. Check against measurements given in **Table 1**.

4. Inspect the primary (A, **Figure 161**) and cam (B, **Figure 161**) chain drive sprockets. If they are worn or damaged, the crankshaft will have to be replaced.

5. Inspect both the drive chains (**Figure 162**). Stretch each chain tight and measure a 20 link length (**Figure 163**). If the length from the 1st pin to the 21st pin exceeds the limit in **Table 1**, install a new chain.

Clutch Housing Inspection

1. Lift the oil pump drive gear (**Figure 164**) off of the clutch housing.

2. Inspect the oil pump drive gear pin (**Figure 165**) for wear or looseness. Also check the gear teeth for wear, flaking or cracks. Replace the gear if necessary.

3. Inspect the pin hole in the clutch housing (**Figure 166**) for enlargement or cracks. Replace the clutch housing if necessary.

4. Check the slots in the clutch housing (**Figure 167**) for cracks, nicks or galling where they come in contact with the clutch friction disc tabs. If severe damage is evident, the housing must be replaced.

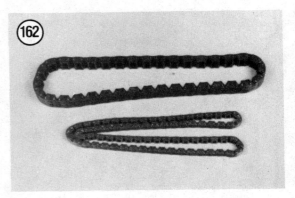

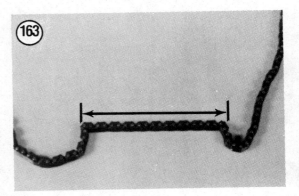

5. Slide the spacer into the clutch housing bushing and check for excessive wear (**Figure 168**). Replace the housing or bushing if necessary.

6. Install the oil pump drive gear onto the clutch housing by reversing Step 1.

Crankshaft Main Bearing Clearance Measurement

1. Check the inside and outside surfaces of the bearing inserts for wear, bluish tint (burned), flaking abrasion and scoring. If the bearings are good, they may be reused. If any insert is questionable, replace the entire set.

2. Clean the bearing surfaces of the crankshaft and the main bearing inserts.

3. Measure the main bearing clearance by performing the following steps.

4. Set the upper crankcase upside down on the workbench on wood blocks.

5. Install the existing main bearing inserts into the upper crankcase.

6. Install the crankshaft into the upper crankcase.

7. Place a piece of Plastigage over each main bearing journal parallel to the crankshaft.

CAUTION
Do not rotate crankshaft while Plastigage is in place.

8. Install the existing bearing inserts into the lower crankcase.

9. Install the lower crankcase over the upper crankcase. Install and tighten the lower crankcase 8 mm bolts as described under *Crankcase Assembly* in this chapter.

10. Remove the 8 mm bolts in the reverse order of installation.

11. Carefully remove the lower crankcase and measure width of flattened Plastigage according to the manufacturer's instructions (**Figure 169**). Measure at both ends of the strip. A difference of 0.025 mm (0.001 in.) or more indicates a tapered crankpin. Confirm with a micrometer. Remove the Plastigage strips from all bearing journals.

12. New bearing clearance should be 0.020-0.044 mm (0.0008-0.0017 in.) with a service limit of 0.08 mm (0.0031 in.). Remove the Plastigage strips from all bearing journals.

13. If the bearing clearance is greater than specified, use the following steps for new bearing selection.

14. If the bearing clearance is between 0.044 mm (0.0017 in.) and 0.08 mm (0.0031 in.), replace the bearing inserts with factory inserts painted blue and recheck the bearing clearance. Always replace all 8 inserts at the same time. The clearance may exceed 0.044 mm (0.0017 in.) slightly but it must not be less than the minimum clearance of 0.020 mm (0.0008 in.) or bearing seizure will occur.

15. If the bearing clearance exceeds the service limit, measure the crankshaft journal OD with a micrometer. See **Table 1** for specifications. If any journal exceeds the wear limit, replace the crankshaft.

16. If the crankshaft has been replaced, determine new bearing inserts as follows:

    a. Purchase a new crankshaft. Then cross-reference the main journal crankshaft diameter markings (**Figure 170**) with the upper crank-

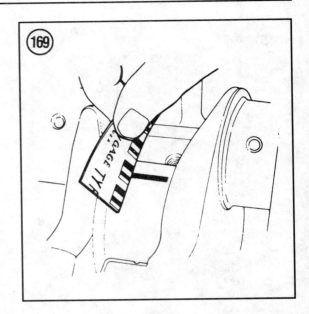

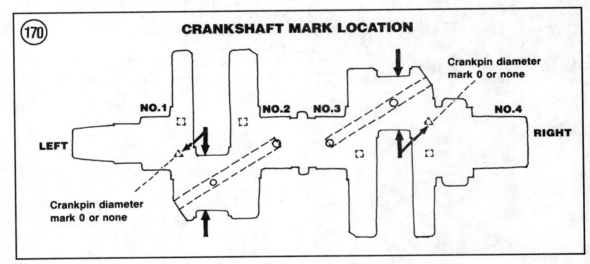

CRANKSHAFT MARK LOCATION

Crankpin diameter mark 0 or none

NO.1 NO.2 NO.3 NO.4

LEFT RIGHT

Crankpin diameter mark 0 or none

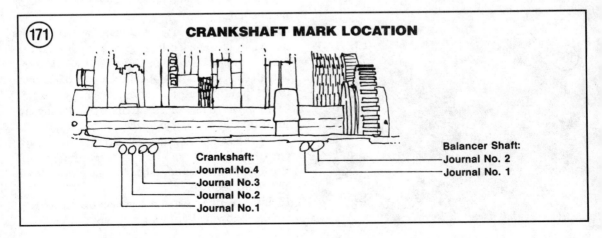

CRANKSHAFT MARK LOCATION

Crankshaft:
Journal No.4
Journal No.3
Journal No.2
Journal No.1

Balancer Shaft:
Journal No. 2
Journal No. 1

case half marks (**Figure 171**). Record these marks and take them to a Kawasaki dealer for new crankshaft main bearing inserts.

b. Recheck the clearance with the new inserts and crankshaft. The clearance should be less than the service limit and as close to the standard as possible, but not less than the standard.

17. Clean and oil the main bearing journals and insert faces.

Connecting Rod Removal/Installation

1. Before disassembly, mark the rods and caps with a "1" and "2" starting from the left-hand side.

2. Remove the connecting rod cap nuts (**Figure 172**) and separate the rods from the crankshaft. Keep each cap with its original rod, with the weight mark on the end of the cap matching the mark on the rod (B, **Figure 173**).

> *CAUTION*
> *Keep each bearing insert in its original place in the crankcase, rod or rod cap. If you are going to assemble the engine with the original inserts, they must be installed exactly as removed in order to prevent rapid wear.*

3. Install by reversing these removal steps while noting the following procedures.

4. Install the bearing inserts into each connecting rod and cap. Make sure they are locked in place correctly.

5. Apply assembly lube to the bearing inserts.

6. If new bearing inserts are going to be installed, check the bearing clearance as described in this chapter.

7. Tighten the connecting rod nuts to torque specifications in **Table 2**.

Connecting Rod Inspection

1. Check each rod for obvious damage such as cracks and burns.

2. Check the piston pin bushing for wear or scoring.

3. Take the rods to a machine shop and have them checked for twisting and bending.

4. Examine the bearing inserts for wear, scoring or burning. They are reusable if in good condition. Make a note of the bearing size (if any) stamped on the back of the insert if the bearing is to be discarded; a previous owner may have used undersize bearings.

5. Remove the connecting rod bearing bolts and check them for cracks or twisting. Replace any bolts as required.

6. Check bearing clearance as described in this chapter.

Connecting Rod Bearing and Clearance Measurement

> *CAUTION*
> *If the old bearings are to be reused, be sure that they are installed in their exact original locations.*

1. Wipe bearing inserts and crankpins clean. Install bearing inserts in rod and cap.

2. Place a piece of Plastigage on one crankpin parallel to the crankshaft.

3. Install rod and cap. Tighten nuts to torque specifications in **Table 2**.

> *CAUTION*
> *Do not rotate crankshaft while Plastigage is in place.*

4. Remove rod cap.

5. Measure width of flattened Plastigage according to the manufacturer's instructions (**Figure 174**). Measure at both ends of the strip. A difference of 0.025 mm (0.001 in.) or more indicates a tapered crankpin; the crankshaft must be replaced. Confirm with a micrometer measurement of the journal OD.

6. If the crankpin taper is within tolerance, measure the bearing clearance with the same strip of Plastigage. Correct bearing clearance is specified in **Table 1**. Remove Plastigage strips.

7. If the bearing clearance is greater than specified, use the following steps for new bearing selection.

8. New bearing clearance should be 0.036-0.066 mm (0.0014-0.0025 in.) with a service limit of 0.10 mm (0.0039 in.). Remove the Plastigage strips from all bearing journals.

9. If the bearing clearance is greater than specified, use the following steps for new bearing selection.

10. If the bearing clearance is between 0.066 mm (0.0025 in.) and 0.10 mm (0.0039 in.), replace the bearing inserts with factory inserts painted blue and recheck the bearing clearance. Always replace all 4 inserts at the same time. The clearance may slightly exceed 0.066 mm (0.0025 in.), but it must not be less than the minimum clearance of 0.036 mm (0.0014 in.) or bearing seizure will occur.

11. If the bearing clearance exceeds the service limit, measure the crankshaft journal OD with a micrometer. See **Table 1** for specifications. If any journal exceeds the wear limit, replace the crankshaft.

12. If the crankshaft has been replaced, determine new bearing inserts as follows:

   a. Purchase a new crankshaft. Then cross-reference the crankpin journal diameter markings (**Figure 170**) with the connecting rod mark (**Figure 175**). The connecting rod will be marked with a 0 around the weight mark or there will be no 0 around the weight mark. Record these marks and take them to a Kawasaki dealer for new bearing inserts.

   b. Recheck the clearance with the new inserts and crankshaft. The clearance should be less

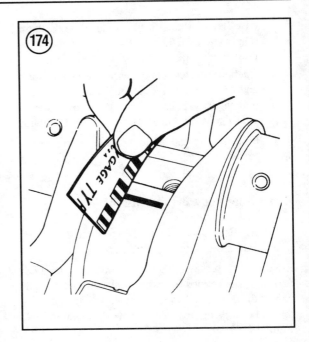

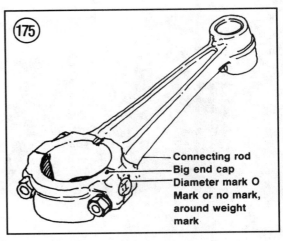

Connecting rod
Big end cap
Diameter mark O
Mark or no mark, around weight mark

than the service limit and as close to the standard as possible, but not less than the standard.

13. Clean and oil the main bearing journals and insert faces.

14. After new bearings have been installed, recheck clearance with Plastigage. If the clearance is out of specifications, either the connecting rod or the crankshaft is worn beyond the service limit. Refer the engine to a dealer or qualified specialist.

BALANCER SHAFT

Removal/Installation

1. Split the crankcase as described in this chapter.

2. Lift the balancer shaft out of the engine (**Figure 176**).

3. If it is necessary to remove the bearing inserts, refer to *Crankcase Disassembly* in this chapter.

4. Installation is the reverse of these steps while noting the following.

5. Apply assembly lube to the balancer shaft bearing inserts before installing the shaft.

⑰

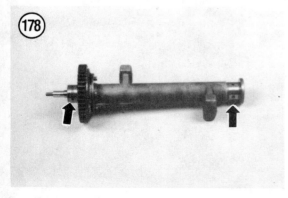

⑱

6. When installing the balancer shaft, align the match mark on the crankshaft drive gear with the match mark on the balancer shaft drive gear. See **Figure 177**.

Balancer Shaft Inspection

1. Clean balancer shaft thoroughly with solvent. Clean oil holes with rifle cleaning brushes; flush thoroughly and dry with compressed air. Lightly oil all oil journal surfaces immediately to prevent rust.

2. Inspect each journal (**Figure 178**) for scratches, ridges, scoring, nicks, etc.

3. If the surface on all journals is satisfactory, measure the journals with a micrometer and check out-of-roundness, taper and wear on the journals. Check against measurements given in **Table 1**.

Balancer Shaft Bearing Clearance Measurement

1. Check the inside and outside surfaces of the bearing inserts for wear, bluish tint (burned), flaking, abrasion and scoring. If the bearings are good, they may be reused. If any insert is questionable, replace the entire set.

2. Clean the bearing surfaces of the balancer shaft and the bearing inserts.

3. Measure the balancer shaft bearing clearance by performing the following steps.

4. Set the upper crankcase upside down on the workbench on wood blocks.

5. Install the existing balancer shaft inserts into the upper crankcase.

6. Install the balancer shaft into the upper crankcase.

7. Place a piece of Plastigage over each main bearing journal parallel to the balancer shaft.

> *CAUTION*
> *Do not rotate balancer shaft while Plastigage is in place.*

8. Install the existing bearing inserts into the lower crankcase.

9. Install the lower crankcase over the upper crankcase. Install and tighten the lower crankcase 8 mm bolts as described under *Crankcase Assembly* in this chapter.

10. Remove the 8 mm bolts in the reverse order of installation.

11. Carefully remove the lower crankcase and measure width of flattened Plastigage according to the manufacturer's instructions (**Figure 174**). Measure at both ends of the strip. A difference of 0.025 mm (0.001 in.) or more indicates a tapered journal. Confirm with a micrometer. Remove the Plastigage strips from all bearing journals.

12. New bearing clearance should be 0.020-0.050 mm (0.0008-0.0019 in.) with a service limit of 0.09 mm (0.0035 in.). Remove the Plastigage strips from all bearing journals.

13. If the bearing clearance is greater than specified, use the following steps for new bearing selection.

14. If the bearing clearance is between 0.050 mm (0.0019 in.) and 0.08 mm (0.003 in.), replace the bearing inserts with factory inserts painted blue and recheck the bearing clearance. Always replace all 4 inserts at the same time. The clearance may slightly exceed 0.050 mm (0.0019 in.), but it must not be less than the minimum clearance of 0.020 mm (0.0008 in.) or bearing seizure will occur.

15. If the bearing clearance exceeds the service limit, measure the balancer shaft journal OD with a micrometer. See **Table 1** for specifications. If any journal exceeds the wear limit, replace the balancer shaft.

16. If the balancer shaft has been replaced, determine new bearing inserts as follows:

 a. Purchase a new balancer shaft. Then cross-reference the journal balancer shaft diameter markings (**Figure 179**) with the upper crankcase half marks (**Figure 171**). Record these marks and take them to a Kawasaki dealer for new balancer shaft bearing inserts.

 b. Recheck the clearance with the new inserts and balancer shaft. The clearance should be less than the service limit and as close to the standard as possible, but not less than the standard.

17. Clean and oil the bearing journals and insert races.

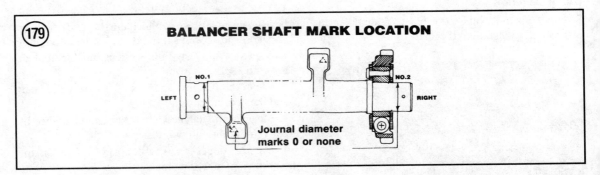

(179)

BALANCER SHAFT MARK LOCATION

NO.1

LEFT

NO.2

RIGHT

Journal diameter marks 0 or none

Table 1 ENGINE SPECIFICATIONS

	Standard mm (in.)	Wear limit mm (in.)
Cam lobe height	35.635-35.761 (1.403-1.408)	35.55 (1.3996)
Camshaft bearing clearance	0.030-0.071 (0.0011-0.0027)	0.16 (0.0006)
Camshaft journal diameter	24.950-24.970 (0.9822-0.9831)	24.92 (0.9811)
Camshaft bearing inside diameter (Cylinder head-to-bearing cap)	25.000-25.021 (0.9842-0.9851)	25.08 (0.9874)
Camshaft runout		0.1 (0.0039)
Camshaft chain (20 link)		128.9 (5.075)
Primary chain 20-link length	190.50-190.97 (7.50-7.52)	193.4 (7.61)
Starter driven gear chain 20-link length	155.5-155.9 (6.12-6.14)	159 (6.26)
Rocker arm inside diameter	12.500-12.518 (0.4921-0.4928)	12.55 (0.4941)
Rocker arm shaft outer diameter	12.466-12.484 (0.4907-0.4915)	12.44 (0.4897)
Cylinder Taper (max.)		0.05 (0.002)
Out of round		0.01 (0.0004)
Cylinder head warpage		0.05 (0.002)
Cylinder diameter	74.000-74.012 (2.9133-2.9138)	74.11 (2.9177)
Piston diameter	73.942-73.957 (2.9110-2.9116)	73.79 (2.9051)
Piston-to-cylinder clearance	0.044-0.070 (0.0017-0.0027)	0.17 (0.0066)
Piston ring groove clearance Top	0.03-0.07 (0.0012-0.0027)	0.17 (0.0067)
Second	0.02-0.06 (0.0007-0.0024)	0.16 (0.0063)
Piston ring groove width Top	0.82-0.86 (0.0322-0.0338)	0.92 (0.0362)
Second	1.01-1.03 (0.0397-0.0405)	1.12 (0.0440)
Oil	2.01-2.03 (0.0791-0.0799)	2.11 (0.0830)
Piston ring thickness Top	0.770-0.790 (0.0303-0.0311)	0.70 (0.0275)
Second	0.97-0.99 (0.0382-0.0389)	0.90 (0.0354)
Piston ring end gap Top and second	0.2-0.35 (0.0078-0.0138)	0.7 (0.0275)
Oil	0.2-0.7 (0.0078-0.275)	1.0 (0.3937)

(continued)

Table 1 ENGINE SPECIFICATIONS (continued)

	Standard mm (in.)	Wear limit mm (in.)
Valve head thickness		
Intake		0.25 (0.0098)
Exhaust		0.7 (0.0276)
Valve stem diameter		
Intake	5.475-5.490 (0.2155-0.2161)	5.46 (0.2149)
Exhaust	5.455-5.470 (0.2148-0.2153)	5.44 (0.2142)
Valve stem runout		0.05 (0.002)
Valve guide inside diameter	5.500-5.512 (0.4915-0.4926)	5.58 (0.4986)
Valve spring free length		
Inner	36.3 (1.429)	35 (1.378)
Outer	40.4 (1.590)	39 (1.535)
Connecting rod side clearance	0.13-0.33 (0.0051-0.0129)	0.50 (0.0197)
Connecting rod bearing clearance	0.036-0.066 (0.0014-0.0025)	0.10 (0.0039)
Crankpin wear limit		37.97 (1.4948)
Crankshaft runout		0.05 (0.002)
Crankshaft journal clearance	0.020-0.044 (0.0008-0.0017)	0.08 (0.0031)
Crankshaft main journal diameter	35.96 (1.4157)	
Crankshaft thrust clearance	0.05-0.25 (0.0019-0.0098)	0.40 (0.0157)
Balancer shaft bearing clearance	0.020-0.050 (0.0008-0.0019)	0.09 (0.0035)
Balancer shaft journal diameter		27.96 (1.1007)
Oil pump		
Inner rotor clearance		0.20 (0.0078)
Pump body clearance		0.30 (0.0118)
Outer rotor diameter		40.45 (1.5925)
Body inside diameter		40.80 (1.6062)
Rotor end clearance		0.12 (0.0047)

Table 2 ENGINE TIGHTENING TORQUES

	N·m	ft.-lb.
Rocker arm shafts	39	29
Rocker arm bearing caps	12	9
Cylinder head cover bolts	9.8	7.2
Cylinder head bolts		
6 mm	9.8	7.2
10 mm	39	29
	(continued)	

Table 2 ENGINE TIGHTENING TORQUES (continued)

	N•m	ft.-lb.
Camshaft cap bolts	12	106 in.-lb.
Camshaft chain tensioner bolts	8.8	78 in.-lb.
Cam sprocket bolts	15	12
Oil line banjo bolts		
At cylinder head	12	106 in.-lb.
At crankcase	20	15
Connecting rod nuts	36	27
Rotor bolts	69	51
Crankcase bolts		
6 mm	12	106 in.-lb.
8 mm	27	20
Allen bolts	12	106 in.-lb.
Engine mount bolts		
Long bolts	39	29
Short bolts	24	18
Oil pan bolts	12	106 in.-lb.

4

CHAPTER FIVE

CLUTCH AND PRIMARY CHAIN

This chapter provides complete service procedures for the clutch and primary chain. **Table 1** (end of chapter) lists clutch wear limits.

CLUTCH AND PRIMARY CHAIN

Removal/Installation

Refer to **Figure 1** for this procedure.

1. Place the bike on the centerstand.
2. Drain the engine oil as described in Chapter Three.
3. Loosen the clutch lever adjustment nut at the handlebar and slacken the clutch cable (**Figure 2**).
4. Remove the bolts securing the clutch cover in place and remove it. See **Figure 3**.

NOTE
It is not necessary to remove the clutch release when removing the clutch cover.

5. Loosen the 5 pressure plate screws in a crisscross pattern. Then remove the screws and springs (**Figure 4**).
6. Remove the pressure plate (**Figure 5**).

7. Remove a friction disc (**Figure 6**) and a clutch plate (**Figure 7**). Continue until all discs and plates are removed. Stack discs and plates in order.

NOTE
*To keep the clutch housing from turning when removing the clutch hub nut in Step 8, use the special tool shown in **Figure 8**. Clutch holding tools are available from K&L Supply Co. dealers.*

8. Straighten out the locking tab on the clutch nut and remove the clutch nut (**Figure 9**).
9. Remove the clutch boss (**Figure 10**) and thrust washer (**Figure 11**).
10. The clutch housing and primary chain (**Figure 12**) cannot be removed until the engine is removed and the crankcase disassembled. Refer to *Crankshaft Removal/Installation* in Chapter Four.
11. Inspect the clutch components as described in this chapter.
12. Installation is the reverse of these steps. Note the following.
13. Because the clutch nut is a self-locking nut, Kawasaki recommends replacing the nut every time it is removed. Install a new clutch nut (**Figure 9**). Tighten the nut to 130 N·m (96 ft.-lb.).

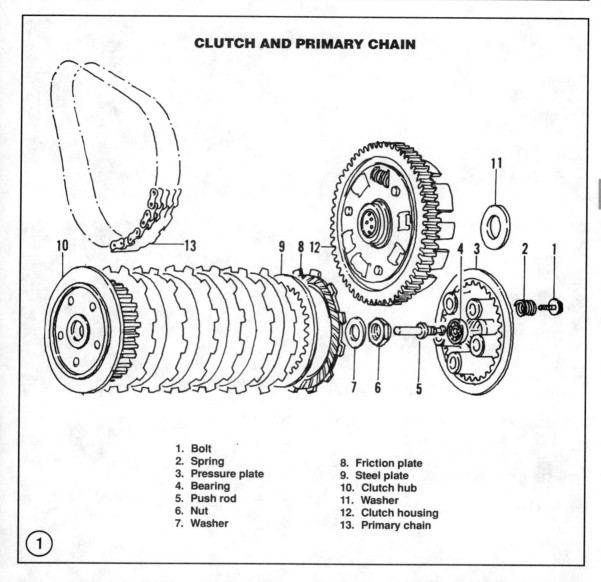

CLUTCH AND PRIMARY CHAIN

1. Bolt
2. Spring
3. Pressure plate
4. Bearing
5. Push rod
6. Nut
7. Washer
8. Friction plate
9. Steel plate
10. Clutch hub
11. Washer
12. Clutch housing
13. Primary chain

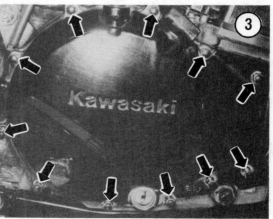

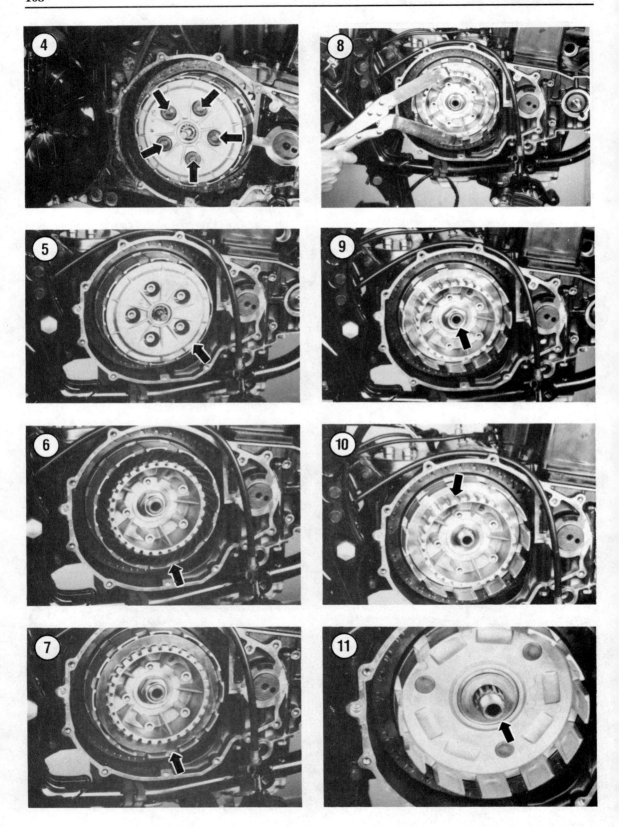

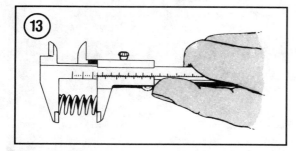

NOTE
Use the same tool as during removal to prevent the clutch boss from turning when tightening the clutch nut.

14. Install the friction plates so that the grooves on the side of the plate, facing to the right-hand side, run in a counterclockwise direction.

15. Tighten the clutch spring bolts to 9.3 N•m (82 in.-lb.).

16. Refill the engine oil as described in Chapter Three.

17. Adjust the clutch as described in Chapter Three.

Inspection

1. Clean all clutch parts in a petroleum-based solvent such as kerosene, and thoroughly dry with compressed air.

2. Measure the free length of each clutch spring as shown in **Figure 13**. Replace any springs (**Figure 14**) that are too short (**Table 1**).

3. Measure the thickness of each friction disc at several places around the disc as shown in **Figure 15**. See **Table 1** for specifications. Replace all friction discs if any one is found too thin. Do not replace only 1 or 2 discs.

4. Check the clutch metal plates (**Figure 16**) for warpage as shown in **Figure 17**. If any plate is warped more than specified (**Table 1**), replace the entire set of plates. Do not replace only 1 or 2 plates.

5. Inspect the clutch boss assembly (**Figure 18**) for cracks or galling in the grooves where the clutch friction disc tabs slide. They must be smooth for chatter-free clutch operation.

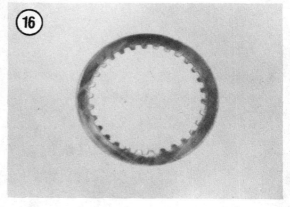

6. Inspect the shaft splines in the clutch boss assembly. If damage is only a slight amount, remove any small burrs with a fine cut file; if damage is severe, replace the assembly.

7. Inspect the clutch release bearing (A, **Figure 19**) and pushrod (**Figure 20**) for wear or damage. Rotate the bearing race and check for excessive play or roughness. Replace if necessary.

8. Inspect the pressure plate (B, **Figure 19**) for signs of wear or damage; replace if necessary.

Primary Chain Removal/Installation

Refer to Chapter Four. Refer to *Crankshaft Removal/Installation*.

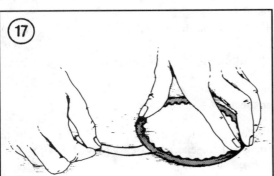

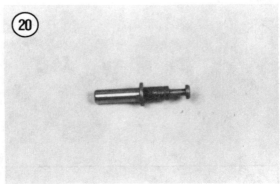

Table 1 CLUTCH WEAR LIMITS

	mm (in.)	limits mm (in.)
Clutch spring free length	34.2 (1.346)	33.1 (1.303)
Friction plate thickness	2.9-3.1 (0.114-0.122)	2.75 (0.108)
Clutch plate warpage		
Friction	less than 0.2 (0.007)	0.3 (0.011)
Steel	less than 0.2 (0.007)	0.3 (0.011)
Friction plate tangs clutch		
housing finger clearance	*	*

* Not specified by Kawasaki

5

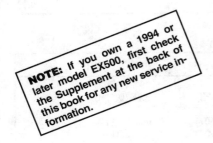
NOTE: If you own a 1994 or later model EX500, first check the Supplement at the back of this book for any new service information.

CHAPTER SIX

TRANSMISSION

This chapter describes complete transmission service procedures. **Table 1** (end of chapter) lists transmission wear limits.

SHIFT MECHANISM

Refer to **Figure 1** for this procedure.

Removal/Installation

1. Remove the front sprocket. Refer to Steps 3-6 under *Drive Chain Removal/Installation* in Chapter Eleven.

2. Drain the engine oil as described in Chapter Three.

3. Remove the linkage rod boot and shift linkage rod (**Figure 2**).

4. Remove the circlip from the shift shaft (A, **Figure 3**).

5. Disconnect the neutral switch electrical connector (**Figure 4**).

6. Remove the bolts securing the shift shaft cover and remove the cover (B, **Figure 3**).

7. Remove the 2 shift shaft cover dowel pins (**Figure 5**) and gasket.

8. Disengage the shift mechanism arm from its position on the shift drum cam by pulling the mechanism arm down (**Figure 6**). Then pull the shift shaft out of the engine together with its arm, spring, shaft return spring and spacer. See **Figure 7**.

9. Remove the gear positioning lever assembly in the following order:
   a. Bolt (A, **Figure 8**).
   b. Washer (**Figure 9**).
   c. Gear positioning lever (**Figure 10**).
   d. Spring (**Figure 11**).
   e. Washer (**Figure 12**).

10. Inspect the shift mechanism assembly as described in this chapter.

11. To install, reverse these steps. Note the following.

12. The gear positioning lever spacer must be installed so that the spacer's small diameter faces toward the crankcase.

13. Align the center of the shift mechanism spring (**Figure 11**) with the pin in the crankcase (B, **Figure 8**) when installing the shift mechanism.

14. Apply a high temperature brake grease to the shift shaft cover seal lips.

15. Tighten front sprocket retaining bolts to 9.8 N·m (87 in.-lb.).

16. Refill the engine oil as described in Chapter Three.

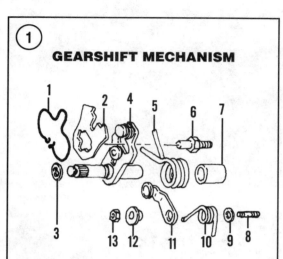

GEARSHIFT MECHANISM

1. Spring
2. Spring mechanism arm
3. Circlip
4. Shift shaft
6. Locating pin
7. Spacer
8. Stud
9. Washer
10. Spring
11. Gear positioning lever
12. Washer
13. Nut

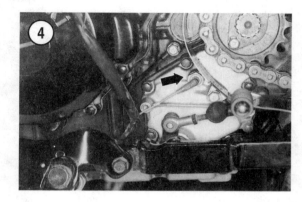

6

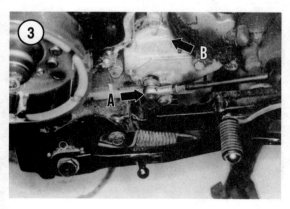

Inspection

1. Check the shift shaft for bending or spline damage (**Figure** 7). If the shaft is bent, it may be straightened by a machine shop. If the splines are damaged, the shaft must be replaced.

2. Check the springs for weakness or damage.

3. Check the shift mechanism arm (**Figure** 7) for distortion or damage.

4. Inspect the shift drum cam and neutral holder for wear or damage.

5. Inspect the gear positioning lever for wear, breakage or distortion.

6. Replace any worn or damaged parts.

TRANSMISSION

Removal/Installation

Refer to **Figure 13** for this procedure.

1. Split the crankcase as described in Chapter Four.

2. Remove the transmission countershaft (**Figure 14**).

3. Lift the clutch housing (A, **Figure 15**) and remove the mainshaft (B, **Figure 15**) from the clutch housing. Set the clutch housing back into the crankcase.

4. Remove the washer (**Figure 16**) and spacer (**Figure 17**) from the clutch housing.

5. Install by reversing these steps. Note the following.

  a. Before installing any components, coat all bearing surfaces with assembly oil.

  b. Install the spacer (**Figure 17**) and washer (**Figure 16**) into the clutch housing.

  c. When installing the transmission shaft assemblies, make sure the dowel pins (A, **Figure 18**) and both 1/2 circlips (B, **Figure 18**) are in

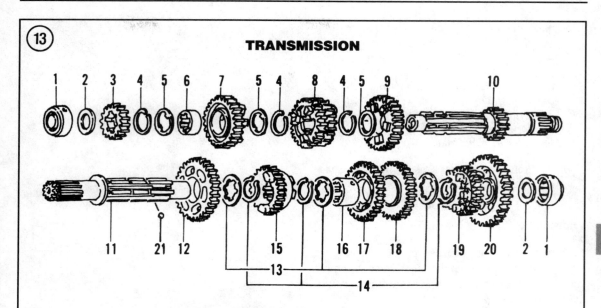

TRANSMISSION

1. Bearing
2. Washer
3. Main shaft 2nd gear
4. Circlip
5. Washer
6. Bearing
7. Main shaft 6th gear
8. Main shaft 3rd/4th gear combination
9. Main shaft 5th gear
10. Main shaft/1st gear
11. Countershaft
12. Countershaft 2nd gear
13. Washers
14. Circlips
15. Countershaft 6th gear
16. Bearing
17. Countershaft 4th gear
18. Countershaft 3rd gear
19. Countershaft 5th gear
20. Countershaft 1st gear

6

place in the upper crankcase before installing the transmission assemblies.

CAUTION
If the mainshaft and countershaft bearings do not engage the dowel pins and 1/2 circlips correctly, there will be no clearance between the crankcase and the outer bearing races.

d. Assemble the crankcase as described in Chapter Four.

Transmission Service Notes

1. A divided container such as an egg carton (**Figure 19**) can be used to help maintain correct alignment and positioning of the parts as they are removed from the transmission shafts.

2. The circlips are a tight fit on the transmission shafts. It is recommended to replace all circlips during reassembly.

3. When removing and installing circlips, they have a tendency to turn sideways and make removal and installation difficult. To ease replacement, open the

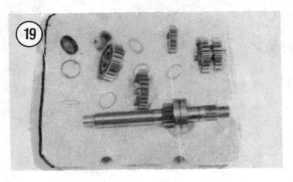

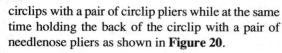

circlips with a pair of circlip pliers while at the same time holding the back of the circlip with a pair of needlenose pliers as shown in **Figure 20**.

Mainshaft Disassembly/Assembly

Refer to **Figure 13** for the following procedure.

1. Remove the seal (**Figure 21**) and bearing (**Figure 22**).

2. Remove the washer (**Figure 23**) and slide off 2nd gear (**Figure 24**).

3. Remove the circlip and washer (**Figure 25**).

4. Slide off 6th gear (**Figure 26**).

5. Remove the washer and circlip (**Figure 27**) and slide off the 4th/3rd gear combination (**Figure 28**).

6. Remove the circlip and washer (**Figure 29**) and slide off 5th gear (**Figure 30**).

7. If necessary, remove the mainshaft bearing (**Figure 31**) with a bearing puller.

8. Inspect the mainshaft assembly as described in this chapter.

9. Assemble by reversing these disassembly steps. Note the following.

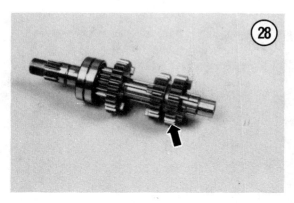

10. Install the splined washers and circlips as shown in **Figure 32**.

11. Align the 6th gear bushing oil hole with the hole in the mainshaft (**Figure 33**).

12. Refer to **Figure 34** for correct placement of the gears.

13. Make sure each gear engages properly to the adjoining gear where applicable.

Countershaft Disassembly/Assembly

Refer to **Figure 13** for the following procedure.

1. Slide the needle bearing (**Figure 35**) off the countershaft.

2. Remove the washer (**Figure 36**) and slide off 1st gear (**Figure 37**).

3. Remove 5th gear (**Figure 38**) as follows. The 5th gear (**Figure 39**) has 3 steel balls located between the gear and the shaft. These are used for NEUTRAL location when shifting from 1st gear. To remove the gear, spin the shaft in a vertical position while holding onto 3rd gear. Pull 5th gear up and off the shaft.

4. Remove the circlip and washer (**Figure 40**).

5. Slide off 3rd (**Figure 41**).

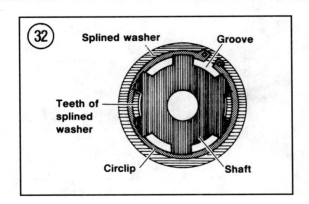

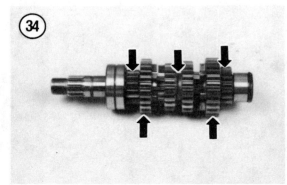

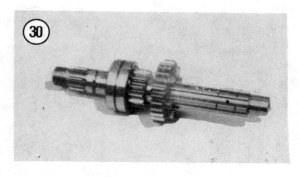

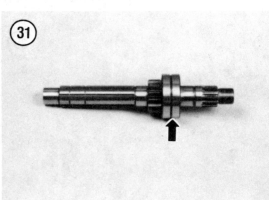

6. Slide off 4th gear (**Figure 42**) and its bushing (**Figure 43**).

7. Remove the washer and circlip (**Figure 44**) and slide off 6th gear (**Figure 45**).

8. Remove the circlip and washer (**Figure 46**) and slide off 2nd gear (**Figure 47**).

9. Remove the oil seal (A, **Figure 48**).

10. If necessary, remove the bearing (B, **Figure 48**) with a bearing puller.

11. Inspect the countershaft assembly as described in this chapter.

12. Assemble by reversing these disassembly steps. Note the following.

13. Install the splined washers and circlips as shown in **Figure 32**.

14. Align the 4th gear bushing oil hole with the hole in the countershaft (**Figure 43**).

15. When installing the 3 balls (**Figure 39**) into the 5th gear, *do not use grease* to hold them in place. The balls must be able to move freely during normal transmission operation.

16. Refer to **Figure 49** for correct placement of the gears.

17. Make sure each gear engages properly to the adjoining gear where applicable.

Inspection

1. Clean all parts in cleaning solvent and dry thoroughly.

2. Inspect the gears visually for cracks, chips, broken teeth and burnt teeth. Check the lugs (**Figure 50**) on ends of gears to make sure they are not rounded off. If lugs are rounded off, check the shift forks as

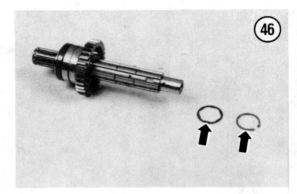

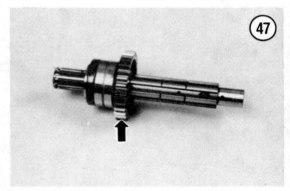

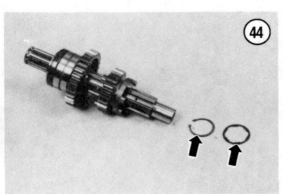

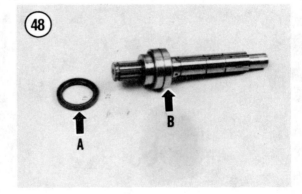

described later in this chapter. More than likely one or more of the shift forks is bent.

> *NOTE*
> *Defective gears should be replaced. It is a good idea to replace the mating gear even though it may not show as much wear or damage. Remember that accelerated wear to new parts is normally caused by contact from worn parts.*

3. Inspect all free wheeling gear bearing surfaces for wear, discoloration and galling. Inspect the mating shaft bearing surface also. If there is any metal flaking or visible damage, replace both parts. See **Figure 51**.

4. Inspect the mainshaft and countershaft splines for wear or discoloration. Check the mating gear internal splines also. If no visible damage is apparent, install each sliding gear on its respective shaft and work the gear back and forth to make sure gear operates smoothly.

5. Replace any washers that show wear.

6. Discard the circlips and replace them during assembly.

7. Inspect the needle bearings and their housings (**Figure 52**) for wear or damage. Replace if necessary.

8. Check the countershaft slot (**Figure 53**) where the 5th gear ball bearings engage. If the slot is worn or damaged, the countershaft must be replaced.

6

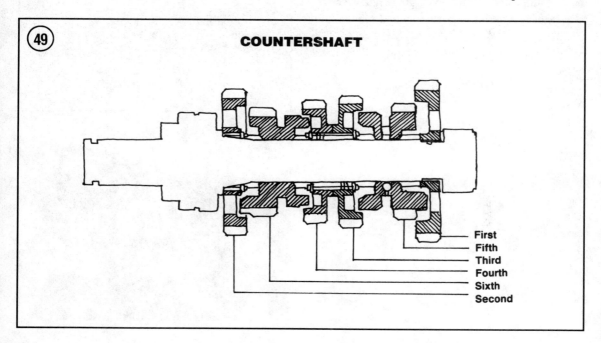

(49) **COUNTERSHAFT**

First
Fifth
Third
Fourth
Sixth
Second

(50)

(51)

Shift Drum and Forks Removal/Installation

Refer to **Figure 54**.

1. Remove the mainshaft and countershaft as described in this chapter.

2. Remove the shift drum mounting bolts (A, **Figure 55**).

NOTE
Label the shift forks so that they can be reinstalled in their original positions.

3. Remove the shift fork shaft (B, **Figure 55**) and remove the 2 shift forks (**Figure 56**) from the lower crankcase. See **Figure 57**.

4. Remove the cotter pin (**Figure 58**). Then remove the 3rd/4th gear shift fork guide pin (**Figure 59**).

5. Pull the shift drum out partway and remove the 3rd/4th gear shift fork (**Figure 60**).

6. Pull the shift drum (**Figure 61**) out of the crankcase.

7. Inspect the shift drum and fork assembly as described in this chapter.

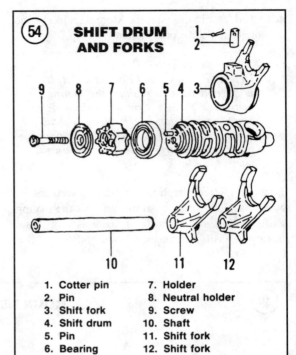

54 SHIFT DRUM AND FORKS

1. Cotter pin	7. Holder
2. Pin	8. Neutral holder
3. Shift fork	9. Screw
4. Shift drum	10. Shaft
5. Pin	11. Shift fork
6. Bearing	12. Shift fork

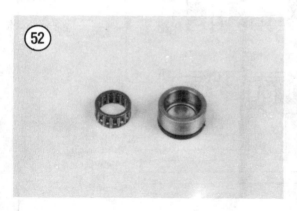

8. Insert the shift drum partway into the crankcase (**Figure 61**).

9. Install the 3rd/4th gear shift fork onto the shift drum so that the long end faces toward the neutral switch (**Figure 60**).

10. Push the shift drum in all the way (**Figure 62**).

11. Apply Loctite 242 (blue) to the shift drum mounting bolts and tighten them securely. See A, **Figure 55**.

12. Align the guide pin hole in the shift fork with the middle shift drum groove. Then install the guide pin (**Figure 59**) and secure it with a new cotter pin. Bend the cotter pin over to lock it. See **Figure 58**.

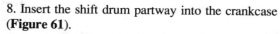

NOTE
When bending the cotter pin over, spread the cotter pin so that the long end faces inward.

13. Place the shift forks into the upper crankcase so that the long end of each fork faces toward the external shift mechanism. See **Figure 56**.

14. Slide the shift shaft through the crankcase and engage both shift forks.

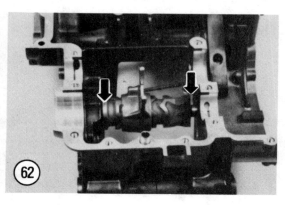

Shift Drum Disassembly

1. Remove the screw (**Figure 64**) from the end of the shift drum. Then remove the following parts:
   a. Neutral holder (**Figure 65**).
   b. Shift drum cam (**Figure 66**).
   c. Ball bearing (**Figure 67**).
   d. Dowel pin (**Figure 68**).

2. Inspect the shift drum as described in this section.

3. Install the dowel pin (**Figure 69**) into the largest hole in the end of the shift drum.

4. Install the ball bearing (**Figure 67**).

5. Align the groove in the end of the shift drum cam (**Figure 70**) with the dowel pin (**Figure 68**) and install the cam.

6. The shift drum cam has 6 points, of which 1 point is higher than the other 5 (**Figure 71**). Align the highest point with the back of the neutral holder and install the neutral holder (**Figure 65**).

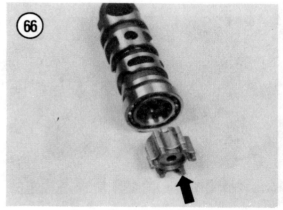

> *NOTE*
> *If the neutral holder is installed incorrectly, the neutral indicator light will not light when the transmission is in NEUTRAL.*

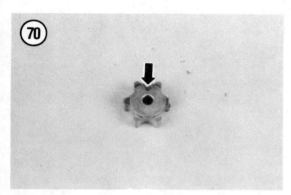

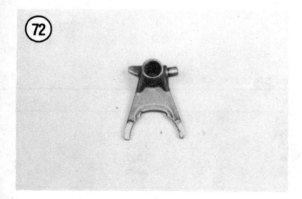

7. Apply Loctite 242 (blue) to the screw and install it into the shift drum. Tighten the screw securely.

Inspection

1. Inspect each shift fork for signs of wear or cracking. See **Figure 72** and **Figure 73**. Examine the shift forks at the points where they contact the slider gear. This surface should be smooth with no signs of wear or damage. Make sure the forks slide smoothly on the shaft (**Figure 74**) or shift drum (**Figure 63**). Make sure the shaft is not bent. This can be checked by removing the shift forks from the shaft and rolling the shaft (**Figure 75**) on a piece of plate glass. Any clicking noise detected indicates that the shaft is bent.

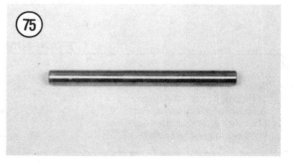

2. Measure the thickness of each shift fork finger. Compare to the specifications in **Table 1**. Replace a shift fork if the finger thickness is too thin.

3. Check grooves in the shift drum (**Figure 76**) for wear or roughness. Measure the grooves with a vernier caliper. Replace the shift drum if any groove is too wide (**Table 1**).

4. Measure the shift fork guide pin diameters with a micrometer. Replace the shift fork if the guide pin diameter is too small (**Table 1**).

5. Check the shift drum bearing. Make sure it operates smoothly with no signs of wear or damage.

6. Inspect the neutral holder (**Figure 77**) for wear, damage or roughness. Replace if necessary.

Table 1 TRANSMISSION SPECIFICATIONS

	mm	in.
Gear backlash	0.23	0.009
Shift fork finger thickness	4.8	0.189
Gear shift fork groove width	5.3	0.208
Shift fork guide pin diameter	7.8	0.307
Shift drum groove width	8.3	0.3267

CHAPTER SEVEN

FUEL, EMISSION CONTROL AND EXHAUST SYSTEM

This chapter describes complete procedures for servicing the fuel, emission control and exhaust systems. **Table 1** (end of chapter) lists carburetor specifications.

FUEL TANK

Removal/Installation

1. Remove the seat.
2. Remove the bolt (**Figure 1A**) at the rear of the fuel tank.
3. Remove the left and right side covers.
4. Remove the outer side fairing screws located underneath the rear of the fairing.
5. Turn fuel valve to "OFF" position.

WARNING
Make sure work area is well ventilated. Keep fuel at least 50 feet from any open flame. Do not smoke. Wipe up spills immediately.

6. Remove hoses from tank and fuel valve.
7. *California models*: Plug the fuel return fitting to prevent gasoline from flowing into the canister.

8. Tilt the rear of the tank upward, then remove the tank from the frame by lifting toward the rear.
9. Reverse removal procedure to install the fuel tank.
10. Securely tighten tank retaining bolt (**Figure 1A**).
11. Check for fuel leaks and repair immediately if noted.

AIR FILTER HOUSING

Removal/Installation

1. Remove the seat and side covers.
2. Remove the junction box bracket and pull the junction box to one side.
3. Remove the air cleaner housing side covers.
4. Disconnect battery terminals (negative side first) and remove the battery.
5. Disconnect the air suction valve hose (U.S. models) from the air filter housing.
6. Remove the rear tension springs (**Figure 2**) from their grooves and remove the carburetor-to-air filter housing rubber boots.
7. Remove the engine breather hose.
8. Pull out air cleaner housing.

9. Installation is the reverse of these steps.

AIR FILTER ELEMENT CLEANING

Refer to *Air Filter Cleaning/Inspection* in Chapter Three.

CARBURETOR

Removal/Installation

1. Park the motorcycle on the centerstand.
2. Remove fairing assembly, side rails and both side covers. See Chapter Thirteen.
3. Remove the fuel tank.
4. Loosen all front carburetor boot clamps (**Figure 1B**) and remove rear tension springs from grooves (**Figure 2**).
5. Remove the carburetor-to-air filter rubber boots.
6. Label and disconnect all hoses at the carburetor (**Figure 3**).
7. Disconnect the accelerator and decelerator throttle cables (A, **Figure 4**) and the choke cable (B, **Figure 4**).
8. Slide the carburetors downward and to the right to disconnect them from the intake boots.
9. Installation is the reverse of these steps. Adjust the throttle cables as described in Chapter Three.

Disassembly/Reassembly

Refer to **Figure 5** for this procedure.
1. Remove the upper chamber cover (**Figure 6**).
2. Remove the spring and spring seat (**Figure 7**).

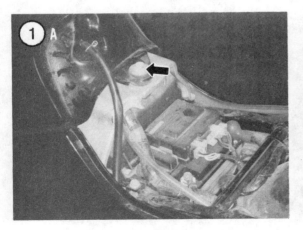

CARBURETOR

1. Cover
2. Screw
3. Spring
4. Holder
5. Jet needle
6. Vacuum piston
7. Choke assembly
8. Body
9. Washer
10. O-ring
11. Spring
12. Pilot screw
13. Plug (U.S. models)
14. Pilot jet
15. Needle jet
16. Needle jet holder
17. Main jet
18. Float valve needle
19. Clip
20. Float
21. Pivot pin
22. O-ring
23. Drain screw
24. O-ring
25. Float bowl
26. Screw

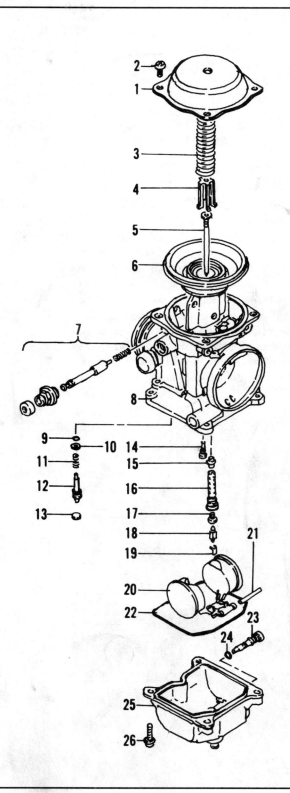

7

3. Remove the diaphragm (**Figure 8**) and jet needle (**Figure 9**).

4. Remove the float bowl (A, **Figure 10**) and gasket.

5. Remove the float pin (B, **Figure 10**) and float (A, **Figure 11**).

> *NOTE*
> *Be sure to catch the float valve needle*
> *and its hanger clip (B, **Figure 11**).*

6. Remove the pilot jet (**Figure 12**).

7. Remove the main jet (**Figure 13**).

8. Remove the needle jet holder (**Figure 14**).

9. Remove the needle jet (**Figure 15**).

10A. *All models except U.S.:* Carefully screw in the mixture screw until it *lightly* seats. Count and record the number of turns so it can be installed in the same position during assembly. Then remove the idle mixture screw (**Figure 16**), spring, washer and O-ring.

10B. *U.S. models:* The idle mixture screw is sealed at the factory. If necessary, remove it as described under *Idle Mixture Screw Removal/Installation* in this chapter.

11. Repeat for the opposite carburetor.

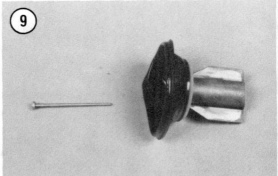

7

12. Separation of the carburetors is not required for cleaning.

13. Clean and inspect the carburetors as described in this chapter.

14. Reassembly is the reverse of these steps. Note the following.

15. Install new O-rings during reassembly.

16. Install the needle jet so that the small diameter end goes in first.

17. When installing the upper chamber cover, push up on the piston just enough so that there is no crease on the diaphragm lip. Install the upper chamber cover and screws.

18. Check the fuel level. See *Fuel Level Measurement* in this chapter.

Idle Mixture Screw Removal/Installation (U.S. Models)

The idle mixture screw is sealed at the factory. When disassembling the carburetors for overhaul, the bonding agent and cover must be removed for access to the screw, O-ring and spring.

1. Carefully scrape out the bonding agent from the recess in the carburetor body.

2. Punch and pry out the plug with a small screwdriver or awl.

3. Carefully screw in the idle mixture screw (**Figure 16**) until it *lightly* seats. Count and record the number of turns so it can be installed in the *same* position during assembly.

4. Remove the mixture screw, O-ring and spring from the carburetor body.

5. Repeat for the other carburetor. Make sure to keep each carburetor's parts separate.

6. Inspect the O-ring and end of the mixture screw; replace if damaged or worn.

7. Install the mixture screws in the same position as noted during removal (Step 3).

8. Install new plugs. Secure the plugs with a small amount of non-hardening bonding agent.

> *CAUTION*
> *Apply only a small amount of bonding agent. Too much may close off the air passage.*

CARBURETOR ADJUSTMENT

Fuel Level Measurement

Carburetors leave the factory with float levels properly adjusted. Rough riding, a worn needle valve or bent float arm can cause the float level to change. To adjust the float level on these carburetors, perform the following.

> *WARNING*
> *Some gasoline will drain from the carburetors during this procedure. Work in a well-ventilated area, at least 50 feet from any open flame. Do not smoke. Wipe up spills immediately.*

1. Remove the carburetors as described in this chapter.

2. Mount the carburetors on a fabricated wooden stand or blocks so that they are in a perfectly vertical position.

3. Remove the fuel tank and place it on wood blocks higher than the carburetors. Then connect a length of fuel hose, 6 mm in diameter and approximately 300 mm long, to the fuel tank and carburetor.

4. Connect a length of hose to the float bowl as shown in **Figure 17**. Connect a fuel level gauge (part No. 57001-1017) to the opposite end of the carburetor so that the "O" line on the gauge is several millimeters higher than the carburetor's bottom edge (**Figure 17**).

5. Turn the fuel valve to PRI. Then turn the carburetor drain plug a few turns out.

6. Wait until the fuel in the gauge settles. Then slowly lower the gauge until the "O" line is even with the bottom edge of the carburetor body (**Figure**

17). The fuel level should be 0.5 ±1 mm (0.002 ±0.004 in.) above the edge of the carburetor body.

7. Turn the fuel valve to the ON position.

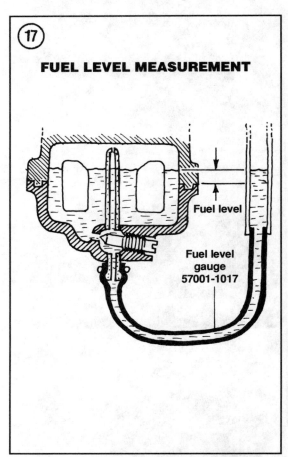

(17)

FUEL LEVEL MEASUREMENT

Fuel level

Fuel level gauge 57001-1017

(18)

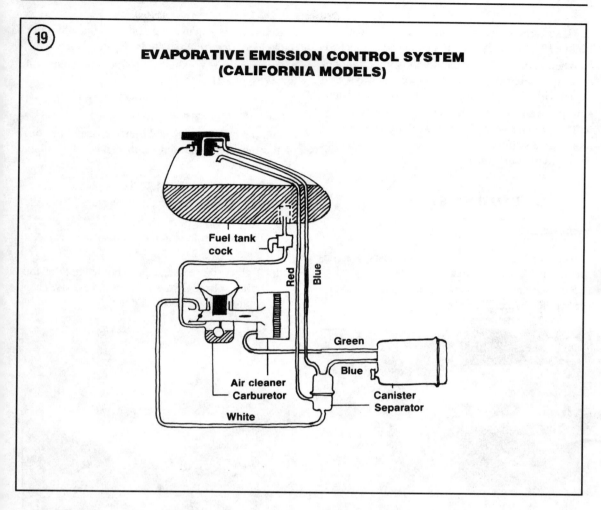

EVAPORATIVE EMISSION CONTROL SYSTEM (CALIFORNIA MODELS)

Fuel tank cock

Red

Blue

Green

Blue

Air cleaner

Carburetor

Canister

Separator

White

7

8. If adjustment is required, remove the carburetor float and bend its tang (**Figure 18**) as required to raise or lower the fuel level.

9. Remove the fuel level gauge when the level is correct.

EMISSION CONTROL
(CALIFORNIA MODELS)

All models sold in California are equipped with an evaporative emission control system to meet the CARB regulations in effect at the time of the model's manufacture. When the engine is running, fuel vapors are routed into the engine for burning; when the engine is stopped, fuel vapors are routed into a canister.

Inspection/Replacement

Maintenance of the evaporative emission control system consists of periodic inspection of the hoses for proper routing and a check of the canister mounting brackets.

When removal or replacement of an emission part is required, refer to **Figure 19**.

WARNING
Because the evaporative emission control system stores fuel vapors, make sure the work area is free of all flames or sparks before working on the emission system.

1. Whenever servicing the evaporative system, make sure the ignition switch is in the OFF position.

2. Make sure all hoses are attached as indicated in **Figure 19** and that they are not damaged or pinched.

3. When removing the separator, it is important not to turn the separator upside down or sideways. Doing so will allow gasoline to flow into the canister.

4. Replace any worn or damaged parts immediately.

5. The canister is capable of working through the motorcycle's life without maintenance, if it is not damaged or contaminated.

EXHAUST SYSTEM

Removal/Installation

1. Remove the lower fairing (if necessary) as described in Chapter Thirteen.

2. Remove the fairing bracket (if necessary) as described in Chapter Thirteen.

3. Remove the exhaust pipe holder nuts and work the holders free from the studs (**Figure 20**).

4. Remove the rear exhaust pipe mounting nuts and bolts (**Figure 21**).

5. Loosen the bolt on the crossover pipe located beneath the engine (**Figure 22**).

6. Pull the exhaust pipe and muffler assemblies out of the cylinder head and remove the split collars (**Figure 23**).

7. Remove the exhaust assembly.

8. To install, reverse the removal steps. Note the following:

    a. Use new gaskets in the cylinder head exhaust ports.

    b. Tighten the exhaust pipe holder nuts at the cylinder head first, gradually and evenly. Then tighten the rear bolts and nuts.

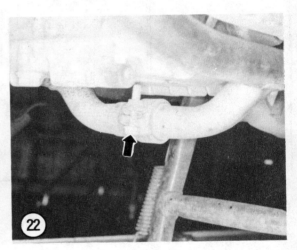

c. Start the engine and check for leakage. Tighten the clamps again after the engine has cooled down.

Maintenance

The exhaust system is vital to the motorcycle's operation and performance. You should periodically inspect, clean and polish (if required) the exhaust system. Special chemical cleaners and preservatives compounded for exhaust systems are available at most motorcycle shops.

Severe dents which cause flow restrictions require replacement of the damaged part.

To prevent internal rust buildup, remove the pipes and turn them to drain any trapped moisture.

Table 1 CARBURETOR SPECIFICATIONS

Carburetor type	Keihin CVK34
Fuel level	0.5 ± 1 mm (0.002 ± 0.004 in.)
Float level	17 mm (21/32 in.)
Main jet	130
Main air jet	100
Jet needle	N36N
Pilot jet	35
Pilot air jet	130
Pilot screw (idle mixture)	pre-set (U.S.; 1 3/4 turns out if altered)
	2 turns out (All models except U.S.)
Starter jet	50

7

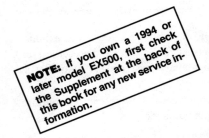

NOTE: If you own a 1994 or later model EX500, first check the Supplement at the back of this book for any new service information.

CHAPTER EIGHT

ELECTRICAL SYSTEMS

This chapter describes service procedures for the electrical system. **Table 1** at the end of the chapter lists electrical specifications.

CHARGING SYSTEM

Before beginning any charging system tests, be sure that the battery is in good condition and that it is at or near full charge.

Regulator/Rectifier Output Voltage Check

Before making any voltage regulator test, be sure that the battery is in good condition and is at or near full charge. Refer to **Figure 1**.

1. Start the bike and allow to warm to normal operating temperature.
2. Turn the engine off and remove the seat.
3. Pull the white/red connector out of its holder to gain access to it (**Figure 1**).

CAUTION
The white/red connector is supplied by current from the battery positive terminal. When attaching the voltmeter lead to the white/red connector, make sure the lead does not touch any part of the chassis.

4. Set a voltmeter to the 25 volt DC range. Attach the red voltmeter lead to the white/red connector and the black lead to the black/yellow connector.

NOTE
To turn the headlight off on U.S. models when performing Step 4, disconnect the headlight connector at the headlight housing.

5. Start the engine and allow to idle. Record the voltage readings at various rpm speeds and with the headlight turned alternately to the ON and OFF positions. The readings should he approximately 14 volts at low rpm and increase to, but not exceed, 15 volts at higher rpms.

6. Turn off the engine and interpret results as follows:

   a. If the voltage is correct as tested in Step 5, the charging system is working correctly.

   b. If the voltage did not rise as the engine speed was increased in Step 5, the regulator/rectifier is defective or the alternator output is insufficient.

   c. If the voltage exceeded 15 volts in Step 5, the regulator/rectifier is damaged or the regulator/rectifier leads are loose or disconnected.

Alternator Checks

1. Turn the ignition switch to the OFF position and remove the seat.
2. Remove the air filter assembly.
3. Disconnect connector 2 from the alternator. See **Figure 1**.
4. Connect the positive terminal of an AC voltmeter to one yellow lead and the negative voltmeter lead to the mating yellow wire.
5. Start the engine and run it at 4,000 rpm.
6. Observe the voltmeter. If it indicates approximately 60 volts, the alternator is operating correctly and the regulator/rectifier is damaged. If the reading is much lower than 60 volts, the alternator is defective.
7. Turn the engine off.
8. Repeat Steps 4-7 for each of the 3 yellow wires.

Stator Test

Use an ohmmeter, set at R × 1, and measure the resistance between the 2 yellow leads from the alternator (**Figure 1**). The value should be about 0.3-0.6

ohms. If the resistance is greater than specified or no meter reading (infinity), the stator has an open and must be replaced.

Change the ohmmeter setting to the highest range and measure the resistance between each yellow lead and the chassis (ground). The meter should read infinity; if it doesn't, this indicates a short and the stator must be replaced.

> *NOTE*
> *If the stator winding resistance is within the specified range, but the voltage output is incorrect, the rotor has probably lost some of its magnetism and must be replaced.*

Voltage Rectifier Tests

1. Remove the seat.
2. Disconnect connector 3. See **Figure 1**. It has 6 wires—1 white/red, 1 brown, 1 black and 3 yellow.
3. Measure and record resistance between the white/red and each yellow lead.

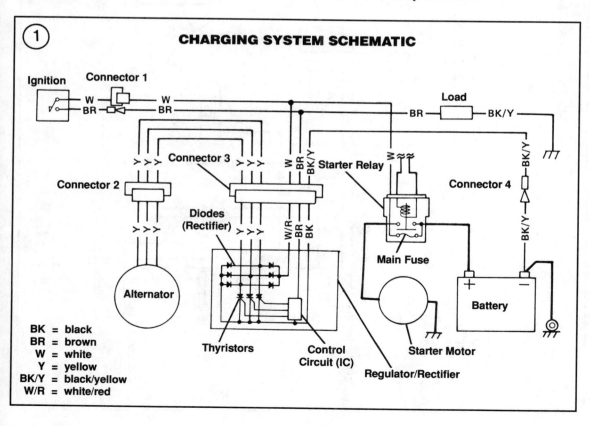

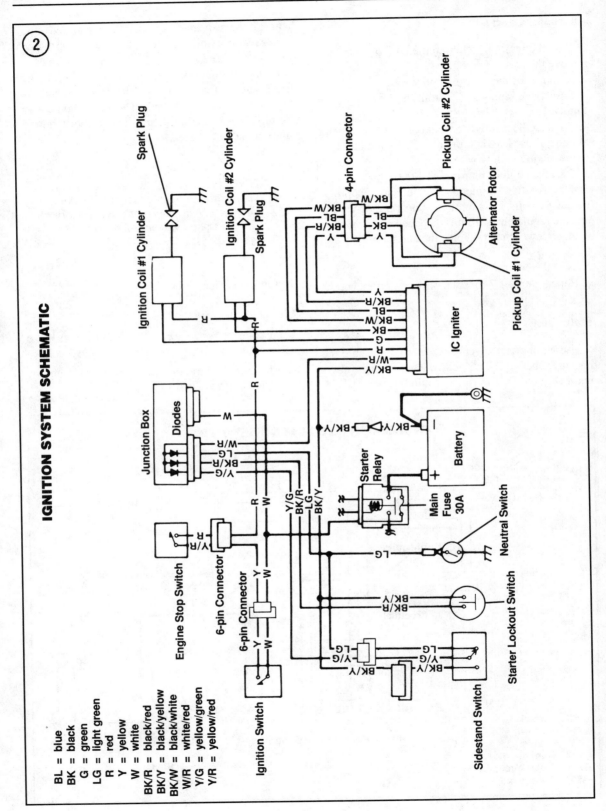

IGNITION SYSTEM SCHEMATIC

BL = blue
BK = black
G = green
LG = light green
R = red
Y = yellow
W = white
BK/R = black/red
BK/Y = black/yellow
BK/W = black/white
W/R = white/red
Y/G = yellow/green
Y/R = yellow/red

Ignition Coil #1 Cylinder
Spark Plug
Ignition Coil #2 Cylinder
Spark Plug
4-pin Connector
Pickup Coil #2 Cylinder
Alternator Rotor
Pickup Coil #1 Cylinder
IC Igniter
Junction Box
Diodes
Engine Stop Switch
6-pin Connector
6-pin Connector
Ignition Switch
Starter Relay
Battery
Main Fuse 30A
Neutral Switch
Starter Lockout Switch
Sidestand Switch

4. Reverse ohmmeter leads, then repeat Step 3. Each pair of measurements must be high with the ohmmeter connected one way and low when the ohmmeter leads are connected the other way. It is not possible to specify exact meter readings, but each pair of measurements should differ by a factor of not less than 10 times.

5. Repeat Steps 3 and 4, but make measurements between each yellow lead and the black lead.

6. Replace the rectifier/regulator if it fails any check of Steps 3, 4 or 5.

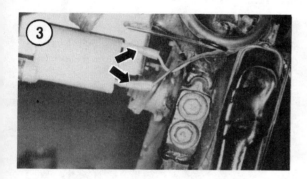

TRANSISTORIZED IGNITION

The ignition system consists of 2 ignition coils, an IC igniter unit and 2 timing pickup units. See **Figure 2**.

Troubleshooting is covered in Chapter Two.

Ignition Coil Removal/Installation

1. Remove the fuel tank.
2. Disconnect the spark plug leads by grasping the leads as near to the plugs as possible and pulling them off the plugs.
3. Disconnect the primary leads to the ignition coil. See **Figure 3**.
4. Remove the coil mounting bolts and the coils and brackets. Note any ground leads that are attached with the bracket bolts.
5. Install by reversing these steps.

Ignition Coil Testing

1. Using an ohmmeter, measure coil primary resistance between both coil primary terminals (**Figure 3**). See **Table 1** for specifications.
2. Measure coil secondary resistance between both spark plug caps. See **Table 1** for specifications.
3. Replace the coil if it did not meet the resistance values in Steps 1 or 2. If the coil exhibits visible damage, it should be replaced.

Pickup Coil Removal/Installation

The pickup coil is located inside the alternator cover.

1. Raise the seat and disconnect the battery negative lead.
2. Disconnect the alternator connectors.
3. Place an oil pan underneath the alternator cover.
4. Remove the alternator cover bolts and remove the cover (**Figure 4**). Note the path of the wire harness as it must be routed through the same path during installation.
5. Remove the screws securing the pickup coils and remove the coils. See **Figure 5**.
6. Install by reversing these steps while noting the following.
7. Install a new alternator cover gasket and the 2 dowel pins.

8

8. Apply silicone sealant, such as RTV, to the new gasket and underneath the rubber wiring grommet in the cover (**Figure 6**).

Pickup Coil Inspection

1. Remove the fuel tank.

2. Disconnect the 2-pole pickup coil/IC igniter connector.

3. With an ohmmeter set at R × 100, measure the resistance between the pickup coil leads. The resistance should be about 400-490 ohms.

4. Set the ohmmeter at its scale and check the resistance between either lead and the chassis ground. The reading should be infinite.

5. If the pickup coil fails either of these tests, check the wiring to the coil. Replace the coil if the wiring is okay.

IC Igniter Removal/Installation

The IC igniter (**Figure 7**) is attached to the right-hand rear side of the frame underneath the right cover. To replace it, remove the attaching bolts and disconnect the electrical connector. Reverse to install.

IC Igniter Test

The IC igniter on this model should only be tested with a Kawasaki tester. Refer service to a Kawasaki dealer.

Rectifier/Regulator Removal/Installation

The rectifier/regulator assembly (**Figure 8**) is installed on the upper left hand side of the rear frame under the left cover.

1. Turn the ignition switch to the OFF position.

2. Disconnect the electrical connector at the rectifier/regulator.

3. Remove the rectifier/regulator mounting bolts and remove the unit.

4. Reverse these steps to install.

ELECTRIC STARTER

The starter circuit includes the starter button, starter relay, battery and starter motor. **Figure 9** illustrates the typical starter circuit.

Removal/Installation

Refer to Chapter Four.

Disassembly/Reassembly

Starter motor repair is generally a job for electrical shops or a Kawasaki dealer. The following procedure describes how to check starter brush condition.

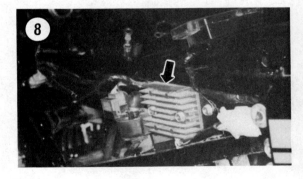

1. Referring to **Figure 10**, disassemble the starter motor.

2. Measure the length of each brush with a vernier caliper (**Figure 11**). If the length is less than specified in **Table 1**, it must be replaced. Replace the brushes as a set even though only one may be worn to this dimension.

3. Inspect the commutator. The mica in a good commutator is below the surface of the copper bars. On a worn commutator, the mica and copper bars may be worn to the same level. See **Figure 12**. If necessary, have the commutator serviced by a dealer or electrical repair shop.

4. Use an ohmmeter and check for continuity between the commutator bars (**Figure 13**); there should be continuity between pairs of bars. Also

check continuity between the commutator bars and the shaft (**Figure 14**); there should be no continuity. If the unit fails either of these tests, the armature is faulty and must be replaced.

5. Use an ohmmeter and inspect the field coil by checking continuity between the starter cable terminal and the starter case; there should be no continuity. Also check continuity between the starter cable terminal and each brush wire terminal; there should be continuity. If the unit fails either of these tests, the case/field coil assembly must be replaced.

6. Connect one probe of an ohmmeter to the brush holder plate and the other probe to each of the positive (insulated) brush holders; there should be no continuity. If the unit fails at either brush holder, the brush holder assembly should be replaced.

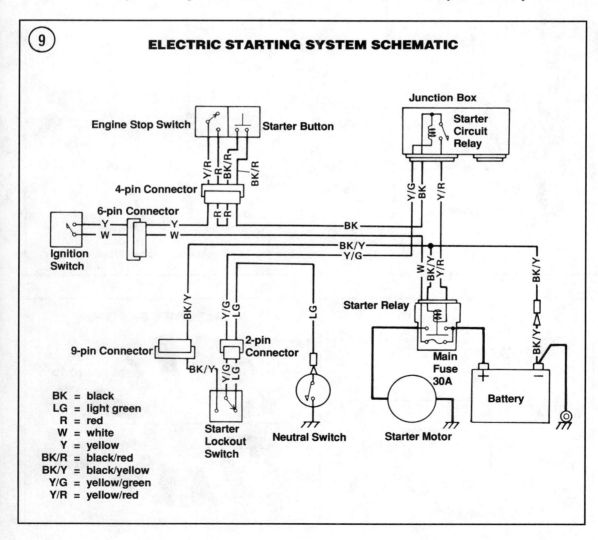

ELECTRIC STARTING SYSTEM SCHEMATIC

BK = black
LG = light green
R = red
W = white
Y = yellow
BK/R = black/red
BK/Y = black/yellow
Y/G = yellow/green
Y/R = yellow/red

Starter Relay
Removal/Installation

The starter relay (A, **Figure 15**) is installed on the upper left-hand side of the rear frame next to the rectifier/regulator. To replace it, make sure the ignition switch is in the OFF position. Then label and disconnect the wires at the starter relay and pull it out of its holder. Remove any attaching screws, if necessary. Reverse to install.

Starter Relay Testing

1. Disconnect the starter motor lead and the battery positive cable from the starter relay terminal.

2. Connect an ohmmeter across the relay terminals.

3. Press the starter button. The relay should click and the ohmmeter should indicate zero resistance. If the relay clicks, but the meter indicates any value greater than zero, replace the relay.

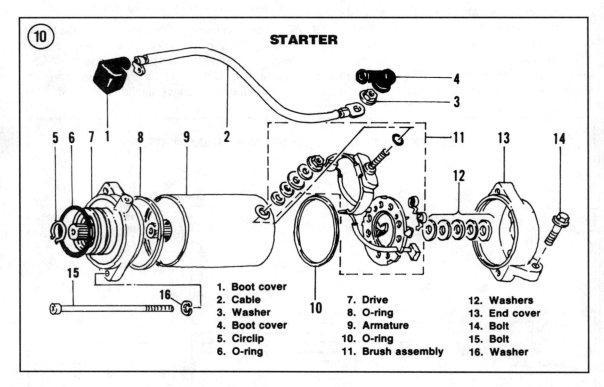

STARTER

1. Boot cover
2. Cable
3. Washer
4. Boot cover
5. Circlip
6. O-ring
7. Drive
8. O-ring
9. Armature
10. O-ring
11. Brush assembly
12. Washers
13. End cover
14. Bolt
15. Bolt
16. Washer

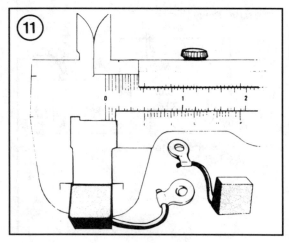

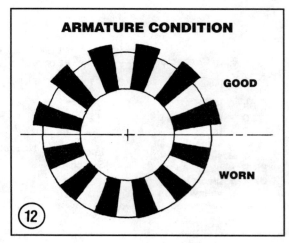

ARMATURE CONDITION

GOOD

WORN

4. If the relay does not click, disconnect the remaining wires, then measure resistance across the relay coil terminals. If the resistance is not close to zero resistance, the relay is defective.

5. If the resistance is close to zero, the relay may be good but inoperative because no current is reaching it. Connect the positive voltmeter lead to the black wire and negative voltmeter lead to the black/yellow wire, then press the starter switch. If the meter indicates battery voltage, the relay is defective. If

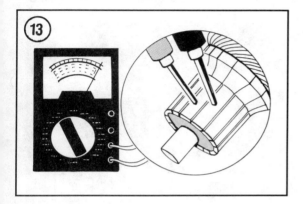

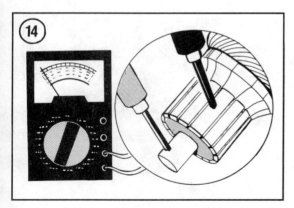

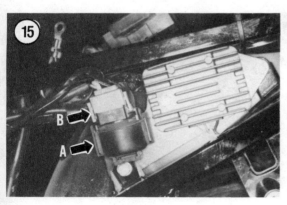

there is no voltage reading, the switch or wiring is defective.

Starter Circuit Relay Testing

All models have a starter circuit relay in the starting circuit. The starter circuit relay (B, **Figure 15**) is located beside the starter relay.

1. Disconnect the wires at the starter circuit relay and remove it.

2. Connect an ohmmeter and a 12-volt battery to the starter circuit relay as shown in **Figure 16**. Interpret the results as follows:

    a. When the battery is connected, the ohmmeter should read zero resistance.

    b. When the battery is disconnected, the ohmmeter should read infinite resistance.

3. If the test results in Step 2 were incorrect, replace the starter circuit relay.

LIGHTING SYSTEM

The lighting system consists of the headlight, taillight/brakelight combination, directional signals, warning lights and speedometer, tachometer and cooling system illumination lights. In the event of trouble with any light, the first thing to check is the affected bulb itself. If the bulb is good, check all wiring and connections with a test light.

Headlight Replacement

1. Remove the two screws and cover (**Figure 17**) underneath the fairing for easier access.

2. Disconnect the connector at the bulb (**Figure 18**).

3. Lift the rubber dust cover away from around the bulb by pulling on the tab (**Figure 19**).

4. Lift the hook spring up and pivot it away from the bulb (**Figure 20**).

> *WARNING*
> *If the headlight has just burned out or turned off, it will be hot. Do **not** touch the bulb until it cools off.*

> *CAUTION*
> *Do not touch the quartz-halogen bulb glass with your fingers because traces of oil on the bulb will drastically reduce the life of the bulb. Clean any traces of*

oil from the bulb with a cloth moistened in alcohol or lacquer thinner.

5. Lift the bulb (A, **Figure 21**) out of the headlight assembly.

6. Install by reversing these steps. Note the following:

    a. Align the tabs on the bulb with the notches in the bulb socket when installing the bulb.

    b. Make sure to lock the hook spring into the bulb socket.

    c. Install the dust cover so that the end labeled TOP (if present) faces up.

Headlight Adjustment

Adjust the headlight horizontally and vertically according to the Department of Motor Vehicles regulations in your area.

1. There are 2 adjustments: horizontal (B, **Figure 21**) and vertical (C, **Figure 21**).

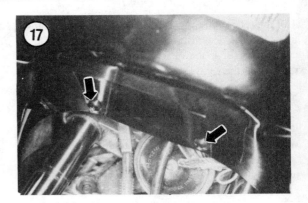

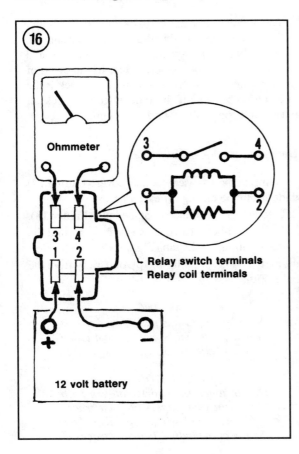

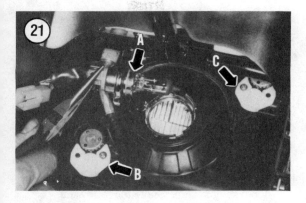

2. When performing this procedure, make sure the tire pressure is correct and that the fuel tank is approximately 1/2 full to full. Have an assistant sit on the seat.

3. *Horizontal adjustment*: Perform the following:
   a. Insert a screwdriver into the horizontal adjuster guide (**Figure 22**).
   b. Turn the adjuster clockwise or counterclockwise until the headlight beam points straight ahead.

4. *Vertical adjustment*: Perform the following:
   a. Insert a screwdriver into the vertical adjuster guide (**Figure 23**).
   b. Turn the adjuster clockwise or counterclockwise to adjust the headlight beam vertically.

Taillight Replacement

1. Remove the seat.
2. Pull the socket assembly out of the taillight housing (**Figure 24**).
3. Replace the bulb.

License Plate Light Bulb Replacement

1. Remove the socket mounting screws and lens.
2. Replace the bulb.
3. Install the socket and lens so that the TOP mark on the lens is facing up.

Directional Signal Light Replacement

1. Remove the two screws securing the lens (**Figure 25**) and remove it.
2. Wash out the inside and outside of the lens with a mild detergent.

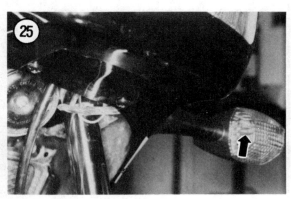

3. Replace the bulb.

4. Install the lens; do not overtighten the screws or the lens will crack.

Instrument Panel Illumination Bulb Replacement

1. Disconnect the speedometer or tachometer cables.

2. Remove the bolts securing the speedometer/tachometer brace and pull it away from the steering head.

3. Remove the outside cover (if necessary) to gain access to the bulb.

4. Remove the bulb from the connector and install a new one.

5. Installation is the reverse of these steps.

SWITCHES

Switches can be tested for continuity with an ohmmeter, as described in Chapter One, or with a test light at the switch connector plug by operating the switch in each of its operating positions and comparing results with the switch operation. For example, **Figure 26** shows a continuity diagram for a typical horn button switch. It shows which terminals should show continuity when the horn button is in a given position.

When the horn button is pushed, there should be continuity between terminals BK/W and BK/Y. This is indicated by the line on the continuity diagram. An ohmmeter connected between these 2 terminals should indicate little or no resistance and a test lamp should light. When the horn button is free, there should be no continuity between the same terminals.

If a switch doesn't perform properly, replace it. Refer to **Figure 27** when testing the switches.

When testing switches, note the following:

a. First check the fuse.

b. Check the battery as described in Chapter Three and bring the battery to the correct state of charge, if required.

(26)

HORN SWITCH

POSITION	Wire color	
	BK/W	BK/Y
PUSH	●——————●	
OFF		

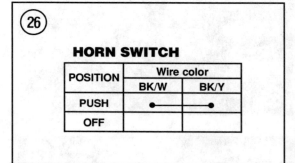

(27)   SWITCHES

HEADLIGHT SWITCH

Switch position	Wire color			
	R/W	R/Bl	Bl	Bl/Y
Off				
☐	●——————●			
On	●——————●		●——————●	

IGNITION SWITCH

Switch position	Wire color						
	Br	W	Y	Bl	R	W/Bk	O/G
Off, lock							
On	●——●——●		●——●——●			●——●	
Park		●————————————●				●——●	

DIMMER SWITCH (U.S.)

Switch position	Wire color			
	Bl/Y	Bl/O	R/Y	R/Bk
High	●——————————————————●			
		●——————●		
Low	●——————●			
		●——————————●		

DIMMER SWITCH (ALL OTHERS)

Switch position	Wire color		
	R/Bk	Bl/Y	R/Y
High	●——————●		
Low		●——————●	

c. When separating 2 connectors, pull on the connector housings and not the wires.

d. After locating a defective circuit, check the connectors to make sure they are clean and properly connected. Check all wires going into a connector housing to make sure each wire is properly positioned and that the wire end is not loose.

e. To engage connectors properly, push them together until they click into place.

f. When replacing handlebar switch assemblies, make sure the cables are routed correctly so that they are not crimped when the handlebar is turned from side to side.

HORN

Removal/Installation

1. Disconnect the horn electrical connector.

2. Remove the bolts securing the horn.

3. Installation is the reverse of these steps.

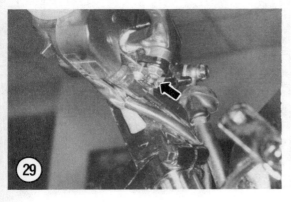

Testing

1. Disconnect horn wires from harness.

2. Connect horn wires to 12-volt battery. If it is good, it will sound.

Ignition Switch Replacement

1. Remove the upper fairing assembly as described in Chapter Thirteen.

2. Disconnect the ignition switch electrical connector.

3. Remove the bolts securing the ignition switch to the steering stem and remove the switch (**Figure 28**).

4. Installation is the reverse of these steps.

Neutral Switch Replacement

Refer to *Neutral Switch Removal/Installation* in Chapter Four.

Oil Pressure Switch Replacement

Refer to *Oil Level Switch Removal/Installation* in Chapter Four.

Front Brake Light Switch Replacement

The front brake switch is mounted underneath the front brake master cylinder (**Figure 29**). Disconnect the connector and remove the switch screw. Reverse to install. Check switch operation. The rear brake light should come on when applying the front brake lever.

Rear Brake Light Switch

The rear brake switch is mounted on the right-hand side next to the rear brake pedal mount (**Figure 30**).

1. Disconnect the electrical connector at the switch.

2. Disconnect the spring at the switch.

3. Unscrew the switch and remove it.

4. Screw a new switch into the switch mount. Attach the spring, then plug in the connector.

5. Adjust the rear brake switch as described under *Rear Brake Light Switch Adjustment* in Chapter Three.

8

Sidestand Switch Replacement

The sidestand switch is mounted on the sidestand (**Figure 31**).

1. Place the bike on its centerstand.

2. Pull the sidestand down to gain access to the switch.

3. Disconnect the connector and remove the switch screws.

4. Install by reversing these steps.

WIRING AND CONNECTORS

Many electrical troubles can be traced to damaged wiring or connectors that are contaminated with dirt and oil. Connectors can be serviced by disconnecting them and cleaning with electrical contact cleaner. Multiple pin connectors should be packed with a dielectric silicone grease (available at most automotive supply stores).

Wiring Check

1. Inspect all wiring for fraying, burning, etc.

2. Connectors can be serviced by disconnecting them and cleaning with electrical contact cleaner. Multiple pin connectors should be packed with dielectric silicone grease.

3. Check wiring continuity of individual circuits as follows:

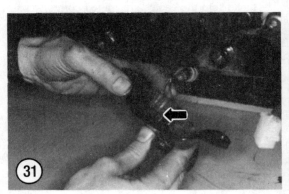

   a. Disconnect the negative cable from the battery.

> *NOTE*
> *When making a continuity test, it is best not to disconnect a connector. Instead, insert the test leads into the back of the connectors and check both sides. Because corrosion between the connector contacts may be causing an open circuit, your trouble may be at the connector instead of with the wiring.*

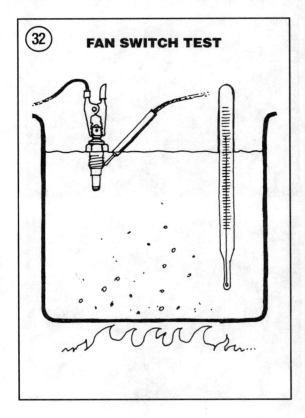

FAN SWITCH TEST

   b. Zero the ohmmeter according to the manufacturer's instructions. Switch the meter to the R × 1 scale.

   c. Attach the test leads to the circuit you want to check.

   d. There should be continuity (indicated low resistance). If there is no continuity, there is an open (break or bad connection) in the circuit.

THERMOSTATIC FAN SWITCH

Testing

The fan switch controls the radiator fan according to engine coolant temperature.

1. Remove the fan switch as described in Chapter Nine.

2. Fill a beaker or pan with water and place on a stove.

3. Mount the fan switch so that the temperature sensing tip and the threaded portion of the body are submerged as shown in **Figure 32**.

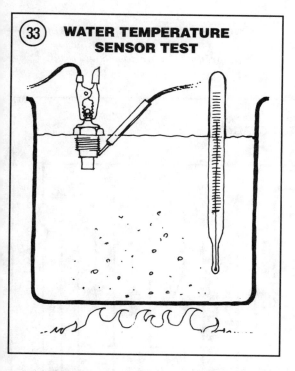

33 WATER TEMPERATURE SENSOR TEST

4. Place a thermometer in the pan of water (use a cooking or candy thermometer that is rated higher than the test temperature).

5. Attach one ohmmeter lead to the fan switch terminal and the other lead to the body as shown in **Figure 32**. Check resistance as follows:
   a. Gradually heat the water.
   b. When the temperature rises from 201-212° F (94-100° C), the resistance reading should be 0.5 ohms or less.
   c. Gradually reduce the heat.
   d. When the temperature falls to approximately 194° F (90° C), the ohmmeter should read 1 ohm or higher.

6. Replace the fan switch if it failed to operate as described in Step 5.

WATER TEMPERATURE SENSOR

Testing

1. Remove the water temperature sensor as described in Chapter Nine.

2. Fill a beaker or pan with water and place on a stove.

3. Mount the water temperature sensor so that the temperature sensing tip and the threaded portion of the body are submerged as shown in **Figure 33**.

4. Place a thermometer in the pan of water (use a candy or cooking thermometer that is rated higher than the test temperature).

5. Attach one ohmmeter lead to the water temperature terminal and the other lead to the body as shown in **Figure 33**. Check resistance as follows:
   a. Gradually heat the water.
   b. When the temperature reaches 176° F (80° C), the resistance reading should be approximately 57 ohms.
   c. Continue to heat the water. When the temperature reaches 212° F (100° C), the resistance reading should be approximately 27 ohms.

JUNCTION BOX AND FUSES

The junction box is mounted underneath the seat (**Figure 34**) and houses the fuses, diodes and relays. The junction box circuit is shown in **Figure 35**. The diodes and relays are an integral part of the junction box and cannot be removed. If they fail, the junction box must be replaced.

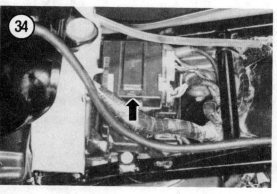

34

Junction Box Removal/Installation

To remove the junction box, remove the fastening screws and disconnect the electrical connectors. Reverse to install.

Fuse Replacement

There are 4 fuses located in the junction box mounted underneath the seat. The fuse functions are:

a. Accessory (10 amp).

b. Fan (10 amp).

c. Taillight (10 amp).

d. Headlight (10 amp).

The main fuse (30 amp) is located near the starter relay at the upper left of the frame.

If a fuse blows, remove the seat and remove the fuse cover (**Figure 36**). Remove the fuse by pulling

it out of the junction box with needlenose pliers. Install a new fuse with the same amperage rating.

NOTE
*The junction box is equipped with one 10-amp and one 30-amp replacement fuse (**Figure 36**). Always carry extra fuses.*

Whenever a fuse blows, find out the reason for the failure before replacing the fuse. Usually, the trouble is a short circuit in the wiring. Check by testing the circuit that the fuse protects. A blown fuse may be caused by worn-through insulation or a disconnected wire shorting to ground.

CAUTION
Never substitute tinfoil or wire for a fuse. Never use a higher amperage fuse than specified. An overload could result in fire and complete loss of the bike.

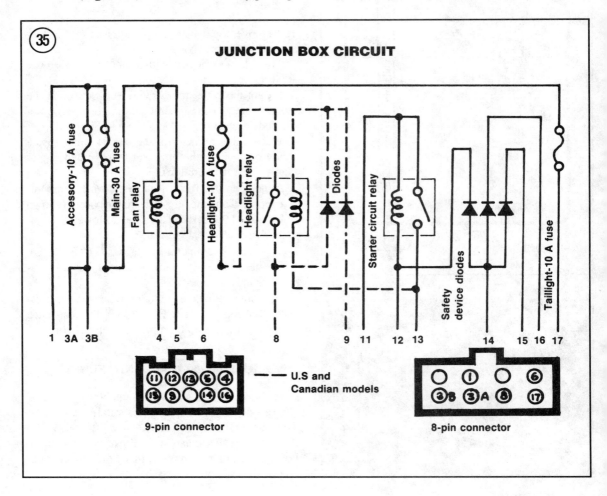

35 **JUNCTION BOX CIRCUIT**

Accessory-10 A fuse · Main-30 A fuse · Fan relay · Headlight-10 A fuse · Headlight relay · Diodes · Starter circuit relay · Safety device diodes · Taillight-10 A fuse

1 3A 3B   4 5 6   8   9 11 12 13   14   15 16 17

--- U.S and Canadian models

9-pin connector   8-pin connector

Junction Box Inspection

This test describes checks for the fuse and relay (fan, starter circuit and headlight) circuits.

1. Remove the junction box as described in this chapter.

2. Check that the connector terminals are clean and straight. If necessary, carefully align any bent terminal.

3. Perform all tests in Steps 4-6 with an ohmmeter set on R × 1.

NOTE
*Refer to **Figure 35** for pin connector locations when performing Steps 4-6.*

4. Check continuity between the fuse circuit terminals listed in **Table 2**. Record readings and compare to those given in **Table 2**.

5. Check continuity between the relay circuit terminals listed in **Table 3**. Record readings and compare to those given in **Table 3**.

6. Check the relay circuit (with battery connected) as follows:

a. Connect a battery and ohmmeter to the junction box terminals as specified in **Table 4**.

b. The correct reading for each test is 0 ohms.

7. Replace the junction box if it failed any of the tests in Steps 4-6.

Diode Circuit Test

Test the diode circuit as follows.

1. With an ohmmeter set on R × 1, check continuity between each of the following terminals (**Figure 35**).

NOTE
Sub-steps a and b are for U.S. models only.

a. 13 and 8.
b. 13 and 9.
c. 12 and 14.
d. 15 and 14.
e. 16 and 14.

2. Switch the ohmmeter leads and recheck the continuity as described in Step 1.

3. For the diode circuit to be normal, the reading should be low in one direction and more than ten times higher with the ohmmeter leads reversed.

4. Replace the junction box if the diode circuit did not test as described in Step 3.

WIRING DIAGRAMS

Wiring diagrams are located at the end of this book.

Tables 1-4 are on the following page.

8

Table 1 ELECTRICAL SPECIFICATIONS

Charging system	
Regulator/rectifier	
output voltage	14-15 volts
Alternator output test	60 volts AC @ 4,000 rpm
Resistance check	0.3-0.6 ohms
Ignition system	
Ignition coil	
Primary	2.2-3.9 ohms
Secondary	10-16 K ohms
Pickup coil resistance	400-490 ohms
Starter motor	
Brush wear limit	6.0 mm (0.236 in.)

Table 2 JUNCTION BOX: FUSE INSPECTION

Meter connection	Meter reading
1 and 3A	0 ohms
6 and 17	0 ohms
3A and 8 *	Infinity
8 and 17 *	Infinity
*U.S. models only	

Table 3 JUNCTION BOX: RELAY CIRCUIT INSPECTION (BATTERY DISCONNECTED)

Meter connection	Meter reading
4 and 5	Infinity
11 and 13	Infinity
12 and 13	Infinity

Table 4 JUNCTION BOX: RELAY CIRCUIT INSPECTION (BATTERY CONNECTED)

Meter connection	Battery connection (+)	(-)	Meter reading
11-13	11	12	0 ohms

CHAPTER NINE

COOLING SYSTEM

The pressurized cooling system consists of the radiator, water pump, radiator cap, thermostat, electric cooling fan and a coolant reservoir tank. **Figure 1** shows the main cooling system components.

It is important to keep the coolant level to the FULL mark on the coolant reservoir tank (**Figure 2**). Always add coolant to the reservoir tank rather than to the radiator.

> *CAUTION*
> *Drain and flush the cooling system at least every 2 years. Refill with a mixture of ethylene glycol antifreeze (formulated for aluminum engines) and purified water. Do not reuse the old coolant as it deteriorates with use. Do **not** operate the cooling system with only purified water (even in climates where antifreeze protection is not required). This is important because the engine is all aluminum; it will not rust but it will oxidize internally and have to be replaced. Refer to **Coolant Change** in Chapter Three.*

> *WARNING*
> *Antifreeze is a toxic waste. Drain into suitable containers and dispose of it according to local regulations. Do not store coolant where it is accessible to children and pets.*

This chapter describes repair and replacement of cooling system components. **Table 1** at the end of the chapter lists all of the cooling system specifications. For routine maintenance of the system, refer to Chapter Three.

> *WARNING*
> *Do not remove the radiator cap when the engine is hot. The coolant is very hot and is under pressure. Severe scalding could result if the coolant comes in contact with your skin.*

> *WARNING*
> *The radiator fan and fan switch are connected to the battery. Whenever the engine is warm or hot, the fan may start even with the ignition switch in the OFF position. Never work around the fan or touch the fan until the engine is completely cool.*

The cooling system must be cooled before removing any component of the system.

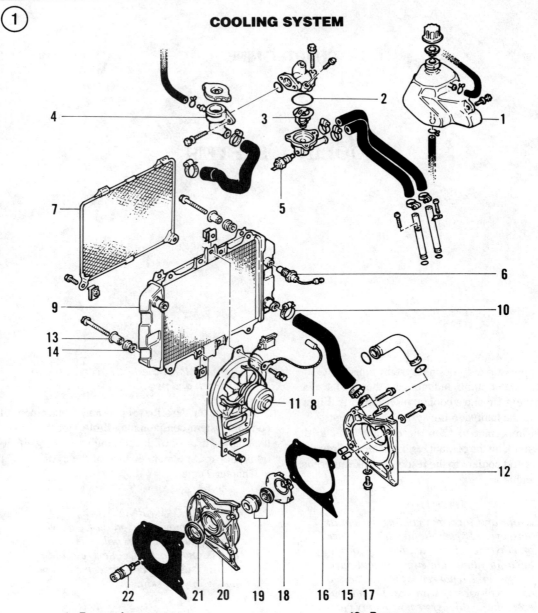

① COOLING SYSTEM

1. Reservoir
2. O-ring
3. Thermostat
4. Thermostat body
5. Water temperature sensor
6. Thermostatic switch *
7. Screen
8. Fan switch ground lead
9. Radiator
10. Hose clamp
11. Fan
12. Pump cover
13. Collar
14. Rubber damper
15. Dowel pin
16. Pump housing gasket
17. Drain plug
18. Impeller
19. Water pump bearing
20. Pump housing
21. Oil seal
22. Impeller shaft

* Located on upper left-hand side of radiator on 1990-on models.

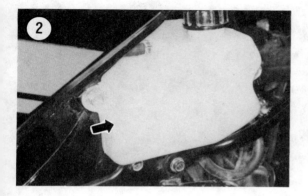

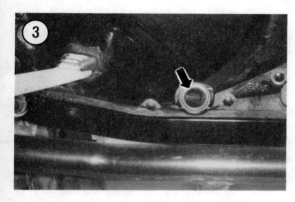

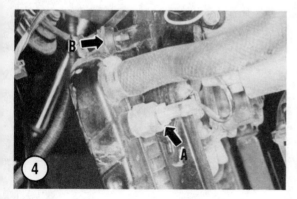

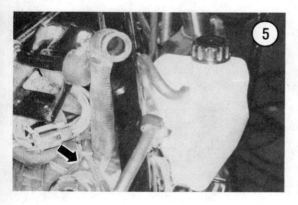

COOLING SYSTEM INSPECTION

1. If a substantial coolant loss is noted, the head gasket may be blown. In extreme cases, sufficient coolant will leak into a cylinder(s) when the bike is left standing for several hours so the engine cannot be turned over with the starter. White smoke (steam) might also be observed at the muffler(s) when the engine is running. Coolant may also find its way into the oil. To check, observe the oil level indicator on the clutch cover (**Figure 3**). If the oil looks like a "green chocolate malt" there is coolant in the oil system. If so, correct the problem immediately.

> *CAUTION*
> *After the problem is corrected, drain and thoroughly flush out the engine oil system to eliminate all coolant residue. Refill with fresh engine oil; refer to **Chapter Three**.*

2. Check the radiator for clogged or damaged fins. If more than 15 percent of the radiator fin area is damaged, repair or replace the radiator.

3. Check all coolant hoses for cracks or damage. Replace all questionable parts. Make sure the hose clamps are tight, but not so tight that they cut the hoses.

4. Pressure test the cooling system as described in Chapter Three.

RADIATOR AND FAN

> *WARNING*
> *The radiator fan and fan switch are connected to the battery. Whenever the engine is warm or hot, the fan may start even with the ignition switch in the OFF position. Never work around the fan or touch the fan until the engine is completely cool.*

Removal/Installation

The radiator and fan are removed as an assembly.

1. Place bike on centerstand.

2. Remove the fairings as described in Chapter Thirteen and fuel tank as described in Chapter Seven.

3. Drain the cooling system as described in Chapter Three.

4. Disconnect the thermostatic fan switch lead (A, **Figure 4**) and the fan motor connector (**Figure 5**).

5. Remove the radiator grille (**Figure 6**) from the front of the radiator.

6. Loosen the clamping screws on the upper and lower (**Figure 7**) radiator hose bands. Move the bands back onto the hoses and off of the necks of the radiator.

7. Remove the radiator mounting bolts (B, **Figure 4**). Disconnect the thermostatic fan switch ground lead from the right-hand side for 1987-89 models (**Figure 1**), or at the left upper radiator mounting screw for 1990-on models.

8. Lower the radiator and remove it and the fan assembly.

9. Replace the radiator hoses if deterioration or damage is noted.

10. Installation is the reverse of these steps. Note the following.

11. Make sure the thermostatic fan switch ground lead is attached as shown in **Figure 1** or at left upper radiator mount.

12. Refill the coolant as described in Chapter Three.

Inspection

1. Flush off the exterior of the radiator with a garden hose on low pressure. Spray both the front and the back to remove all road dirt and bugs. Carefully use a whisk broom or stiff paint brush to remove any stubborn dirt.

> *CAUTION*
> *Do not press too hard or the cooling fins and tubes may be damaged, causing a leak.*

2. Carefully straighten out any bent cooling fins (**Figure 8**, typical) with a broad-tipped screwdriver, or a fin comb.

3. Check for cracks or leakage (usually a moss-green colored residue) at the filler neck, the inlet and outlet hose fittings and the upper and lower tank seams.

Cooling Fan
Removal/Installation

1. Remove the radiator as described in this chapter.

2. Remove the bolts (**Figure 9**, typical) securing the fan shroud and fan assembly and remove the assembly.

3. Installation is the reverse of these steps.

4. Refill the cooling system with the recommended type and quantity of coolant. See Chapter Three.

THERMOSTAT

Removal/Installation

1. Remove the seat and fairing assembly.
2. Remove the fuel tank as described in Chapter Seven.

3. Disconnect the water temperature sensor lead (A, **Figure 10**) at the thermostat housing.
4. Drain the cooling system as described in Chapter Three.
5. Loosen the clamping screws on the 2 radiator hoses at the thermostat housing (**Figure 11**). Slide the clamps down the radiator hoses.
6. Loosen and remove the filler neck mounting bolts (C, **Figure 10**).
7. Loosen and remove the thermostat housing mounting bolts (B, **Figure 10**).
8. Remove the thermostat housing cover (**Figure 12**, typical) and remove the thermostat.
9. Install by reversing these steps while noting the following.
10. Install main wiring harness ground lead under thermostat housing mounting bolt (B, **Figure 10**).
11. Refill the cooling system with the recommended type and quantity of coolant. Refer to Chapter Three.

Inspection

Test the thermostat to ensure proper operation. The thermostat should be replaced if it remains open at normal room temperature or stays closed after the specified temperature has been reached during the test procedure.

Place the thermostat on a small piece of wood in a pan of water (**Figure 13**). Place a cooking thermometer with a heat range higher than the test temperature in the pan of water. Gradually heat the water and continue to stir the water gently until it reaches 176.9-182.3° F (80.5-83.5° C). At this temperature the thermostat should open.

NOTE
Valve operation is sometimes sluggish; it usually takes 3-5 minutes for the valve to operate properly.

If the valve fails to open, the thermostat should be replaced (it cannot be serviced). Be sure to replace it with one of the same temperature rating.

WATER PUMP

Removal/Installation

1. Drain the engine oil as described in Chapter Three.
2. Drain the cooling system as described in Chapter Three.

3. Shift the transmission into first gear.

4. Loosen the clamp on the water pump cover radiator hose (**Figure 7**). Then twist the hose and slide it off the cover neck.

5. With the water pipe attached to the water pump cover, remove cover bolts and cover (**Figure 14**).

> *NOTE*
> *Due to corrosion around the bolts and cover gasket (A, **Figure 15**), the water pump cover may be difficult to remove. Tapping the edges with a rubber mallet will help to free the cover and gasket.*

6. Apply the rear brake.

> *NOTE*
> *The impeller must be turned **clockwise** for removal.*

7. Turn the impeller nut clockwise and remove the impeller (**Figure 16**).

8. Pull the water pump housing from the crankcase (**Figure 17**).

9. Installation is the reverse of these steps. Note the following.

> *NOTE*
> *The impeller must be turned **counter-clockwise** for installation.*

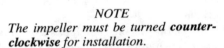

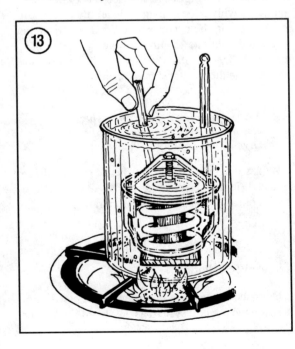

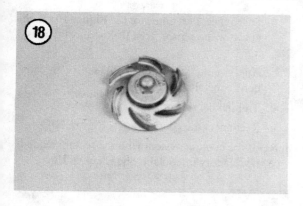

10. Turn the impeller shaft nut counterclockwise to tighten it. Tighten to 9.8 N•m (87 in.-lb.).

11. Install the 2 water pump housing dowel pins (B, **Figure 15**) and a new gasket.

12. Install new O-rings on the water pipe.

13. Refill the cooling system with the recommended type and quantity of coolant. Refer to Chapter Three.

Inspection

1. Inspect the impeller (**Figure 18**) for corrosion or damaged blades. Replace the impeller if necessary.

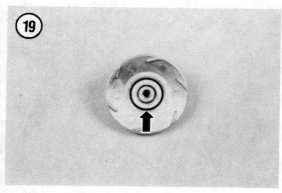

2. Inspect the rubber seal on the backside of the impeller (**Figure 19**). Replace it if worn or damaged by prying it out of the impeller. Clean the seal area with solvent and allow to dry thoroughly. Apply clean coolant to the new seal and install it by hand.

3. Inspect the water pump oil seal (**Figure 20**) and the mechanical seal (**Figure 21**) for wear or damage. If necessary, remove the water pump seal with a hook or screwdriver. The removal of the mechanical seal requires the use of Kawasaki driver (part No. 57001-1139). Install the new seals as follows:

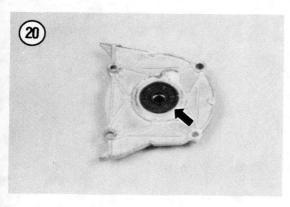

a. *Water pump oil seal:* Install the new seal by driving it into the water pump with a socket of the appropriate size placed on the outside of the seal. Install the seal until it is flush with the housing.

b. *Mechanical seal:* Install the new seal driving it into the water pump housing until the seal flange touches the housing surface.

HOSES

Hoses deteriorate with age and should be replaced periodically or whenever they show signs of cracking or leakage. To be safe, replace the hoses every 2 years. The spray of hot coolant from a cracked hose can injure the rider and passenger. Loss of coolant can also cause the engine to overheat, causing damage.

Whenever any component of the cooling system is removed, inspect the hoses(s) and determine if replacement is necessary.

THERMOSTATIC FAN SWITCH AND WATER TEMPERATURE SENSOR

Removal/Installation

1. Drain the cooling system as described in Chapter Three.

2A. *Thermostatic fan switch*—Perform the following:

    a. Disconnect the connector at the switch (A, **Figure 22**).

    b. Unscrew the switch (B, **Figure 22**) from the right-hand side of the radiator on 1987-1989 models and from the left-hand side of the radiator on 1990-on models. See **Figure 1**.

> *NOTE*
> *Do not use a liquid gasket on the fan switch threads during installation.*

    c. Install the switch and tighten to 7.4 N•m (65 in.-lb.).

2B. *Water temperature sensor*—Perform the following:

    a. Drain the cooling system as described in Chapter Three.

    b. Disconnect the connector (A, **Figure 10**), then unscrew the sensor from the thermostat housing.

    c. Apply a liquid gasket to the sensor threads before installation.

    d. Tighten the sensor to 7.8 N•m (69 in.-lb.).

    e. Reconnect the connector (A, **Figure 10**).

3. Refill the cooling system with the recommended type and quantity of coolant. See Chapter Three.

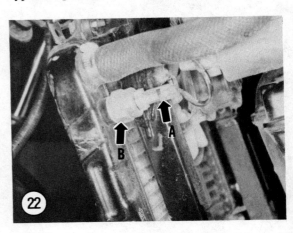

Table 1 COOLING SYSTEM SPECIFICATIONS

Capacity	1.8 L (1.9 qt.)
Coolant type	Antifreeze suited for aluminum engines
Mix ratio	50% purified water:50% coolant
Radiator cap pressure	11-15 psi (0.75-1.05 kg/cm^2)
Thermostat	
Opening temperature	176.9-182.3°F (80.5-83.5°C)
Valve opening lift	Not less than 8 mm (0.315 in.) @ 203°F (95°C)

9

FRONT SUSPENSION AND STEERING

This chapter discusses service operations on suspension components, steering, wheels and related items. **Table 1** lists front suspension wear limits. **Tables 1-2** are at the end of the chapter.

FRONT WHEEL

Removal/Installation

1. Support the motorcycle so that the front wheel is clear of the ground.

2. Loosen the speedometer cable nut (**Figure 1**) and pull the cable out of the speedometer drive unit.

3. Remove the brake caliper's mounting bolts (**Figure 2**) and lift the caliper off of the brake disc. Support the caliper with a bunji cord to prevent stress buildup on the brake hose.

4. Loosen the right-hand axle clamp bolt (**Figure 3**). Then loosen and remove the axle nut on the left-hand side (**Figure 4**).

5. Remove the axle from the right-hand side (**Figure 5**).

6. Pull the wheel forward and remove it.

7. Remove the speedometer drive gear (**Figure 6**) from the left-hand side.

8. Remove the spacer from the right-hand side.

CAUTION
Do not set the wheel down on the disc surface as it may be scratched or warped. Either lean the wheel against a wall or place it on a couple of wooden blocks.

NOTE
Insert a piece of wood in the caliper in place of the disc. This way, if the brake is inadvertently squeezed, the pistons will not be forced out of the cylinder. If this does happen, the caliper might have to be disassembled to reseat the pistons and the system will have to be bled. By

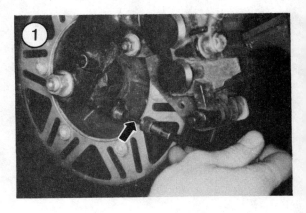

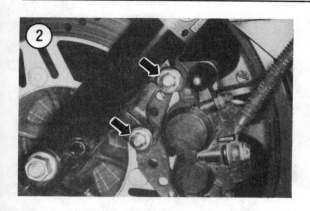

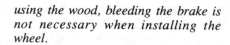

using the wood, bleeding the brake is not necessary when installing the wheel.

9. When servicing the wheel assembly, install the spacer, speedometer drive gear, washer and nut on the axle to prevent their loss. See **Figure 7**.

10. Installation is the reverse of these steps. Note the following.

    a. Align the 2 tabs in the speedometer gear housing (**Figure 8**) with the 2 speedometer drive

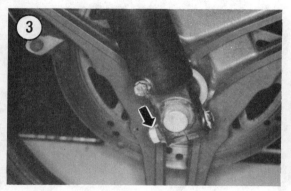

10

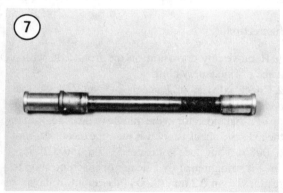

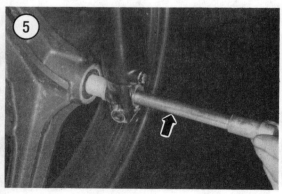

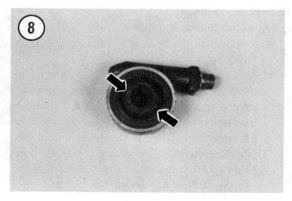

slots (**Figure 9**) in the front wheel and install the gear housing. See A, **Figure 10**.

b. When installing the front wheel, align the tab on the speedometer gear housing (B, **Figure 10**) with the slot in the back of the left-hand fork tube. This procedure locates the speedometer drive gear and prevents it from rotating when the wheel turns.

c. To prevent axle seizure, coat the axle with an anti-seize compound such as Bostik Neverseez lubricating & Anti-seize compound (part No. 49501).

d. Tighten the axle nut to specifications in **Table 2**.

e. Make sure that the speedometer gear housing does not move as the axle nut is tightened.

f. Remove the brake caliper from the bunji cord and carefully align it with the brake disc and install it. Install the 2 caliper bolts and tighten to 32 N•m (24 ft.-lb.).

g. Apply the front brake and compress the front forks several times to make sure the axle is installed correctly without binding the forks. Then tighten the axle clamp bolt to 14 N•m (10 ft.-lb.).

Inspection

1. Remove any corrosion on the front axle with a piece of fine emery cloth.
2. Check axle runout. Place the axle on V-blocks that are set 100 mm (4 in.) apart (**Figure 11**). Place the tip of a dial indicator in the middle of the axle. Rotate the axle and check runout. If runout exceeds 0.2 mm (0.008 in.) but does not exceed 0.7 mm (0.027 in.), have it straightened by a dealer or machine shop to read less than 0.2 mm (0.008 in.) runout. If the axle exceeds 0.7 mm (0.027 in.), replace the axle. Do not attempt to straighten it.
3. Check rim runout as follows:
   a. Remove the tire from the rim as described in this chapter.
   b. Measure the radial (up and down) runout of the wheel rim with a dial indicator. If runout exceeds 0.8 mm (0.03 in.), check the wheel bearings.
   c. Measure the axial (side to side) runout of the wheel rim with a dial indicator as shown in **Figure 12**. If runout exceeds 0.5 mm (0.01 in.), check the wheel bearings.

d. If the wheel bearings are okay, the wheel cannot be serviced and must be replaced.

e. Replace the front wheel bearings as described under *Front Hub* in this chapter.

4. Inspect the wheel rim for dents, bending or cracks. Check the rim and rim sealing surface for cracks or scratches that are deeper than 0.5 mm (0.020 in.). If

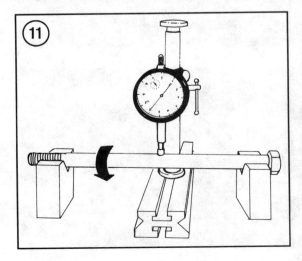

any of these conditions are present, replace the wheel.

Speedometer Gear Lubrication

The speedometer gear should be lubricated with high-temperature grease according to the maintenance schedule (**Table 1**) in Chapter Three.

1. Remove the front wheel from the motorcycle.
2. Clean all old grease from the gear housing (**Figure 8**) and gear. Pack the gear with high-temperature grease.
3. Install the front wheel as described in this chapter.

FRONT HUB

Disassembly/Inspection/Reassembly

Refer to **Figure 13**.
1. Check the wheel bearings by rotating the inner race. Check for bearing roughness, excessive noise or damage. If necessary, replace the bearings as follows. Always replace bearings as a set.

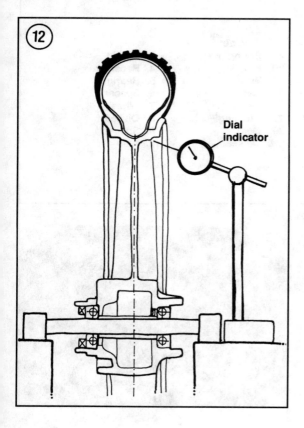

2. Remove the circlip and lift the speedometer gear drive out of the wheel (**Figure 14**).
3. Using a long drift or screwdriver, pry the oil seal from the right-hand side. See **Figure 15**.
4. Remove the circlip from the right-hand side (**Figure 13**).
5. Using a long drift and hammer, tilt the center spacer away from one side of the left-hand bearing (**Figure 16**). Then drive the left-hand bearing out of the hub. See **Figure 16**.
6. Remove the center spacer and remove the right-hand bearing.
7. Clean the axle spacer and hub thoroughly in solvent.
8. Tap the right-hand bearing into place carefully using a suitable size socket placed on the outer bearing race (**Figure 17**).
9. Install the right-hand circlip. Make sure it seats in its groove.
10. Install the center spacer and install the left-hand bearing as described in Step 8.
11. Install the speedometer drive and circlip on the left-hand side. Make sure the circlip seats in its groove. See **Figure 18**.
12. Install a new right-hand grease seal. Drive the seal in squarely with a large diameter socket on the outer portion of the seal. Drive the seal until it seats against the circlip.

WHEEL BALANCE

An unbalanced wheel results in unsafe riding conditions. Depending on the degree of unbalance and the speed of the motorcycle, the rider may experience anything from a mild vibration to a violent shimmy and loss of control.

Weights are attached to the rim (**Figure 19**). Weight kits are available from motorcycle dealers. These kits contain test weights and strips of adhesive-backed weights that can be cut to the desired length and attached directly to the rim. Kawasaki offers weights that can be crimped on the aluminum rims (**Figure 20**).

> *NOTE*
> *Be sure to balance the wheel with the brake disc attached as it also affects the balance.*

Before attempting to balance the wheels, check to be sure that the wheel bearings are in good condition

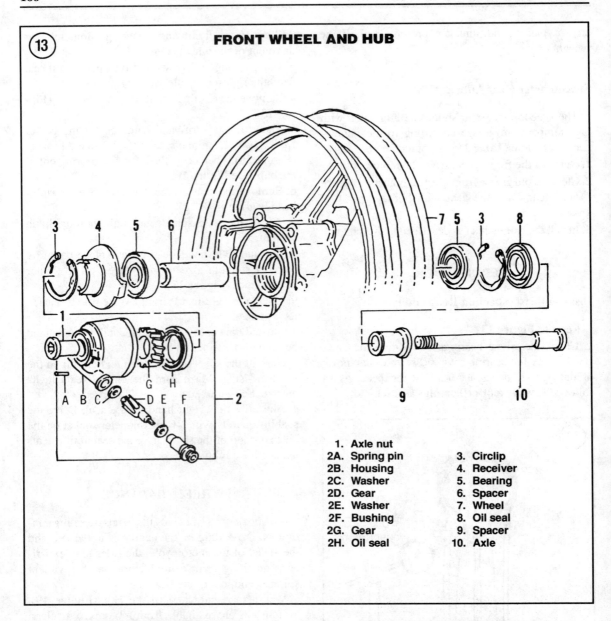

FRONT WHEEL AND HUB

1. Axle nut
2A. Spring pin
2B. Housing
2C. Washer
2D. Gear
2E. Washer
2F. Bushing
2G. Gear
2H. Oil seal
3. Circlip
4. Receiver
5. Bearing
6. Spacer
7. Wheel
8. Oil seal
9. Spacer
10. Axle

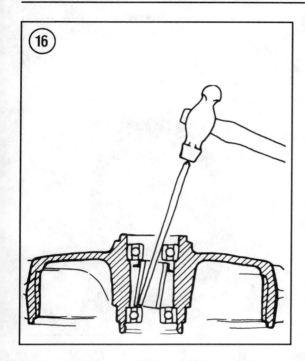

and properly lubricated. The wheel must rotate freely.

1. Remove the wheel as described in this chapter or in Chapter Eleven.

2. Mount the wheel on a fixture such as the one in **Figure 21** so it can rotate freely.

3. Give the wheel a spin and let it coast to a stop. Mark the tire at the lowest point.

4. Spin the wheel several more times. If the wheel keeps coming to rest at the same point, it is out of balance.

5. Tape a test weight to the upper (or light) side of the wheel.

6. Experiment with different weights until the wheel, when spun, comes to rest at a different position each time.

7. Remove the test weight and install the correct size weight.

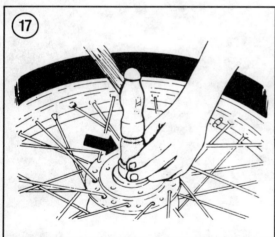

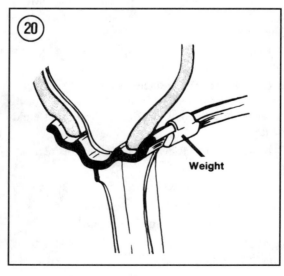

Weight

NOTE
*When installing crimp-type weights to aluminum rims, it may be necessary to let some air out of the tire. After installing the weight, refill the tire to the correct air pressure. See **Tire Pressure** in Chapter Three.*

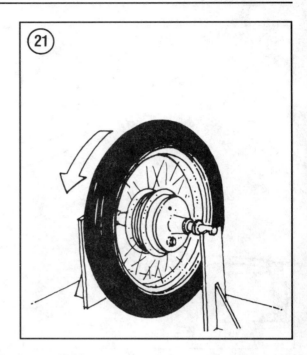

TUBELESS TIRES

WARNING
Do not install an inner tube inside a tubeless tire. The tube will cause an abnormal heat buildup in the tire.

Tubeless tires have the word TUBELESS molded in the tire sidewall (**Figure 22**) and the rims have TUBELESS cast on them (**Figure 23**).

When a tubeless tire is flat, it is best to take it to a motorcycle dealer for repair. Punctured tubeless tires should be removed from the rim to inspect the inside of the tire and to apply a combination plug/patch from the inside. Don't rely on a plug or cord repair applied from outside the tire. They might be okay on a car, but they're too dangerous on a motorcycle.

After repairing a tubeless tire, don't exceed 50 mph (80 kph) for the first 24 hours. Never race on a repaired tubeless tire. The patch could work loose from tire flexing and heat.

Repair

Do not rely on a plug or cord patch applied from outside the tire. Use a combination plug/patch applied from inside the tire (**Figure 24**).

1. Remove the tire from the rim as described in this chapter.

2. Inspect the rim inner flange. Smooth any scratches on the sealing surface with emery cloth. If a scratch is deeper than 0.5 mm (0.020 in.), the wheel should be replaced.

3. Inspect the tire inside and out. Replace a tire if any of the following is found:

    a. A puncture larger than 1/8 in. (3 mm) diameter.

    b. A punctured or damaged sidewall.

    c. More than 2 punctures in the tire.

4. Apply the plug/patch, following the instructions supplied with the patch.

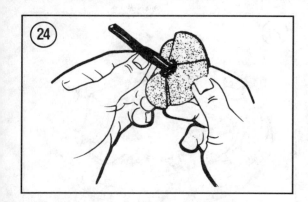

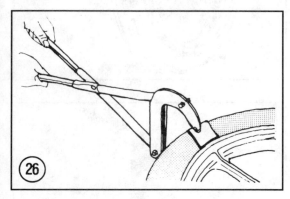

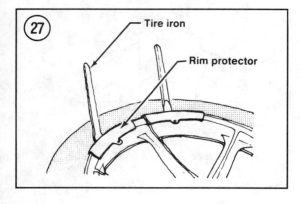

Tire iron

Rim protector

TUBELESS TIRE CHANGING

The wheels can easily be damaged during tire removal. Special care must be taken with tire irons when changing a tire to avoid scratches and gouges to the outer rim surface. Insert scraps of leather between the tire iron and the rim to protect the rim from damage.

The stock cast wheels are designed for use with tubeless tires.

Tire repair is different and is covered under *Tubeless Tires* in this chapter.

When removing a tubeless tire, take care not to damage the tire beads, inner liner of the tire or the wheel rim flange. Use tire levers or flat-handled tire irons with rounded ends.

Removal

NOTE
While removing a tire, support the wheel on 2 blocks of wood so the brake disc doesn't contact the floor.

1. Mark the valve stem location on the tire, so the tire can be installed in the same position for easier balancing. See **Figure 25**.

2. Remove the valve core to deflate the tire.

NOTE
*Removal of tubeless tires from their rims can be very difficult because of the exceptionally tight bead/rim seal. Breaking the bead seal may require the use of a special tool (**Figure 26**). If you have trouble breaking the seal, take the tire to a motorcycle dealer.*

CAUTION
The inner rim and tire bead area are sealing surfaces on a tubeless tire. Do not scratch the inside of the rim or damage a tire bead.

3. Press the entire bead on both sides of the tire into the center of the rim.

4. Lubricate the beads with soapy water.

CAUTION
*Use rim protectors (**Figure 27**) or insert scraps of leather between the tire irons and the rim to protect the rim from damage.*

10

5. Insert the tire iron under the bead next to the valve (**Figure 28**). Force the bead on the opposite side of the tire into the center of the rim and pry the bead over the rim with the tire iron.

6. Insert a second tire iron next to the first to hold the bead over the rim. Then work around the tire with the first tool prying the bead over the rim (**Figure 29**).

NOTE
Step 7 is required only if it is necessary to remove the tire from the rim completely.

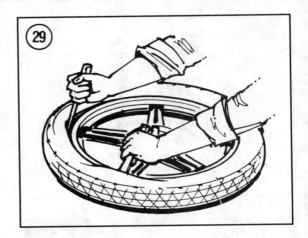

7. Turn the wheel over. Insert a tire tool between the second bead and the same side of the rim that the first bead was pried over (**Figure 30**). Force the bead on the opposite side from the tool into the center of the rim. Pry the second bead off the rim, working around the wheel with 2 tire irons as with the first.

8. Inspect the valve stem seal. Because rubber deteriorates with age, it is advisable to replace the valve stem when replacing a tire. See **Figure 31**.

Installation

1. Carefully inspect the tire for any damage, especially inside.

2. A new tire may have balancing rubbers inside. These are not patches and should not be disturbed. A colored spot near the bead indicates a lighter point on the tire. This spot should be placed next to the valve stem (**Figure 25**). In addition, most tires have directional arrows labeled on the side of the tire that indicate in which direction the tire should rotate (**Figure 32**). Make sure to install the tire accordingly.

3. Lubricate both beads of the tire with soapy water.

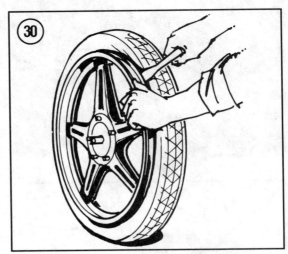

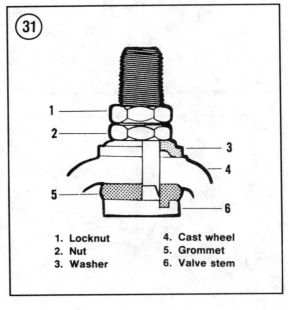

1. Locknut	4. Cast wheel
2. Nut	5. Grommet
3. Washer	6. Valve stem

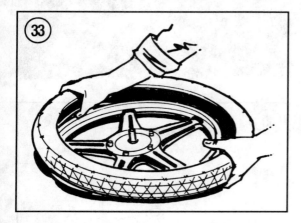

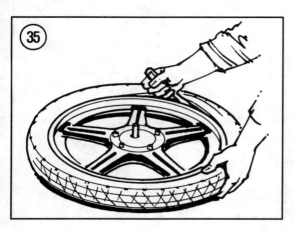

4. Place the backside of the tire into the center of the rim. The lower bead should go into the center of the rim and the upper bead outside. Work around the tire in both directions (**Figure 33**). Use a tire iron for the last few inches of bead (**Figure 34**).

5. Press the upper bead into the rim opposite the valve (**Figure 35**). Pry the bead into the rim on both sides of the initial point with a tire tool, working around the rim to the valve.

6. Check the bead on both sides of the tire for an even fit around the rim.

7. Place an inflatable band around the circumference of the tire. Slowly inflate the band until the tire beads are pressed against the rim. Inflate the tire enough to seat it, deflate the band and remove it.

> **WARNING**
> In the next step, never exceed 56 psi (4.0 k/cm^2) inflation pressure as the tire could burst causing severe injury. Never stand directly over the tire while inflating it.

8. After inflating the tire, check to see that the beads are fully seated and that the tire rim lines (**Figure 36**) are the same distance from the rim all the way around the tire. If the beads won't seat, deflate the tire and relubricate the rim and beads with soapy water.

9. Reinflate the tire to the required pressure. See *Tire Pressure* in Chapter Three. Screw on the valve stem cap.

10. Balance the wheel assembly as described in this chapter.

HANDLEBARS

Removal/Installation

The EX500 uses separate handlebar assemblies (**Figure 37**) that slip over the top of the fork tubes and are bolted directly to the upper fork bridge.

The handlebars can be removed individually by removing the cover plugs and 2 Allen bolts (**Figure 38**) and lifting the handlebar (A, **Figure 39**) off of the upper fork bridge. Allow the handlebar(s) to hang by their control cables while performing service procedures.

Tighten the handlebar Allen bolts to the specifications in **Table 2**.

Inspection

Check the handlebars at their bolt holes and along the entire mounting area for cracks or damage. Replace a bent or damaged handlebar immediately. If the bike is involved in a crash, examine the handlebars, steering stem and front forks carefully.

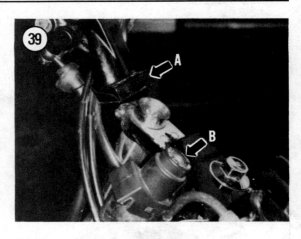

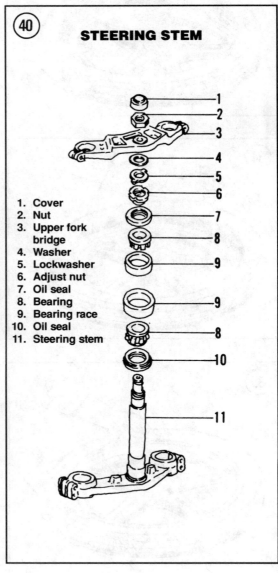

STEERING STEM

1. Cover
2. Nut
3. Upper fork bridge
4. Washer
5. Lockwasher
6. Adjust nut
7. Oil seal
8. Bearing
9. Bearing race
10. Oil seal
11. Steering stem

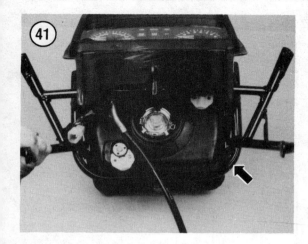

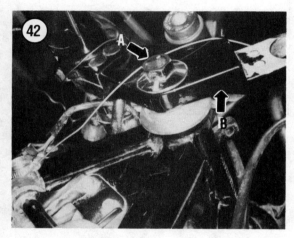

STEERING HEAD

Removal/Disassembly

Refer to **Figure 40**.

1. Support the bike on the centerstand.

2. Remove the upper fairing as described in Chapter Thirteen.

3. Remove the front wheel as described in this chapter.

4. Remove the fuel tank as described in Chapter Seven.

5. Remove the ignition switch bolts and separate the switch (B, **Figure 39**) from the upper fork bridge.

6. Disconnect the speedometer cable.

7. Disconnect headlight and instrument wiring connectors.

8. Remove the front fairing bracket along with the instrument cluster and headlight assembly (**Figure 41**).

9. Remove the handlebars as described in this chapter.

10. Remove the front forks as described in this chapter.

11. Remove the steering nut (A, **Figure 42**) and flat washer.

12. Lift the upper fork bridge (B, **Figure 42**) off the steering stem shaft.

13. Remove the lockwasher and remove the steering adjust nut (**Figure 43**) with a spanner wrench.

14. Remove the bearing cap and pull the steering stem out of the frame (**Figure 44**).

15. Lift the upper bearing from the frame tube.

10

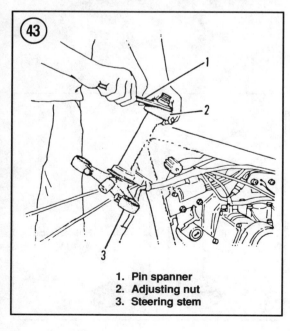

1. Pin spanner
2. Adjusting nut
3. Steering stem

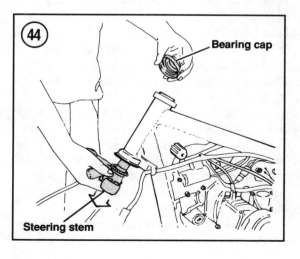

Bearing cap

Steering stem

16. Remove the lower bearing (**Figure 45**) as follows:

   a. Install a bearing puller (**Figure 46**) onto the steering stem and bearing.

   b. Pull the bearing off of the steering stem.

   c. Slide the seal (**Figure 45**) off the steering stem.

Installation

Refer to **Figure 40**.

1. If the lower bearing was removed from the steering stem, install a new bearing as follows:

   a. Clean the steering stem thoroughly in solvent.

   b. Slide a new seal (**Figure 45**) onto the steering stem.

   c. Slide the new bearing onto the steering stem until it stops.

   d. Align the bearing with the machined portion of the shaft and slide a long hollow pipe over the steering stem (**Figure 47**). Drive the bearing until it rests against the seal.

2. Apply a coat of wheel bearing grease to both bearings.

3. Apply a coat of wheel bearing grease to both bearing races.

4. Carefully slide the steering stem up through the frame neck.

5. Install the upper bearing and the bearing cap (**Figure 44**).

6. Install the steering adjust nut and tighten to 7.4 N•m (65 in.-lb.).

7. Turn the steering stem by hand to make sure it turns freely and does not bind. Repeat Step 6 if necessary.

8. Install the lockwasher (5, **Figure 40**).

9. Install the upper fork bridge (B, **Figure 42**).

10. Install the washer and steering stem nut (A, **Figure 42**). Tighten the steering nut to 47 N•m (35 ft.-lb.).

11. Turn the steering stem again by hand to make sure it turns freely and does not bind. If the steering stem is too tight, the bearings can be damaged. If the steering stem is too loose, the steering will become unstable. Repeat Steps 6-10 if necessary.

12. Reverse *Disassembly* Steps 1-10 to complete installation.

13. Recheck the steering adjustment. Repeat if necessary.

14. If brake line was disconnected, bleed the brake system as described under *Bleeding the System* in Chapter Twelve.

Inspection

1. Clean the bearing races in the steering head and both bearings with solvent.

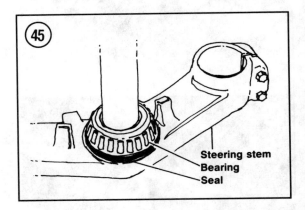

Steering stem
Bearing
Seal

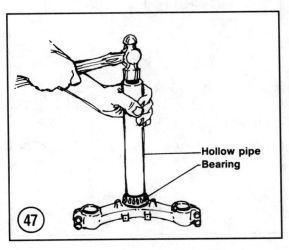

Hollow pipe
Bearing

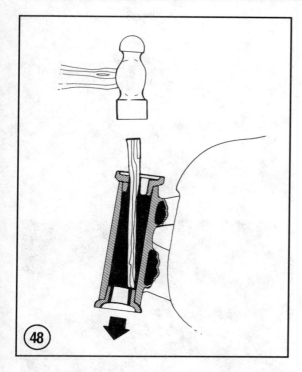

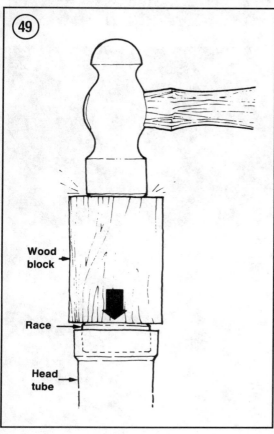

2. Check for broken welds on the frame around the steering head. If any are found, have them repaired by a competent frame shop or welding service familiar with motorcycle frame repair.

3. Check the bearings for pitting, scratches or discoloration indicating wear or corrosion. Replace them in sets if any are bad.

4. Check the upper and lower races in the steering head for pitting, galling and corrosion. If any of these conditions exist, replace them as described in *Bearing Race Replacement* in this chapter.

5. Check steering stem for cracks and check its race for damage or wear. Replace if necessary.

Bearing Race Replacement

The headset and steering stem bearing races are pressed into place. Because they are easily bent, do not remove them unless they are worn and require replacement. Take old races to the dealer to ensure exact replacement.

To remove a headset race, insert a hardwood stick into the head tube and carefully tap the race out from the inside (**Figure 48**). Tap all around the race so that neither the race nor the head tube is bent. To install a race, fit it into the end of the head tube. Tap it slowly and squarely with a block of wood (**Figure 49**).

FRONT FORK

Removal/Installation

1. Place the motorcycle on the centerstand.

2. Remove the front wheel as described in this chapter.

3. Remove the brake caliper as described in Chapter Twelve.

> *NOTE*
> *Insert a piece of wood in the caliper in place of the disc. That way, if the brake lever is inadvertently squeezed, the piston will not be forced out of the caliper. If this happens, the caliper might have to be disassembled to reseat the piston. By using the wood, bleeding the brake is not necessary when installing the wheel.*

4. Remove the handlebars as described in this chapter.

5. Remove the 4 front fender bolts and remove the fender.

6. Loosen the pinch bolts (**Figure 50**) on the upper fork bridge.

> *NOTE*
> *Step 7 describes how to remove the fork cap and spring while the forks are still held in the triple clamps.*

> *WARNING*
> *The fork caps are held under spring pressure. Take precautions to prevent the caps from flying into your face during removal. Furthermore, if the fork tubes are bent, the fork caps will be under considerable pressure. Have them removed by a Kawasaki dealer.*

7. The fork cap and spring are held in position by a circlip (**Figure 51**). To remove the circlip, it is necessary to have an assistant depress the fork cap using a suitable size drift. Then pry the circlip out of its groove in the fork with a suitable tool (**Figure 52**). When the circlip is removed, release tension from

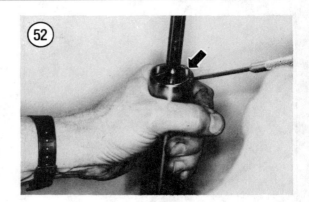

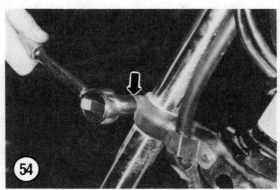

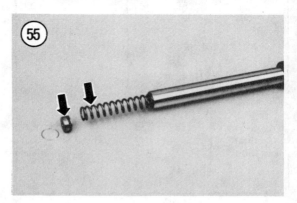

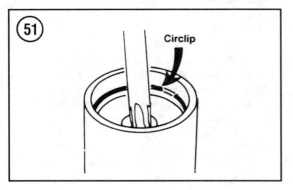

Circlip

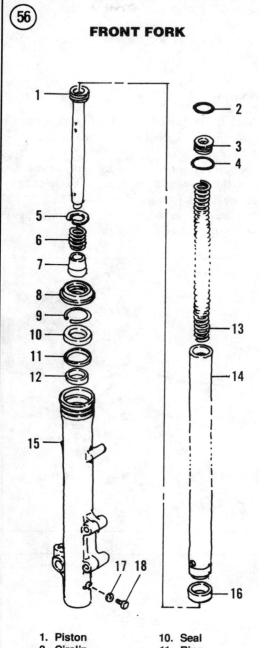

FRONT FORK

56

1. Piston
2. Circlip
3. Fork cap
4. O-ring
5. Ring
6. Spring
7. Oil-lock
8. Oil seal
9. Circlip
10. Seal
11. Ring
12. Ring
13. Spring
14. Inner fork tube
15. Outer fork tube
16. Bushing
17. Washer
18. Drain screw

the fork cap and remove it together with the fork spring (**Figure 53**).

8. Loosen the lower fork bridge bolts. See **Figure 54**.

9. Remove the fork tube. It may be necessary to rotate the tube slightly while removing it.

10. Repeat for the opposite side.

11. Install by reversing these removal steps while noting the following:

   a. Tighten the upper and lower fork bridge pinch bolts to torque specified in **Table 2**.

   b. Install the fork spring and fork cap (**Figure 55**). Have an assistant compress the fork cap and install a new circlip (**Figure 52**).

   c. Make sure the circlip seats fully in the groove in the fork tube before releasing the fork cap.

12. If it is necessary, bleed the brake caliper. See Chapter Twelve.

Disassembly/Reassembly

Refer to **Figure 56** for this procedure.

1. Refer to *Removal/Installation*.

2. Pour the oil out and discard it. Pump the fork several times by hand to expel most of the remaining oil.

3. Remove the Allen bolt and gasket from the bottom of the outer tube. Prevent the cylinder from turning with Kawasaki tools (part Nos. 57001-183 and 57001-1057). See **Figure 57**.

NOTE
The Allen bolt may be removed without holding the cylinder if an impact driver is used.

4. Remove the rubber boot out of the notch in the lower fork tube and slide it off of the upper fork tube.

5. Clamp the slider in a vise with soft jaws.

6. Remove the retainer and washer from the outer tube.

7. Hold the fork tube in a vertical position. Then install the Kawasaki tool (part No. 57001-1091) onto the inner tube and tap the outer tube until it falls off the inner tube. See **Figure 58**.

CAUTION
Do not tap the outer tube when the fork assembly is placed in a horizontal position. Removing the outer tube in this

10

position will damage the inner tube guide bushing.

8. Remove the oil seal, washer and outer tube guide bushing with the oil seal and bearing remover (Kawasaki tool No. 57001-1058). See **Figure 59**.

9. Remove the cylinder base, spring washers and washer from the bottom of the outer tube.

10. Assembly is the reverse of these steps. Note the following.

    a. Tap the oil seal into place using a socket of appropriate diameter.

    b. Apply Loctite 242 (blue) to the Allen bolt during reassembly.

    c. Install the spring so that the end with the tighter coils is upward.

11. Pour in the correct amount of fork oil. See Chapter Three.

Inspection

1. Check the upper fork tube exterior for scratches and straightness. If bent or scratched, it should be replaced.

2. Check the lower fork tube for dents or exterior damage that may cause the upper fork tube to hang up during riding. Replace if necessary.

3. Measure the front fork spring free length. Replace the spring if it is too short (**Table 1**).

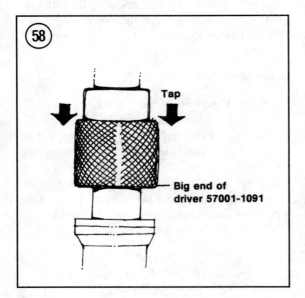

Tap

Big end of driver 57001-1091

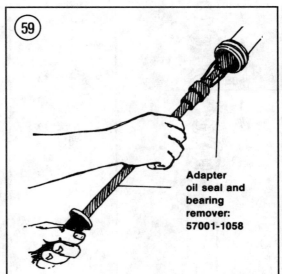

Adapter oil seal and bearing remover: 57001-1058

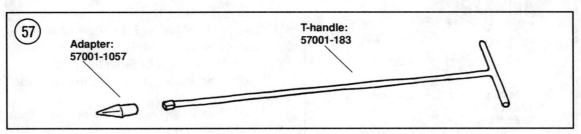

Adapter: 57001-1057

T-handle: 57001-183

Table 1 FRONT SUSPENSION WEAR LIMITS

	mm	in.
Steering stem ball size*	6.35 O.D.	1/4 O.D.
For spring free length	506	19.92
*Quantity: 20 top and 20 bottom		

Table 2 FRONT SUSPENSION TIGHTENING TORQUES

	N•m	ft.-lb.
Front axle nut	88	65
Front fork		
Upper clamp bolts	20	15
Lower clamp bolts	29	21
Bottom Allen bolt	29	21
Handlebar holder/mounting bolts	23	17
Handlebar mounting bolts	12	17
Steering stem head bolt	47	35
Steering stem locknut	7.4	65 in.-lb.

10

CHAPTER ELEVEN

REAR SUSPENSION

This chapter includes repair and replacement procedures for the rear wheel, drive chain and rear suspension components.

Tables 1-3 are at the end of the chapter.

REAR WHEEL

Removal/Installation

1. Support the bike so that the rear wheel clears the ground.
2. Remove the cotter pin, then disconnect the torque link (**Figure 1**) at the rear brake. Then remove the rear brake adjuster nut (**Figure 2**).
3. Loosen the drive chain adjusting locknuts and adjuster bolts (A, **Figure 3**).
4. Remove the cotter pin, rear axle nut and washer (B, **Figure 3**).
5. Slide the axle out of the wheel and allow the wheel to drop to the ground.
6. Remove the axle spacer (**Figure 4**).
7. Lift the drive chain off of the sprocket and remove the rear wheel.
8. If the wheel is going to be taken off for any length of time, or if it is to be taken to a shop for repair, install the chain adjusters and axle spacers on

the axle along with the axle nut to prevent losing any parts.
9. Install by reversing these removal steps. Note the following.
10. Adjust the drive chain as described in Chapter Three.
11. Tighten the torque link nut securely. Secure the nut with a new cotter pin.
12. Tighten the axle nut to specifications in **Table 3**. Secure the nut with a new cotter pin.
13. Adjust the rear brake as described in Chapter Three.
14. Spin the wheel several times to make sure it rotates freely and that the brakes work properly.

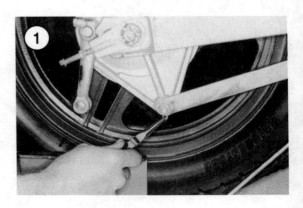

Inspection

Measure the axial and radial runout of the wheel with a dial indicator as shown in **Figure 5**. The maximum allowable axial runout is 0.5 mm (0.019 in.) and the radial runout is 0.8 mm (0.031 in.). If the runout exceeds this dimension, check the wheel bearings. If the wheel bearings are in good condition on cast wheels and no other cause can be found, the wheel will have to be replaced as it cannot be serviced. Inspect the wheel for signs of cracks, fractures, dents or bends.

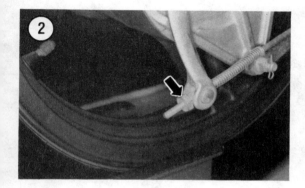

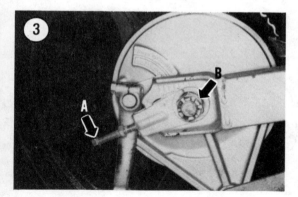

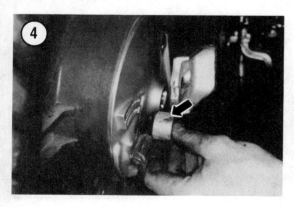

WARNING
Do not try to repair any damage to cast wheels as it will result in an unsafe riding condition.

REAR HUB

Bearing removal usually destroys the bearings. Check the bearings for wear while they are still installed in the hub. Replace any questionable bearings.

Disassembly/Inspection/Reassembly

Refer to **Figure 6**, typical for this procedure.

1. Pull the rear sprocket/coupling assembly from the hub (**Figure 7**).

2. Remove the rubber damper (**Figure 8**).

3. Remove the circlip (**Figure 9**).

4. Insert a long drift punch from the right-hand side and remove the left-hand bearing (**Figure 10**). Tap evenly around the inner race so that the bearing will not get cocked in its bore during removal.

5. Remove the distance collar (11, **Figure 6**).

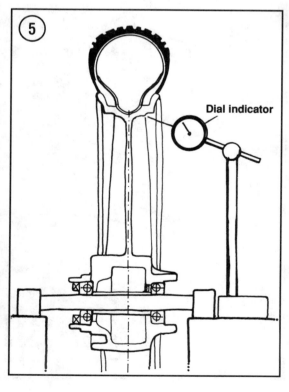

Dial indicator

11

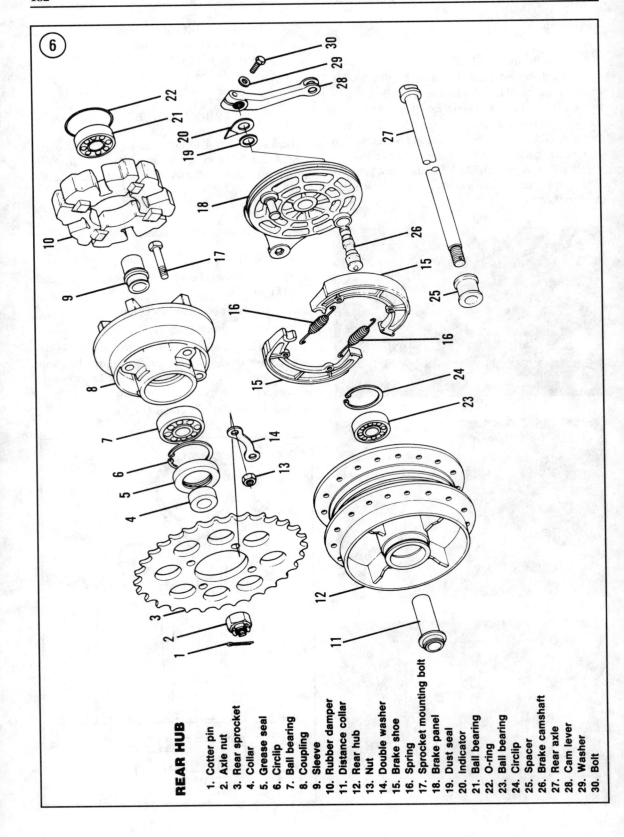

REAR HUB

1. Cotter pin
2. Axle nut
3. Rear sprocket
4. Collar
5. Grease seal
6. Circlip
7. Ball bearing
8. Coupling
9. Sleeve
10. Rubber damper
11. Distance collar
12. Rear hub
13. Nut
14. Double washer
15. Brake shoe
16. Spring
17. Sprocket mounting bolt
18. Brake panel
19. Dust seal
20. Indicator
21. Ball bearing
22. O-ring
23. Ball bearing
24. Circlip
25. Spacer
26. Brake camshaft
27. Rear axle
28. Cam lever
29. Washer
30. Bolt

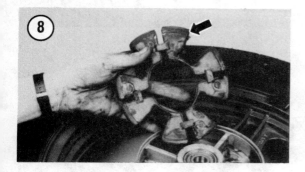

6. Turn the wheel over and repeat Step 4 to drive out the right-hand bearing (**Figure 10**).

7. Clean the hub thoroughly in solvent and check for cracks or damage in the bearing area. Replace the hub if necessary.

8. Blow any dirt or foreign matter out of the hub before installing the bearings.

9. Pack non-sealed bearings with grease before installation.

NOTE
Install the right-hand bearing (23, Figure 6) with the flush side facing outward.

10. Tap the bearing (23, **Figure 6**) into position with a socket placed on the outer bearing race (**Figure 11**). Then install the distance collar (11, **Figure 6**) and install the opposite bearing (21, **Figure 6**).

11. Install the circlip (**Figure 9**) and rubber damper (**Figure 8**).

12. Install the rear sprocket/coupling assembly into the hub.

REAR WHEEL COUPLING

The rear wheel coupling (**Figure 12**, typical) connects the rear sprocket to the rear wheel. Rubber shock dampers installed in the coupling absorb some of the shock that results from torque changes during acceleration or braking.

Removal/Installation

1. Remove the rear wheel as described in this chapter.

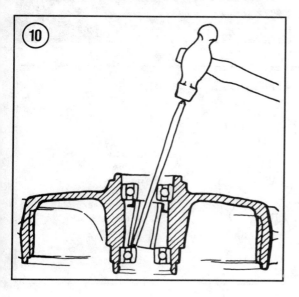

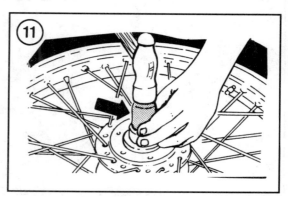

2. Pull the rear wheel coupling assembly (**Figure 7**) up and out of the wheel hub.

3. Pull the dampers out of the housing (**Figure 8**).

4. Remove the spacer (A, **Figure 13**).

5. To remove the sprocket, loosen and remove the nuts and lift the sprocket off of the housing (A, **Figure 14**).

6. Perform *Inspection/Disassembly/Reassembly* as described in this chapter.

7. Install by reversing these steps. Note the following:

    a. Install the sprocket so that the chamfered side faces toward the housing.

    b. Apply Loctite 242 (blue) to the sprocket nuts and tighten them to the specifications in **Table 3**.

Inspection/Disassembly/Reassembly

1. Visually inspect the rubber dampers (**Figure 8**) for damage or deterioration. Replace, if necessary, as a complete set.

2. Inspect the flange assembly housing and damper separators (B, **Figure 13**) for cracks or damage. Replace the coupling housing if necessary.

3. If necessary, replace the coupling housing bearing(s) as follows:

    a. Pry the seal from the housing, (B, **Figure 14**).

    b. Remove the bearing circlips (2, **Figure 12**).

    c. Insert a long drift punch from the right-hand side and remove the bearing. Tap evenly around the inner race so that the bearing will not get cocked in its bore during removal.

    d. Remove the distance collar (center spacer).

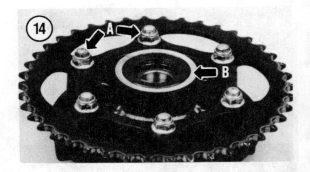

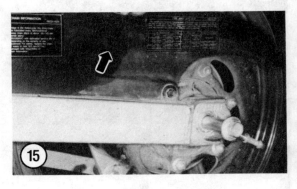

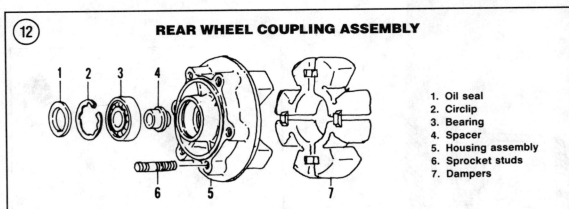

REAR WHEEL COUPLING ASSEMBLY

1. Oil seal
2. Circlip
3. Bearing
4. Spacer
5. Housing assembly
6. Sprocket studs
7. Dampers

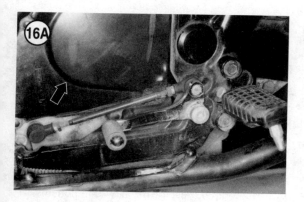

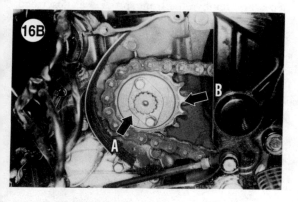

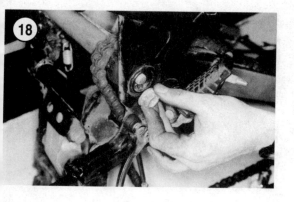

e. Turn the wheel over and repeat Sub-step c to drive out the opposite bearing.

f. Discard the bearings.

g. Clean the housing thoroughly in solvent and check for cracks or damage in the bearing area.

h. Blow any dirt or foreign matter out of the housing before installing the bearings.

i. Pack non-sealed bearings with grease before installation.

j. Tap the bearing into position with a socket placed on the outer bearing race.

k. If necessary, install the spacer and opposite bearing. Install the bearing circlips.

l. If necessary, install a new seal (B, **Figure 14**) by driving it in squarely with a socket and hammer.

DRIVE CHAIN

Because the drive chain is endless (has no master link), the swing arm must be removed to remove the drive chain.

> *WARNING*
> *Kawasaki uses an endless chain on this model for strength and reliability. Do not cut the chain with a chain cutter or install chain with a master link. The chain may fail and rear wheel lockup could result in an accident.*

Removal/Installation

1. Remove the rear wheel as described in this chapter.

2. Remove the chain guard (**Figure 15**).

3. Remove the screws securing the engine sprocket cover (**Figure 16A**) and remove the cover.

> *NOTE*
> *Perform Steps 4 and 5 if front sprocket removal is required.*

4. Remove the two bolts securing the front sprocket.

5. Remove the holding plate (A, **Figure 16B**), then slide the front sprocket (B, **Figure 16B**) off the output shaft.

6. Separate the drive chain from the front sprocket.

7. Remove the swing arm pivot covers (**Figure 17**).

8. Loosen and remove the swing arm pivot shaft nut (**Figure 18**).

9. Remove the following:
  a. Uni-Trak tie-rod upper nuts (**Figure 19**).
  b. Lower shock absorber nut (A, **Figure 20**).
10. Remove the shock absorber bolt, tie rod bolts and swing arm pivot shaft and pull the swing arm toward the rear.
11. Slip the drive chain off the swing arm.
12. Install by reversing the removal steps. Note the following:
  a. Tighten the lower shock absorber shaft and the Uni-Trak nuts to the specifications in **Table 3**.
  b. Tighten the pivot shaft to specifications (**Table 3**).
  c. Adjust the drive chain as described under *Drive Chain Adjustment* in Chapter Three.
  d. Tighten the axle nut to the torque values in **Table 3**.
  e. Rotate the wheel several times to make sure it rotates smoothly. Apply the brake several times to make sure it operates correctly.
  f. Adjust the rear brake as described under *Rear Brake Pedal Height Adjustment* and *Rear Brake Light Switch Adjustment* in Chapter Three.

CLEANING

CAUTION
The factory drive chain is equipped with O-rings between the side plates that seal lubricant between the pins and bushings. To prevent damaging these O-rings, use only kerosene or diesel oil for cleaning. Do not use gasoline or other solvents that will cause the O-rings to swell or deteriorate.

Occasionally, the drive chain should be removed from the bike for a thorough cleaning and soak lubrication. Perform the following:
  a. Brush off excess dirt and grit.
  b. Remove the drive chain as described in this chapter.
  c. Soak the chain in kerosene or diesel oil for about half an hour and clean it thoroughly. Then hang the chain from a piece of wire and allow it to dry.
  d. Install the chain on the motorcycle as described in this chapter

Lubrication

For lubrication of the drive chain, refer to *Drive Chain Lubrication* in Chapter Three.

Sprocket Inspection

Inspect the teeth of the sprockets. If the teeth are visibly worn (**Figure 21**), replace both sprockets and the drive chain. Never replace any one sprocket or chain as a separate item; worn parts will cause rapid wear of the new components. If necessary, remove the front sprocket as described in Steps 3-6 under *Drive Chain Removal/Installation*.

WHEEL BALANCING

For complete information, refer to *Wheel Balancing* in Chapter Ten.

TIRE CHANGING

Refer to *Tubeless Tire Changing* in Chapter Ten.

REAR SHOCK ABSORBER

Removal/Installation

Refer to **Figure 22** for this procedure.

1. Park the bike on its centerstand.

2. Remove the seat and side covers.

3. Loosen, but do not remove, the upper shock absorber nut (**Figure 23**).

4. Remove the following:

   a. Lower shock absorber bolt (A, **Figure 20**).

   b. Lower tie-rod bolt (B, **Figure 20**).

   c. Upper shock absorber nut and bolt (**Figure 23**).

5. Lower the shock absorber and remove it from underneath the swing arm.

6. Install by reversing these steps. Note the following:

   a. Tighten the upper and lower shock absorber nuts to the specifications in **Table 3**.

   b. Tighten the tie-rod nut to the specifications in **Table 3**.

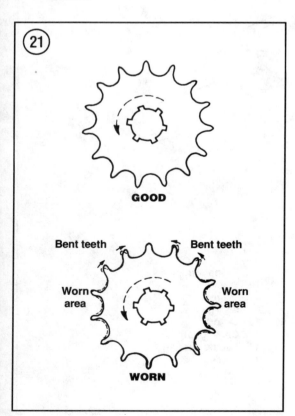

UNI-TRAK PRELOAD ADJUSTMENT

The rear shock absorber can be adjusted to suit various riding conditions by changing the spring preload.

Adjustment

Refer to **Figure 22**.

1. Remove the shock absorber as described in this chapter.

2. Loosen the locknut (A, **Figure 24**) and unscrew the adjusting nut (B, **Figure 24**) until the spring is fully extended.

3. Measure the free length of the shock absorber spring.

4. Turn the adjusting nut in to strengthen (firmer ride) the spring preload or out to weaken (spongy ride) spring preload.

5. Securely tighten the locknut to retain the adjustment setting.

REAR SWING ARM

Removal/Installation

Refer to **Figure 22** for this procedure.

1. Park the motorcycle on its centerstand.

2. Remove the seat and side covers.

3. Remove the mufflers.

4. Remove the chain guard.

5. Remove the rear wheel as described in this chapter.

6. Remove the swing arm pivot shaft covers (**Figure 17**).

7. Remove the following:

   a. Torque arm nut and bolt (**Figure 1**).

   b. Swing arm pivot nut (**Figure 18**).

   c. Uni-Trak upper tie-rod nut (**Figure 19**).

   d. Lower shock absorber nut (**Figure 20**).

8. Remove the shock absorber bolt, tie-rod bolts and swing arm pivot shaft and pull the swing arm toward the rear.

9. Remove the drive chain, if necessary.

10. Installation is the reverse of these steps. Note the following:

   a. Tighten the swing arm pivot nut to specifications in **Table 3**.

   b. Tighten the lower shock absorber nut and upper tie-rod nut to specifications in **Table 3**.

11

㉒ **UNI-TRAK AND SWING ARM ASSEMBLY**

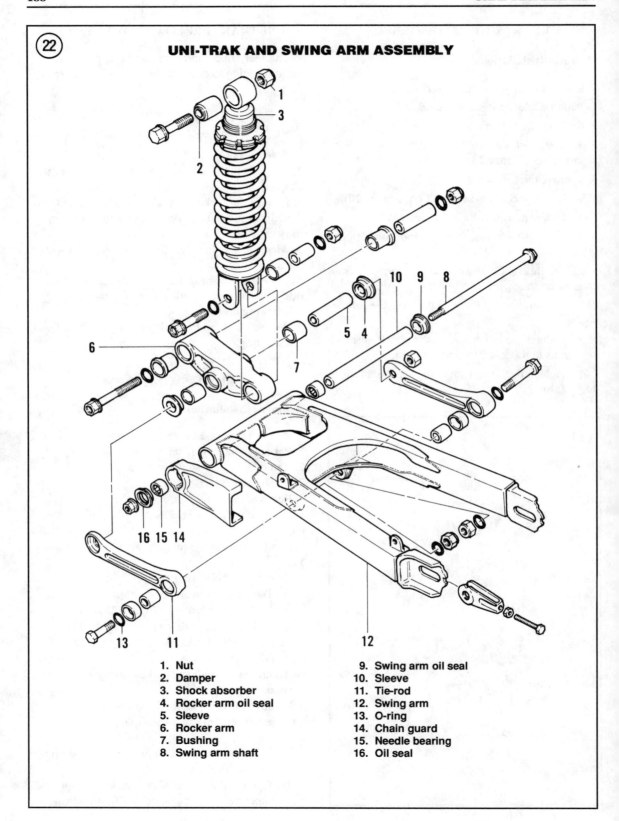

1. Nut
2. Damper
3. Shock absorber
4. Rocker arm oil seal
5. Sleeve
6. Rocker arm
7. Bushing
8. Swing arm shaft
9. Swing arm oil seal
10. Sleeve
11. Tie-rod
12. Swing arm
13. O-ring
14. Chain guard
15. Needle bearing
16. Oil seal

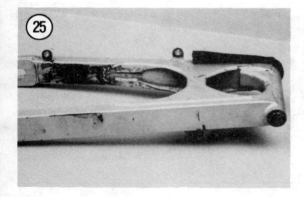

c. Tighten the torque link nut to specifications.

d. Adjust drive chain as described under *Drive Chain Adjustment* in Chapter Three.

Inspection and Bearing Replacement

Refer to **Figure 22**.

1. Check the swing arm (**Figure 25**) for cracks, twisting, weld breakage or other damage. Refer repair to a competent welding shop.

2. Pry the bearing seals (A, **Figure 26**) out of the swing arm.

3. The roller bearings (B, **Figure 26**) wear very slowly and the wear is difficult to measure. Turn the bearings by hand. Make sure they rotate smoothly. Check the rollers for evidence of wear, pitting or color change indicating heat from lack of lubrication. In severe instances, the needles will fall out of the bearing cage.

4. Replace the bearings as follows:

a. Using a long metal rod or drift punch, tap one of the bearings out of the swing arm (**Figure 27**).

b. Remove the center sleeve and remove opposite bearing.

c. Clean the swing arm bearing bore with solvent and allow to dry.

d. Lubricate the bearings with oil before installation.

e. Install the new bearings with a hydraulic press. Make sure to install the center sleeve

11

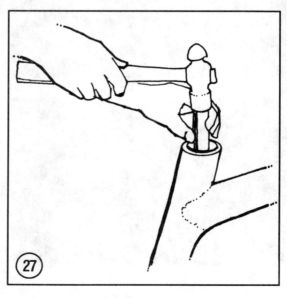

after installing the first bearing. If a press is not available, a bearing installer can be fabricated with a piece of pipe and a long threaded rod. See **Figure 31**.

> *WARNING*
> *Never reinstall a needle bearing that has been removed. During removal it is damaged and no longer true to alignment. If installed, it will damage the sleeve and create an unsafe riding condition.*

f. Apply a coat of molybdenum disulfide grease to the inner needle bearing surface.

Tie-Rod Removal/Installation

The tie-rods can be removed without having to remove the swing arm. Refer to **Figure 22**.
1. Place the motorcycle on its centerstand.
2. Remove the lower tie-rod bolt (A, **Figure 28**) at the rocker arm and the upper tie-rod bolt at the swing arm (B, **Figure 28**).
3. Remove the other tie-rod.

4. Installation is the reverse of these steps. Tighten the tie-rod nuts and bolts to the torque specifications in **Table 3**.

Rocker Arm Removal/Installation

The rocker arm can be removed without having to remove the swing arm. Refer to **Figure 22**.
1. Place the motorcycle on the centerstand.
2. Remove the lower tie-rod bolt (A, **Figure 28**) and lower shock absorber pivot bolt (**Figure 20**).
3. Remove the rocker arm pivot bolt at the frame (**Figure 29**) and remove the rocker arm.
4. Install by reversing these steps. Tighten all Uni-Trak nuts to the specifications in **Table 3**.

Rocker Arm and Tie-Rod Inspection

The rocker arm is equipped with bushings (A, **Figure 30**) and O-rings (B, **Figure 30**) where pivoting takes place. Check the bushings for evidence of wear, pitting or color change indicating heat from lack of lubrication. Replace O-rings if cracking or swelling exists.

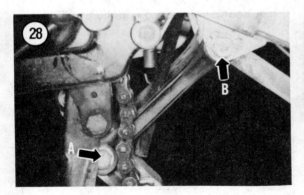

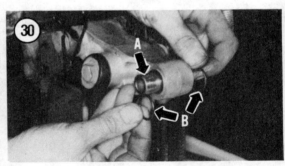

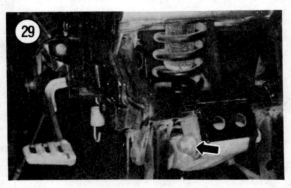

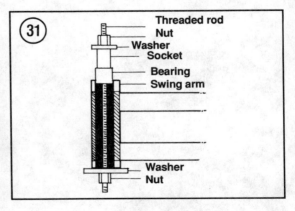

Table 1 REAR SUSPENSION WEAR LIMITS

	mm	in.
Rim runout	2	0.078
Axle runout	0.7	0.027

Table 2 DRIVE CHAIN SPECIFICATIONS

Manufacturer	Enuma endless
Size	EK250 MV-O 104 links
20 link length	
Standard	317.5-318.4 mm (12.50-12.54 in.)
Service limit	323 mm (12.72 in.)
Chain slack	35-40 mm (1.37-1.57 in.)

Table 3 REAR SUSPENSION TIGHTENING TORQUES

	N•m	ft.-lb.
Rear axle nut	110	81
Front sprocket bolt	9.8	87 in.-lb.
Rear sprocket nuts	88	65
Shock absorber bolts and nuts	49	36
Pivot shaft nut	88	65
Uni-Trak nuts	49	36
Brake stay arm nuts	29	21

11

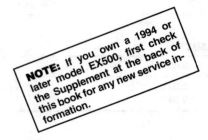
NOTE: If you own a 1994 or later model EX500, first check the Supplement at the back of this book for any new service information.

CHAPTER TWELVE

BRAKES

The EX500 is equipped with a dual-piston front disc brake and a rear drum brake. This chapter describes repair and replacement procedures for all brake components.

Refer to **Table 1** for brake wear limits. **Tables 1-2** are found at the end of the chapter.

FRONT DISC BRAKES

The front disc brake is actuated by hydraulic fluid controlled by the hand lever on the right-hand side of the handlebar. As the brake pads wear, the brake fluid level drops in the master cylinder reservoir and automatically adjusts for pad wear. However, brake lever free play must be maintained. Refer to *Front Brake Lever Adjustment* in Chapter Three.

When working on a hydraulic brake system, it is necessary that the work area and all tools be absolutely clean. Any tiny particles of foreign matter or grit on the caliper assembly or the master cylinder can damage the components. Also, sharp tools must not be used inside the caliper or on the caliper pistons. If there is any doubt about your ability to correctly and safely carry out major service on the brake components, take the job to a Kawasaki dealer or brake specialist.

When adding brake fluid, use only a type clearly marked DOT 3 and use it from a sealed container. Brake fluid will draw moisture which greatly reduces its ability to perform correctly, so it is a good idea to purchase brake fluid in small containers and discard what is not used.

Whenever *any* component has been removed from the brake system, the system is considered "opened" and must be bled to remove air bubbles. Also, if the brake feels "spongy" this usually means there are air bubbles in the system and it must be bled. For safe brake operation, refer to *Bleeding the System* in this chapter for complete details.

> *CAUTION*
> *Disc brake components rarely require disassembly, so do not disassemble unless absolutely necessary. Do not use solvents of any kind on the brake system's internal components. Solvents will cause the seals to swell and distort. When disassembling and cleaning brake components, except brake pads, use new brake fluid.*

FRONT BRAKE PAD REPLACEMENT

There is no recommended mileage interval for changing the friction pads on the disc brakes. Pad wear depends greatly on riding habits and conditions. The pads should be checked for wear at specified intervals. See Chapter Three.

Service Notes

Observe the following service notes before replacing brake pads.

1. Brake pads should be replaced only as a set.

2. Disconnecting the hydraulic brake hose is not required for brake pad replacement. Disconnect the hose only if caliper removal is required.

3. When new pads are installed in the caliper, the master cylinder brake fluid level will rise as the caliper pistons are repositioned. Clean the top of the master cylinder of all dirt and foreign matter. Remove the cap (**Figure 1**) and diaphragm. Then slowly push the caliper pistons into the caliper. Constantly check the reservoir to make sure brake fluid does not overflow. Remove fluid, if necessary, before it overflows. The pistons should move freely. If they don't, and there is evidence of them sticking in the cylinder, the caliper should be removed and serviced as described under *Caliper Rebuilding* in this chapter.

4. Push the caliper pistons in to allow room for the new pads.

5. Refill the master cylinder reservoir, if necessary, to maintain the correct fluid level. Install the diaphragm and top cap.

WARNING
Use brake fluid clearly marked DOT 3 from a sealed container. Other types

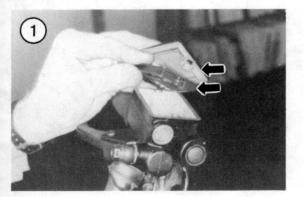

may vaporize and cause brake failure. Always use the same brand name; do not intermix brake fluids. Many brands are not compatible.

WARNING
*Do not ride the motorcycle until you are sure the brake is operating correctly. If necessary, bleed the brake as described under **Bleeding the System** in this chapter.*

Pad Replacement

Refer to **Figure 2**.

1. Remove the 2 caliper bolts and lift the caliper off the front fork (**Figure 3**).

WARNING
*When working on the brake system, do **not** inhale brake dust. It may contain asbestos, which can cause lung injury and cancer. Wear a disposable face mask and wash your hands thoroughly after completing work.*

2. Lift the inner pad (A, **Figure 4**) out of the caliper.

3. Push the caliper holder (B, **Figure 4**) toward the caliper pistons. Then remove the outer brake pad (C, **Figure 4**).

4. Lift the anti-rattle spring (A, **Figure 5**) out of the caliper.

5. Check the caliper holder to make sure the clips (B, **Figure 5**) are installed. **Figure 6** shows the caliper holder (A) and clips (B) with the holder removed for clarity.

6. Remove the cap and diaphragm from the master cylinder (**Figure 1**) and slowly push the pistons into the caliper while checking the reservoir to make sure it doesn't overflow. The pistons should move freely. You may need to use a C-clamp to push the pistons back into the caliper. If the pistons stick, remove the caliper as described in this chapter and have it rebuilt.

7. Install a new anti-rattle spring into the caliper (A, **Figure 5**).

8. Align the holes in the outer brake pad plate and install it onto the caliper holder (C, **Figure 4**).

9. Drop the inner brake pad (A, **Figure 4**) into the caliper.

12

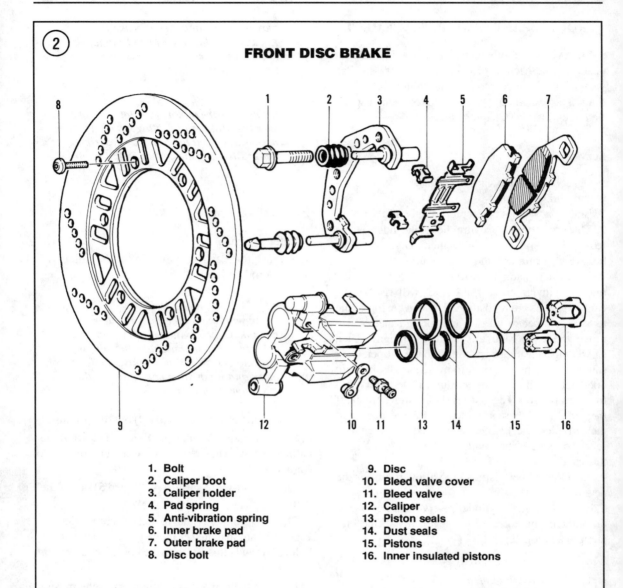

FRONT DISC BRAKE

1. Bolt
2. Caliper boot
3. Caliper holder
4. Pad spring
5. Anti-vibration spring
6. Inner brake pad
7. Outer brake pad
8. Disc bolt
9. Disc
10. Bleed valve cover
11. Bleed valve
12. Caliper
13. Piston seals
14. Dust seals
15. Pistons
16. Inner insulated pistons

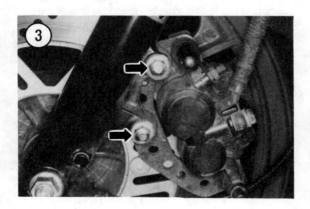

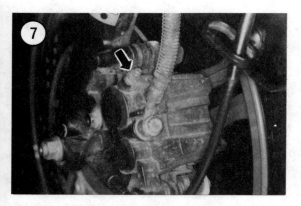

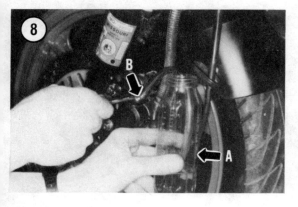

NOTE
Install the pads with the friction material toward the disc.

10. Carefully align the brake pads with the brake disc and install the caliper. Install the caliper bolts (**Figure 3**) and tighten to specifications in **Table 2**.

11. Support the motorcycle with the wheel off the ground. Spin the wheel and pump the brake until the pads are seated against the disc.

12. Refill the master cylinder with brake fluid, if necessary, and replace the diaphragm and top cap. See *Service Notes*.

WARNING
Use brake fluid clearly marked DOT 3 from a sealed container. Other types may vaporize and cause brake failure. Always use the same brand name. Do not intermix brake fluids. Many brands are not compatible.

WARNING
Do not ride the motorcycle until you are sure the brakes are working correctly.

FRONT CALIPER

Removal/Installation

1. Drain the master cylinder as follows:
   a. Attach a hose to the brake caliper bleed screw (**Figure 7**).
   b. Place the end of the hose in a clean container (A, **Figure 8**).
   c. Open the bleed screw (B, **Figure 8**) and operate the brake lever to drain all brake fluid from the master cylinder reservoir.
   d. Close the bleed screw (**Figure 7**) and disconnect the hose.
   e. Discard the brake fluid.

WARNING
Dispose of brake fluid according to local EPA regulations—never reuse brake fluid. Contaminated fluid can cause brake failure.

2. Remove the bolt and copper sealing washers attaching the brake hose to the caliper. To prevent loss of fluid, cap the end of the brake hose and tie it up to the fender. Be sure to cap or tape the ends to prevent the entry of moisture and dirt.

12

3. Remove the brake pads as described under *Brake Pad Replacement* in this chapter.

4. Installation is the reverse of these steps. Note the following:

    a. Torque the caliper attaching bolts to specifications in **Table 2**.

    b. Install the brake hose using new copper washers.

    c. Tighten the brake hose banjo bolt to specifications in **Table 2**.

    d. Bleed the brakes as described under *Bleeding the System* in this chapter.

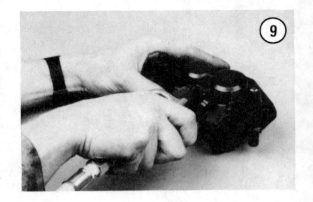

> *WARNING*
> *Do not ride the motorcycle until you are sure that the brakes are operating properly.*

Caliper Rebuilding

If the caliper leaks, the caliper should be rebuilt. If the piston sticks in the cylinder, indicating severe wear or galling, the entire unit should be replaced.

Refer to **Figure 2**.

1. Remove the brake caliper as described in this chapter.

2. Pull the caliper out of the holder.

> *WARNING*
> *When working on the brake system, do **not** inhale brake dust. It may contain asbestos, which can cause lung injury and cancer. Wear a disposable face mask and wash your hands thoroughly after completing work.*

> *NOTE*
> *Compressed air will be required to remove the pistons.*

> *WARNING*
> *Keep your fingers and hand out of the caliper bore area when removing the pistons in Step 3. The pistons will fly out of the bore with considerable force and could crush your hand or fingers.*

3. Pad the pistons with shop rags or wooden blocks. Then apply compressed air through one of the caliper ports and blow the pistons out of the caliper (**Figure 9**).

4. Remove the dust seals (**Figure 10**) and piston seals (**Figure 11**) from the caliper bore.

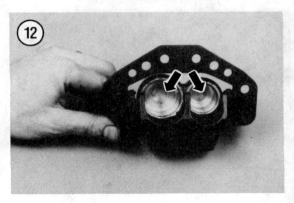

5. Clean all caliper parts (except brake pads) in new DOT 3 brake fluid. Place the cleaned parts on a lint-free cloth while performing the following inspection procedures.

6. Check the caliper bores (**Figure 12**) for cracks, deep scoring or excessive wear.

7. Check the caliper pistons (**Figure 13**) for deep scoring, excessive wear or rust.

8. Replace the caliper housing or pistons if necessary.

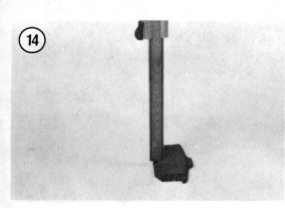

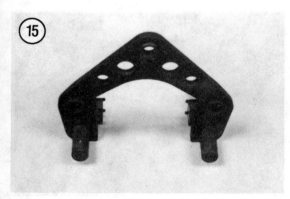

9. The piston seal (**Figure 11**) maintains correct brake pad-to-disc clearance. If the seal is worn or damaged, the brake pads will drag and cause excessive pad wear and brake fluid temperatures. Replace the piston seals (**Figure 11**) and dust seals (**Figure 10**) if the following conditions exist:

    a. Brake fluid leaks around the inner brake pad.

    b. The piston seal (**Figure 11**) is stuck in the caliper groove.

    c. There is a large difference in inner and outer brake pad wear (**Figure 4**).

10. Measure the brake pad friction material with a ruler or caliper (**Figure 14**) and compare to wear limits in **Table 1**. Replace both brake pads if any one pad is too thin.

11. Check the caliper holder (**Figure 15**) for cracks or other damage. Replace the support if necessary.

FRONT MASTER CYLINDER

Removal/Installation

> *CAUTION*
> *Cover the fuel tank, front fender and instrument cluster with a heavy cloth or plastic tarp to protect them from accidental spilling of brake fluid. Wash any spilled brake fluid off any painted or plated surfaces immediately as it will destroy the finish. Use soapy water and rinse completely.*

1. Drain the master cylinder as follows:

    a. Attach a hose to the brake caliper bleed screw (**Figure 7**).

    b. Place the end of the hose in a clean container (A, **Figure 8**).

    c. Open the bleed screw (B, **Figure 8**) and operate the brake lever to drain all brake fluid from the master cylinder reservoir.

    d. Close the bleed screw and disconnect the hose.

    e. Discard the brake fluid.

2. Disconnect the brake switch wires at the master cylinder.

3. Remove the bolt securing the brake hose to the master cylinder (**Figure 16**). Remove the brake hose and both copper sealing washers. Cover the end of the hose to prevent the entry of foreign matter and moisture. Tie the hose end up to the handlebar to prevent the loss of brake fluid.

12

4. Remove the two clamping bolts (A, **Figure 17**) and clamp securing the master cylinder to the handlebar and remove the master cylinder (B, **Figure 17**).

5. Install by reversing these removal steps. Note the following:

    a. Install the master cylinder clamp with the arrow facing upward, if so marked.

    b. Tighten the upper clamp bolt first, then the lower bolt to specifications in **Table 2**. There should be a gap at the lower part of the clamp after tightening.

    c. Install the brake hose onto the master cylinder. Be sure to place a copper sealing washer on each side of the hose fitting and install the banjo bolt. Tighten the banjo bolt to the specification listed in **Table 2**.

    d. Bleed the brake system as described under *Bleeding the System* in this chapter.

WARNING
Do not ride the motorcycle until the front brake is operating correctly.

Disassembly/Reassembly

Refer to **Figure 18**.

1. Remove the master cylinder as described in this chapter.

2. Remove the screws securing the reservoir cap and diaphragm. Pour out the remaining brake fluid and discard it. *Never* reuse brake fluid.

3. Remove the rubber boot from the area where the hand lever actuates the internal piston.

4. Remove the brake lever.

5. Remove the dust cover.

CAUTION
Do not remove the secondary cup from the piston when removing the piston assembly in Step 6. Removing the secondary cup from the piston will damage the cup.

6. Remove the piston assembly and spring as shown in **Figure 18**. Remove the primary cup from the piston assembly.

7. Inspect the master cylinder assembly as described in this chapter.

8. Assembly is the reverse of these steps. Note the following:

    a. Soak the new cups in fresh brake fluid for at least 15 minutes to make them pliable. Coat the inside of the cylinder with fresh brake fluid before assembling the parts.

CAUTION
When installing the piston assembly, do not allow the cups to turn inside out as they will be damaged and allow brake fluid to leak within the cylinder bore.

    b. Install the master cylinder piston assembly in the order shown in **Figure 18**. Make sure the dust cover is firmly seated in the groove in the cylinder.

Inspection

1. Clean all parts in fresh DOT 3 brake fluid. Inspect the cylinder bore and piston contact surfaces for signs of wear or damage. If either part is less than perfect, replace it.

2. Place the master cylinder on a clean lint-free cloth when performing the following inspection procedures.

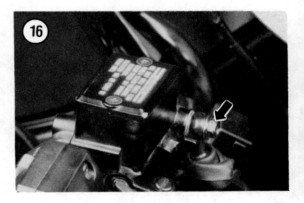

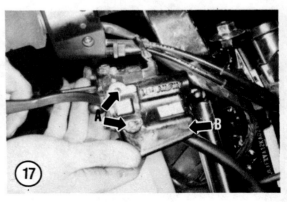

3. Check the end of the piston for wear caused by the hand lever. Replace the entire piston assembly if any portion of the piston requires replacement.

4. Check the secondary cup (on the piston) for damage, softness or for swollen conditions. Replace the piston assembly if necessary.

5. Check the primary cup for the same conditions in Step 3. Replace the primary cup if necessary.

6. Inspect the pivot hole in the hand lever. If worn, it must be replaced.

7. Make sure the passages in the bottom of the brake fluid reservoir are clear. Check the reservoir cap and diaphragm for damage and deterioration. Replace if necessary.

8. Inspect the threads in the master cylinder body where the brake hose banjo bolt screws in. If the threads are damaged or partially stripped, replace the master cylinder body.

FRONT BRAKE HOSE REPLACEMENT

Brake hoses should be replaced whenever signs of cracking, leakage or damage are apparent. The deterioration of rubber by ozone and other atmospheric elements may require hose replacement every 4 years.

CAUTION
Cover the front wheel, fender and fuel tank with a heavy cloth or plastic tarp to protect it from the accidental spilling of brake fluid. Wash any spilled brake fluid off of any painted or plated surface immediately, as it will destroy the finish. Use soapy water and rinse completely.

1. Before replacing a brake hose, inspect the routing of the old hose carefully, noting any guides and grommets the hose may go through.

2. Drain the master cylinder as described under *Front Master Cylinder Removal/Installation* in this chapter.

3. Disconnect the banjo bolts securing the hose at either end and remove the hose with its banjo bolts and 2 washers at both ends.

4. Disconnect the hose from the clamp on the fork.

5. Install new brake hose, copper sealing washers and bolts in the reverse order of removal. Be sure to install the new sealing washers in their correct positions. Tighten all banjo bolts to specifications in **Table 3**.

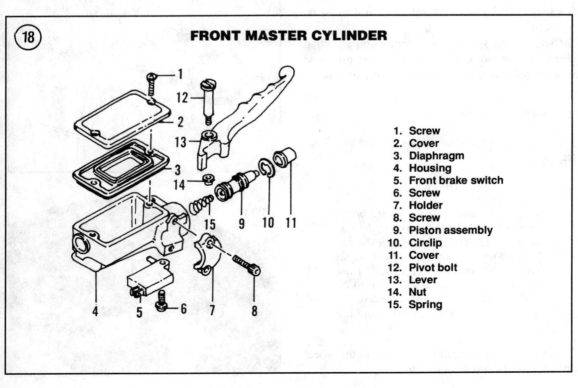

FRONT MASTER CYLINDER

1. Screw
2. Cover
3. Diaphragm
4. Housing
5. Front brake switch
6. Screw
7. Holder
8. Screw
9. Piston assembly
10. Circlip
11. Cover
12. Pivot bolt
13. Lever
14. Nut
15. Spring

6. Refill the master cylinder with fresh brake fluid clearly marked DOT 3. Bleed the brake as described under *Bleeding the System* in this chapter.

> *WARNING*
> *Do not ride the motorcycle until you are sure that the brakes are operating properly.*

FRONT BRAKE DISC

Inspection

It is not necessary to remove the disc from the wheel to inspect it. Small marks on the disc are not important, but deep radial scratches, deep enough to snag a fingernail, reduce braking effectiveness and increase brake pad wear. If these grooves are found, the disc should be resurfaced or replaced.

1. Measure the thickness around the disc at several locations with vernier calipers or a micrometer. The disc must be replaced if the thickness at any point is less than the minimum specified in **Table 1**.

2. Make sure the disc bolts are tight prior to performing this check. Check the disc runout with a dial indicator as shown in **Figure 19**. Slowly rotate the wheel and watch the dial indicator. If the runout is 0.3 mm (0.012 in.) or greater, the disc must be replaced.

3. Clean the disc of any rust or corrosion and wipe clean with lacquer thinner. Never use an oil-based solvent that may leave an oil residue on the disc.

Removal/Installation

1. Remove the front wheel as described in this chapter.

> *NOTE*
> *Place a piece of wood in the caliper in place of the disc. This way, if the brake lever is inadvertently squeezed, the piston will not be forced out of the cylinder. If this does happen, the caliper might have to be disassembled to reseat the piston and the system will have to be bled. By using the wood, bleeding the system is not necessary when installing the wheel.*

2. Remove the bolts securing the disc to the wheel and remove the disc (**Figure 20**).

3. Install by reversing these removal steps. Note the following:

   a. Apply Loctite 242 (blue) to the bolts before installation.

   b. Tighten the disc bolts to the specifications in **Table 2**.

BLEEDING THE SYSTEM

This procedure is necessary only when the brakes feel spongy, there is a leak in the hydraulic system, a component has been replaced or the brake fluid has been replaced.

1. Remove the dust cap from the brake air bleed valve (**Figure 7**).

2. Connect a length of clear tubing to the air bleed valve (B, **Figure 8**) on the caliper. Place the other end of the tube into a clean container (A, **Figure 8**). Fill the container with enough fresh brake fluid to

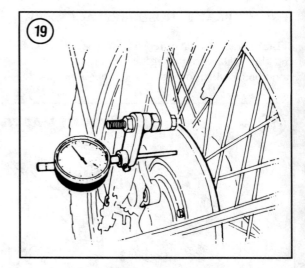

keep the end submerged. The tube should be long enough so that a loop can be made higher than the bleeder valve to prevent air from being drawn into the caliper during bleeding. See **Figure 21**.

> *CAUTION*
> *Cover the front wheel, fender and fuel tank with a heavy cloth or plastic tarp to protect it from the accidental spilling of brake fluid. Wash any spilled brake fluid off of any painted or plated surface immediately, as it will destroy the finish. Use soapy water and rinse completely.*

3. Clean the top of the master cylinder of all dirt and foreign matter. Remove the cap and diaphragm (**Figure 22**). Fill the reservoir to about 10 mm (3/8 in.) from the top. Install the diaphragm to prevent the entry of dirt and moisture.

> *WARNING*
> *Use only fluid clearly marked DOT 3. Others may vaporize and cause brake failure. Always use the same brand name. Do not intermix the brake fluids, as many brands are not compatible.*

4. Slowly apply the brake lever several times. Hold the lever in the applied position and open the bleeder valve about 1/2 turn. Allow the lever to travel to its limit. When this limit is reached, tighten the bleeder screw. As the brake fluid enters the system, the level will drop in the master cylinder reservoir. Maintain the level at about 10 mm (3/8 in.) from the top of the reservoir to prevent air from being drawn into the system.

5. Continue to pump the lever and fill the reservoir until the fluid emerging from the hose is completely free of air bubbles.

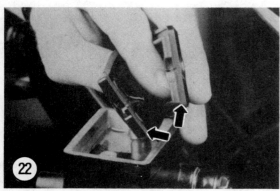

> *NOTE*
> *If bleeding is difficult, it may be necessary to allow the fluid to stabilize for a few hours. Repeat the bleeding procedure when the tiny bubbles in the system settle out.*

6. Hold the lever in the applied position and tighten the bleeder valve. Remove the bleeder tube and install the bleeder valve dust cap.

7. If necessary, add fluid to correct the level in the master cylinder reservoir. It must be above the LOWER level line (**Figure 23**).

12

8. Install the diaphragm and cap. Tighten the retaining screws.

9. Test the feel of the brake lever. It should feel firm and should offer the same resistance each time it's operated. If it feels spongy, it is likely that air is still in the system and it must be bled again. When all air has been bled from the system, and the brake fluid level is correct in the reservoir, double-check for leaks and tighten all fittings and connections.

> *WARNING*
> *Before riding the motorcycle, make certain that the brake is operating correctly by operating the lever several times. Then make the test ride a slow one at first to make sure the brake is operating properly.*

REAR DRUM BRAKE

Removal/Installation

Refer to **Figure 24**.

1. Remove the rear wheel as described in Chapter Eleven.

2. Pull the brake assembly (**Figure 25**) straight up and out of the brake drum.

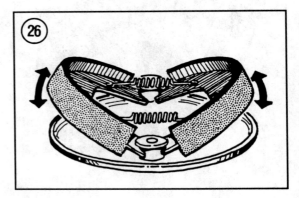

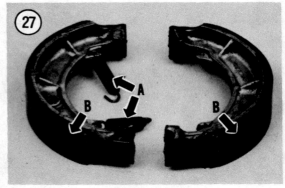

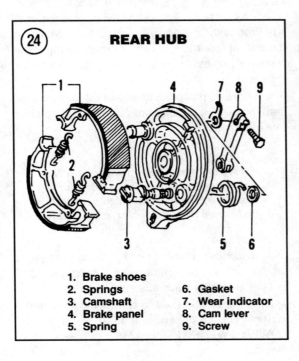

REAR HUB

1. Brake shoes
2. Springs
3. Camshaft
4. Brake panel
5. Spring
6. Gasket
7. Wear indicator
8. Cam lever
9. Screw

When working on the brake system, do
not *inhale brake dust. It may contain*
asbestos, which can cause lung injury
and cancer. Wear a disposable face
mask and wash your hands thoroughly
after completing the work.

NOTE
Before performing Step 3, mark the left
and right shoe. If the shoes are to be
reused, they must be installed in their
original position.

3. Pull the brake shoes (**Figure 26**) and springs up
and off the guide pins and camshaft.

4. Remove the return springs (A, **Figure 27**) and
separate the shoes (B, **Figure 27**). If the shoes will

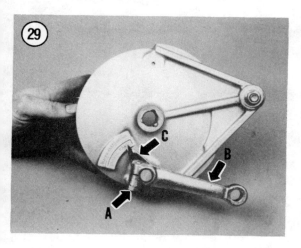

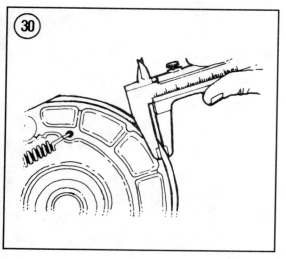

be reused, place a clean shop rag around the linings
to protect them from oil and grease while removed.

5. Mark the position of the cam lever (**Figure 28**) on
the camshaft so that it will be installed at the same
angle.

6. Loosen the clamping bolt (A, **Figure 29**) and
remove the brake arm (B, **Figure 29**).

7. Remove the wear indicator (C, **Figure 29**), dust
seal and camshaft.

8. Assemble the brake by reversing the disassembly
steps while noting the following.

9. Grease the camshaft and anchor posts with a light
coat of molybdenum disulfide grease; avoid getting
any grease on the brake plate where the linings come
in contact with it.

10. When installing the brake arm onto the brake
camshaft, be sure to align the punch marks on the
brake lever and housing and tighten the bolt securely.

11. Insert the brake panel assembly (**Figure 25**) into
the brake drum.

12. Install the rear wheel as described in Chapter
Eleven.

13. Adjust the rear brake as described in Chapter
Three.

Inspection

1. Thoroughly clean and dry all parts except the
linings.

2. Check the contact surface of the drum for scoring.
If there are grooves deep enough to snag a fingernail,
the drum should be reground and new shoes fitted.
This type of wear can be avoided to a great extent if
the brakes are disassembled and thoroughly cleaned
after riding the motorcycle in water, mud or deep
sand.

NOTE
If oil or grease is on the drum surface,
clean it off with a clean rag soaked in
lacquer thinner—do not use any solvent
that may leave an oil residue.

3. Use a vernier caliper (**Figure 30**) and measure the
thickness of each brake shoe. They should be replaced if lining thickness is less than the minimum
specified in **Table 1**.

4. Inspect the linings for embedded foreign material.
Dirt can be removed with a stiff wire brush. Check

12

for traces of oil or grease. If the linings are contaminated, they must be replaced as a set.

5. Inspect the cam lobe and pivot pin area of the shaft for wear and corrosion. Minor roughness can be removed with fine emery cloth.

6. Inspect the brake shoe return springs for wear or distortion. Replace the springs if they are too long. If they are stretched, they will not fully retract the brake shoes from the drum, resulting in a power-robbing drag on the drums and premature wear of the linings. Replace as necessary and always replace as a pair.

NOTE
Kawasaki does not specify brake spring free length.

Table 1 BRAKE SPECIFICATIONS

	Standard mm (in.)	Wear limit mm (in.)
Front brake disc		
Runout		0.3 (0.012)
Thickness	4.8-5.1 (0.189-0.200)	4.5 (0.177)
Rear brake drum inside		
diameter	160.160.16 (6.299-6.305)	160.75 (6.328)
Rear brake shoe lining		
thickness	4.0-4.5 (0.157-0.177)	2 (0.078)
Front brake pade lining		
thickness	4.5 (0.177)	1 (0.039)
Brake pedal free length	0-20 (0-0.78)	

Table 2 BRAKE TIGHTENING TORQUES

	N•m	ft.-lb.
Front brake disc bolts	23	17
Front brake caliper bolts	32	23
Union (banjo) bolts	29	21
Torque link nuts	29	21
Brake lever pivot nut	5.9	52 in.-lb.
Front master cylinder bolts	11	97 in.-lb.
Bleed valve	7.8	69 in.-lb.

12

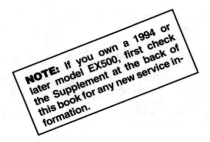

NOTE: If you own a 1994 or later model EX500, first check the Supplement at the back of this book for any new service information.

CHAPTER THIRTEEN

FAIRING

This chapter contains removal and installation procedures for the fairing assembly (**Figure 1**).

When removing a fairing component, it is best to reinstall all mounting hardware onto the removed part or store it in plastic bags taped to the inside of the fairing. After removal, fairing components should be placed away from the service area to prevent accidental damage.

Upper Fairing
Removal/Installation

Refer to **Figure 1**.

1. Park the motorcycle on its centerstand.
2. Remove the inner fairing screws and remove the left- and right-hand inner fairings (**Figure 2**). Place tape on the J-nuts as these are springs and are easily lost.
3. Remove the outer side fairing screws located underneath the rear of the fairing (**Figure 3**).
4. Pull back the rubber mirror boots and remove the left- and right-hand mirror bolts at the fairing (**Figure 4**).

5. Remove turn signal wire connector (**Figure 5**).
6. Lift the fairing slightly and remove by pulling it gently forward.
7. Install by reversing these steps. Note the following.
8. Connect the turn signal wire connector before installing the upper fairing all the way in.

Lower Fairing and Stay Removal/Installation

The 1990-on EX500 models can be equipped with a lower fairing.

1. Remove the lower fairing screws and remove the fairing (**Figure 6**).
2. Remove the fairing stay screws and remove the stay (**Figure 7**) from the left and right frame tube.
3. Install by reversing these steps.

Windshield

The windshield can be replaced by removing the mounting screws (**Figure 8**).

① **FAIRING ASSEMBLY**

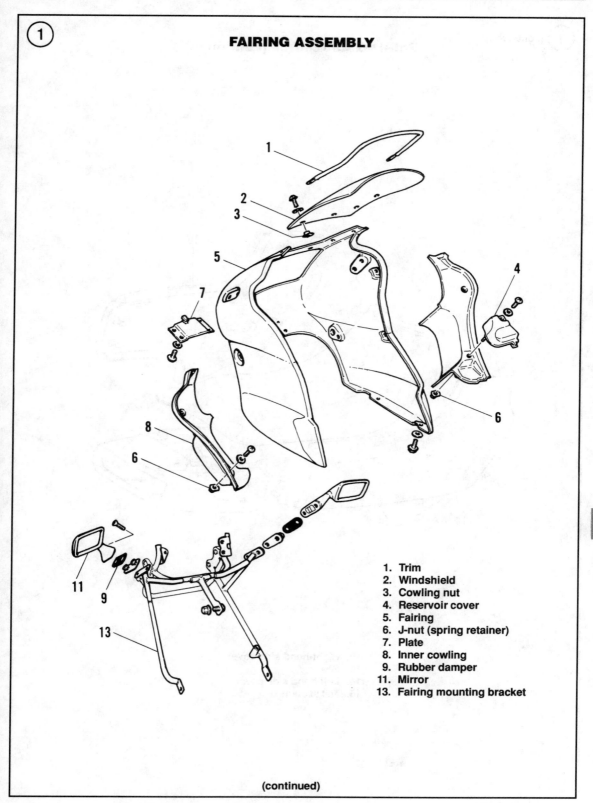

1. Trim
2. Windshield
3. Cowling nut
4. Reservoir cover
5. Fairing
6. J-nut (spring retainer)
7. Plate
8. Inner cowling
9. Rubber damper
11. Mirror
13. Fairing mounting bracket

13

(continued)

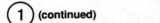

FAIRING ASSEMBLY (continued)

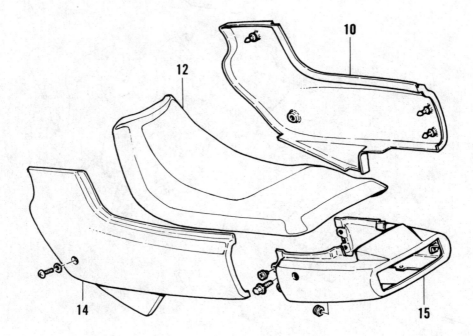

10. **Right-hand side cover**
12. **Seat**
14. **Left-hand side cover**
15. **Tail section**

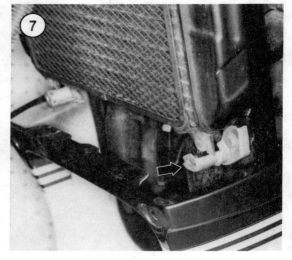

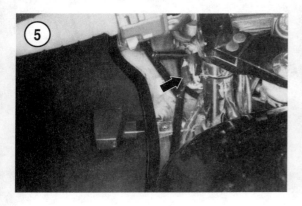

13

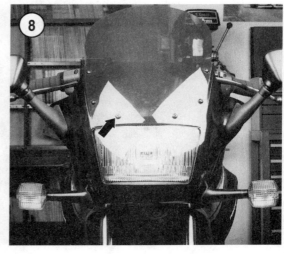

Windshield Cleaning

Be very careful when cleaning the windshield (**Figure 8**) as it can be scratched or damaged. Do not use a cleaner with an abrasive, a combination cleaner and wax or any solvent that contains ethyl or methyl alcohol. Never use gasoline or cleaning solvent. These products scratch or destroy the surface of the windshield.

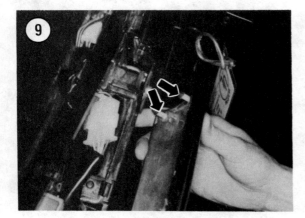

To remove oil, grease or road tar, use isopropyl alcohol. Then wash the windshield with a solution of mild soap and water. Dry *gently* with a soft cloth or chamois.

NOTE
When removing road tar, make sure there are no small stones or sand imbedded in it. Carefully remove any abrasive particles before performing any rubbing action with a cleaner. This will help minimize scratching.

Many commercial windshield cleaners are available. If using a cleaner, make sure it is safe for use on plastic and test it on a small area first.

Side Covers

Refer to **Figure 1**.
1. Remove side cover screws.
2. Pull rear of cover straight out to avoid breaking cover pins (**Figure 9**).
3. Reverse to install.

SUPPLEMENT

1994 AND LATER
SERVICE INFORMATION

This supplement contains all procedures and specifications unique to the EX500 (Ninja 500R) from 1994 through 2002. If specific procedures are not included, refer to the procedures in the prior chapters of the main body of this book.

This supplement is divided into sections that correspond to the chapters in the main body of the book. Refer to the index to quickly locate the desired section. Specifications are located in the Tables at the end of the supplement.

CHAPTER ONE

GENERAL INFORMATION

**Table 1 ENGINE AND FRAME SERIAL NUMBERS
(U.S. MODELS)**

Model and Year	Frame serial number	Engine serial number
EX500 D1 1994	JKAEXVD1-RA00001-009000	EX500 AE01800-on
EX500 D2 1995	JKAEXVD1-SA00001-025000	EX500 AE01800-on
EX500 D3 1996	JKAEXVD1-TA00001-035000	EX500 AE01800-on
EX500 D4 1997	JKAEXVD1-VA00001-040000	EX500 AE01800-on
EX500 D5 1998	JKAEXVD1-WA00001-on	EX500 AE01800-on
EX500 D6 1999	JKAEXVD1-XA00001-on	EX500 AE01800-on
EX500 D7 2000	JKAEXVD1-YA00001-on	EX500 AE01800-on
EX500 D8 2001	JKAEXVD1-1A00001-on	EX500 AE01800-on
EX500 D9 2002	JKAEXVD1-2A00001-on	EX500 AE01800-on

CHAPTER THREE

PERIODIC LUBRICATION, MAINTENANCE AND TUNE-UP

PERIODIC MAINTENANCE

Drive Chain Inspection/Adjustment

1. Place the motorcycle on the centerstand.
2. Turn the rear wheel and check the chain for its tightest point. Mark this spot and turn the wheel so the mark is located on the chain's lower run, midway between both the drive and driven sprockets.
3. With a thumb and forefinger, lift up then press down the chain at this point, measuring the distance the chain moves vertically.
4. The drive chain should have 35-40 mm (1 3/8-1 9/16 in.) of vertical travel (free play) at midpoint (**Figure 1**). If necessary, adjust the chain as follows:

5. Remove the cotter pin (A, **Figure 2**) and loosen the rear axle nut (B).
6. Loosen the drive chain adjuster locknut (C, **Figure 2**) on both sides of the wheel.

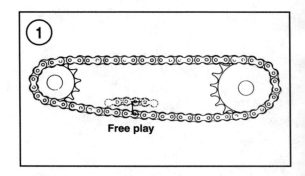

Free play

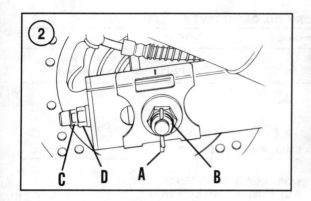

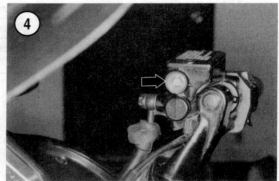

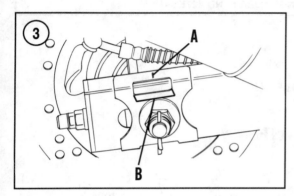

7. Turn each adjuster nut (D, **Figure 2**) and equal number of turns to obtain the correct drive chain slack. Check the alignment to make sure the alignment notch (A, **Figure 3**) is pointing to the same mark (B) on each side of the swing arm. Readjust if necessary to achieve the correct amount of slack while maintaining alignment.

8. Tighten the rear axle nut to 110 N·m (81 ft.-lb.).

9. Install a *new* cotter pin (A, **Figure 2**) and bend the ends over completely.

Rear Brake Pedal Height Adjustment

1. Place the motorcycle on the centerstand.

2. Check to make sure the pedal is in the at-rest position.

3. The correct height position from the top of the footpeg is 50 mm (1.97 in.).

4. To adjust, loosen the locknut on the master cylinder pushrod. Rotate the pushrod until the pedal height is correct. Tighten the locknut to 18 N·m (13 ft.-lbs.).

5. Adjust the rear brake light as described in Chapter Three.

Clutch Lever Adjustment

The clutch lever is equipped with a five-position adjuster so the lever can be adjusted to suit the rider's hand. Push the clutch lever forward, then align the adjuster number mark with the triangle on the lever holder. The minimum distance from the lever to the grip is the No. 5 position and the maximum distance is the No. 1 position.

Front Fork Oil Change

The fork oil change procedure is identical to prior years; however, the oil capacity and oil level are different. Refer to **Table 2** for specifications.

Disc Brake Fluid Level Inspection

1. Place the motorcycle on level ground on the centerstand.

2. Turn the handlebar so the front master cylinder is level.

3. The brake fluid must be kept above the lower level on both reservoirs. Refer to **Figure 4** for the front brake and through the right side of the rear side cover for the rear brake.

TUNE-UP

Correct Spark Plug Heat Range

Spark plug service is identical to prior years with the exception of the spark plug heat range specification. Refer to **Table 3**.

14

Table 2 FRONT FORK OIL CAPACITY

	Oil capacity	Oil level
Oil change capacity	300 mL	115-118 mm (4.53-4.65 in.)
Rebuild capacity	348-356 mL	115-118 mm (4.53-4.65 in.)

Table 3 TUNE-UP SPECIFICATIONS

Spark plug (standard heat range)	
U.S.	NGK D9EA or ND X27ES-U
Canada	NGK DR9EA or ND X27ESR-U
Other than U.S. & Canada	NGK D9EA or ND X27ES-U

CHAPTER FOUR

ENGINE

CYLINDER HEAD AND CAMSHAFTS

Camshaft Inspection

Inspection of the camshafts is identical to prior years with the exception of new lobe height specification as follows:

a. Standard height: 35.649-35.765 mm (1.4035-1.4081 in.).

b. Wear limit: 35.55 mm (1.3996 in.).

Cylinder Head Installation

Cylinder head installation is identical to prior years with the exception of the bolt torque specifications for the cylinder head and oil pipe bolts. See **Table 4**.

Table 4 ENGINE TIGHTENING TORQUES

Item	N•m	in.-lbs.	ft.-lbs.
Chain tensioner bolt	11	97	—
Cylinder head bolt (10 mm)	51	—	38
Engine drain plug	29	—	21
Oil pipe banjo bolts			
6 mm	7.8	69	—
8 mm	12	106	—
10 mm	20	—	15

CHAPTER FIVE

CLUTCH AND PRIMARY CHAIN

CLUTCH AND PRIMARY CHAIN

Removal/Installation

Removal and installation of the clutch assembly is identical to prior years with the exception of the clutch spring screws torque specification. Tighten the clutch screws to 8.8 N·m (78 in.-lb.).

CHAPTER SIX

TRANSMISSION

SHIFT MECHANISM

Removal and installation of the shift mechanism assembly is identical to prior years with the exception of the installation of the shift shaft cover. Prior to installing a *new* cover gasket, apply a light coat of silicone sealant to the shaded area of the crankcase shown in **Figure 5**.

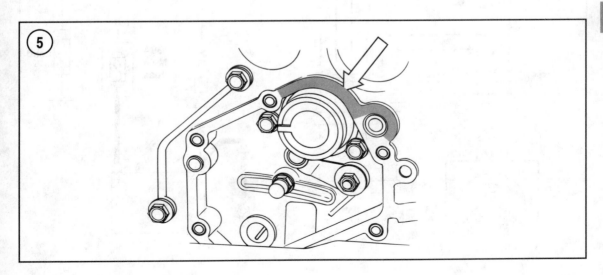

CHAPTER EIGHT

ELECTRICAL SYSTEM

Electrical specifications are in **Tables 5-7** at the end of this section.

CHARGING SYSTEM

Refer to **Figure 6** for the charging system schematic for these models.

Regulator/Rectifier Output Voltage Check

The *Number 1* electrical connector on prior models is no longer in the new circuit. The output voltage check must be made at the battery.

Before making any voltage regulator test, make sure the battery is fully charged and in good condition before performing any tests. Clean and test the battery as described in Chapter Three. Make sure all electrical connectors are tight and free of corrosion.

1. Start the engine, and let it reach normal operating temperature; shut off the engine.
2. Remove the seat.
3. Start the engine and let it idle.
4. On U.S., Canada and Australia models, turn OFF the headlight. Remove the 10A headlight fuse at the junction box.
5. Connect a 0-15 DC voltmeter to the battery negative and positive terminals (**Figure 7**).
6. Increase the engine speed and measure the voltage. It should be within 14-15 volts.
7. Turn OFF the engine and interpret the results as follows:
   a. If the voltage is correct, the charging system is working correctly.
   b. If the voltage did not rise as the engine speed increased, the regulator/rectifier is defective or the alternator output is insufficient.

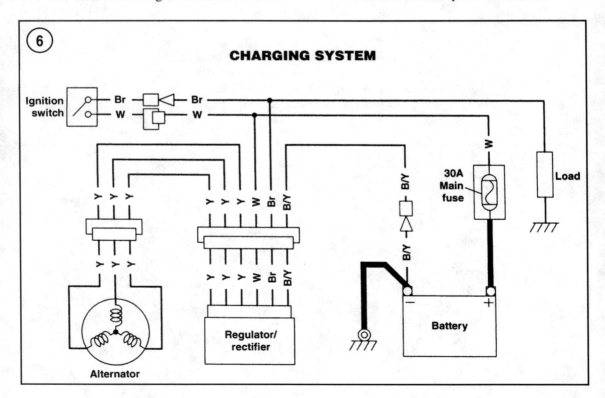

c. If the voltage exceeded 15 volts, the regulator/rectifier is damaged or the regulator/rectifier electrical leads are loose or disconnected.

8. After the test is completed, perform the following:

a. Disconnect the voltmeter.

b. On U.S., Canada and Australia models, install the 10A headlight fuse at the junction box.

c. Install the seat.

Voltage Rectifier Test

1. Remove the seat and the left side frame cover.
2. Disconnect the six-pin electrical connector (**Figure 8**) from the voltage regulator/rectifier.
3. Measure and record the resistance between the white/red and each yellow terminal.
4. Measure and record the resistance between the black and each yellow terminal.
5. Reverse ohmmeter lead, then repeat Steps 3 and 6. Each pair of measurements must be high with the ohmmeter connected one way and low when the ohmmeter leads are connected the other way. It is

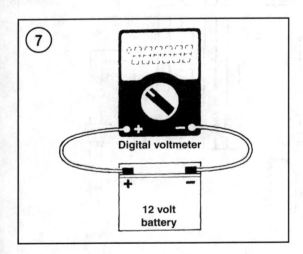

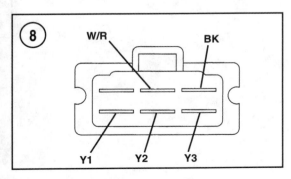

not possible to specify exact ohmmeter readings, but each pair of measurements should differ by a factor of not less than 10 times.

IGNITION SYSTEM

Refer to **Figure 9** for the ignition system schematic for these models.

Ignition Coil Testing

Ignition coil testing is identical to prior years with the exception of the resistance specifications. The specifications are as follows:

a. Primary resistance: 2.3-3.5 ohms.

b. Secondary resistance: 12-18K ohms.

STARTING SYSTEM

Refer to **Figure 10** for the electric starting system schematic these models.

Starter Relay

The starter relay is now an integral part of the junction box. Testing is part of the *Junction Box Inspection* in this section of the supplement.

JUNCTION BOX AND FUSES

The junction box is mounted underneath the seat and houses the fuses, diodes and relays. The junction box circuits are shown in **Figure 11** and **12** for these models. The diodes and relays are an integral part of the junction box and cannot be removed. If they fail, the junction box must be replaced.

Junction Box Removal/Installation

To remove the junction box, remove the seat, then remove the mounting screws. Disconnect the two electrical connectors. Reverse to install.

Junction Box Inspection

This test describes checks for the fuse and relay (fan, starter and headlight) circuits.

Refer to **Figures 11** and **12** for this procedure.

1. Remove the junction box as described in this section of the supplement.

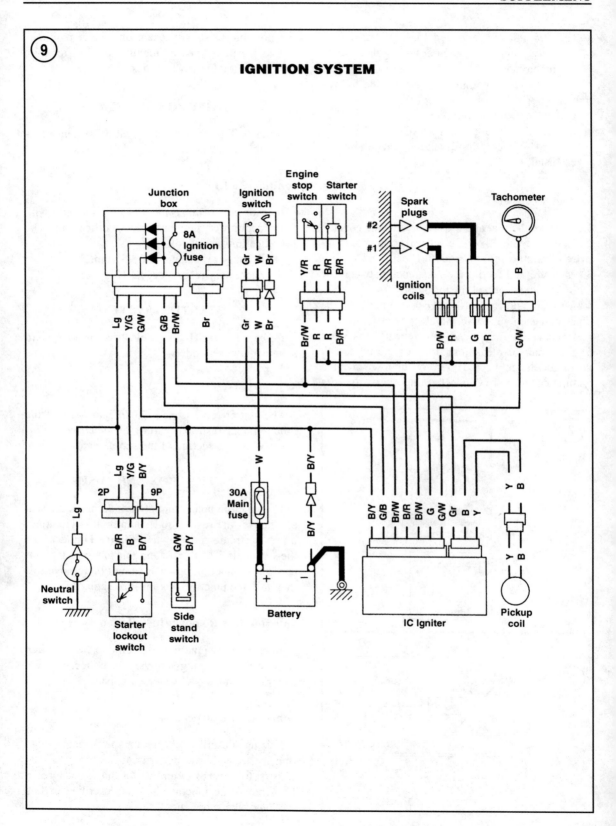

9

IGNITION SYSTEM

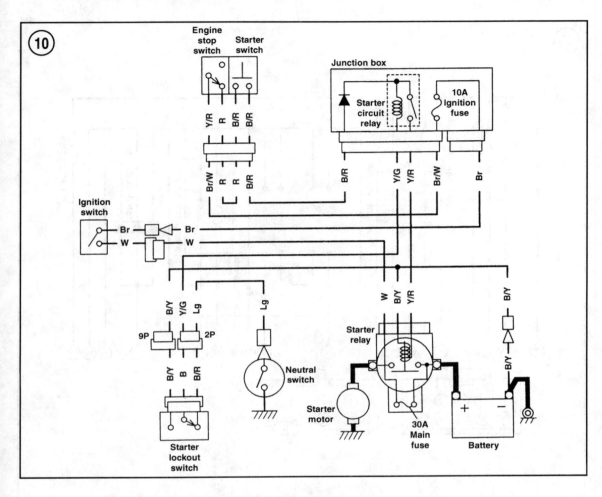

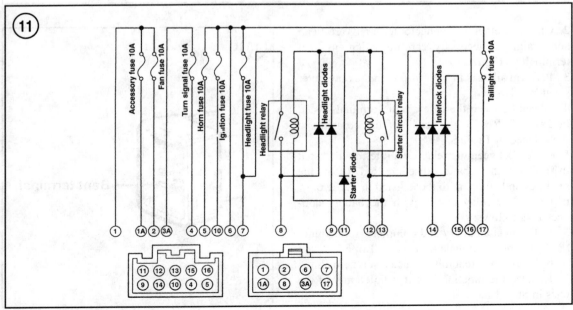

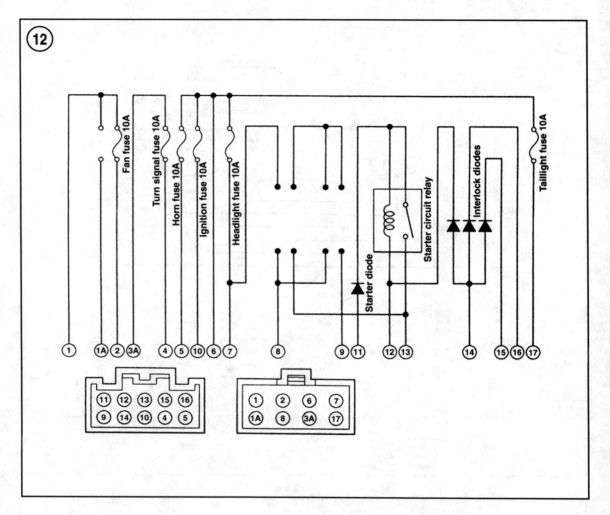

2. Check whether the connector terminals are clean and straight. If necessary, carefully align any bent terminal(s) (**Figure 13**).

3. Perform all tests in Steps 4-6 with the ohmmeter set at R × 1.

4. Check between the fuse circuit terminals listed in **Table 5**. Record the readings and compare to those listed in **Table 5**.

5. Check between the relay circuit terminals listed in **Table 6** with the battery disconnected. Record the readings and compare to those listed in **Table 6**.

6. Check the relay circuit with the battery connected as follows:

    a. Connect a battery and ohmmeter to the junction box terminals as listed in **Table 7**.

    b. The correct reading for each test is zero ohm.

7. Replace the junction box if it failed any of the tests in Step 4-6.

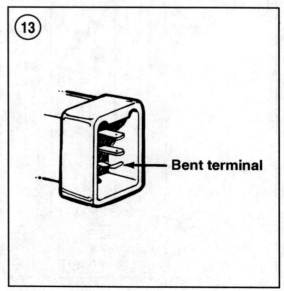

Bent terminal

Table 5 JUNCTION BOX: FUSE INSPECTION

Meter connection	Meter reading
1 and 1A	0 ohm
1 and 2	0 ohm
3A and 4	0 ohm
6 and 5	0 ohm
6 and 10	0 ohm
6 and 7	0 ohm
6 and 17	0 ohm
1A and 8	Infinity
2 and 8	Infinity
3A and 8	Infinity
6 and 2	Infinity
6 and 3A	Infinity
17 and 3A	Infinity

Table 6 JUNCTION BOX: CIRCUIT INSPECTION (BATTERY DISCONNECTED)

Meter connection	Meter reading
Headlight relay*	
7 and 8	Infinity
7-13	Infinity
13 (+) and 9 (-)	Other than infinity
Starter relay	
9 and 11	Infinity
12 and 13	Infinity
13 (+) and 11 (-)	Infinity
12 (+) and 11 (-)	Other than infinity
* U.S., Canada and Australia models only.	

Table 7 JUNCTION BOX: CIRCUIT INSPECTION (BATTERY CONNECTED)

	Meter connection	Battery connection	Meter reading
Headlight relay*	7 and 8	9 (+) and 13 (-)	0 ohm
Starter relay	13 (+) and 11 (-)	11 (+) and 12 (-)	Other than infinity
* U.S., Canada and Australia			

14

CHAPTER NINE

COOLING SYSTEM

THERMOSTATIC FAN SWITCH AND WATER TEMPERATURE SENSOR

Removal/Installation

Thermostatic fan switch removal and installation is identical to prior years with the exception of the switch torque specification. Tighten the switch to 18 N·m (13 ft.-lbs.).

CHAPTER TEN

FRONT SUSPENSION AND STEERING

STEERING HEAD

Removal/Installation

The removal and installation of the steering head is identical to prior years with the exception of the steering stem nut torque specification.

Tighten the nut to the specification in **Table 8** in this supplement.

FRONT FORK

Removal/Installation

The removal and installation of the front fork assemblies are identical to prior years with the exception of the fork clamps bolt and bottom Allen bolt torque specification.

Tighten these bolts to the specification in **Table 8**.

Table 8 FRONT SUSPENSION TIGHTENING TORQUES

Item	N•m	in.-lbs.	ft.-lbs.
Front axle clamp bolt	20	—	15
Front fork			
Upper clamp bolt	20	—	15
Lower clamp bolt	34	—	25
Lower Allen bolt	20	—	15
Steering stem head bolt	44	—	32

CHAPTER ELEVEN

REAR SUSPENSION

Suspension torque specifications are in **Table 9** at the end of this section.

REAR WHEEL

Removal/Installation

1. Support the motorcycle so the rear wheel clears the ground.
2. Remove the cotter pin (A, **Figure 14**) and loosen the rear axle nut (B).

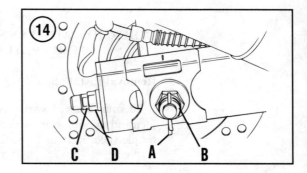

3. Loosen the drive chain adjuster locknut (C, **Figure 14**) on both sides of the wheel.

4. Loosen the adjuster nut (D, **Figure 14**) to allow slack in the drive chain.

5. Slide the axle out of the wheel and allow the wheel to drop to the ground.

6. Remove the axle spacer from the right side.

7. Lift the drive chain off the sprocket.

8. Move the rear wheel toward the rear while holding onto the rear caliper assembly.

9. Remove the rear wheel.

10. Secure the rear caliper assembly to the frame with wire or Bungee cord.

NOTE
Insert a piece of wood in the caliper in place of the disc. This way, if the brake pedal is inadvertently applied, the piston will not be forced out of the caliper. If this happens, the caliper may have to be disassembled to reseat the piston.

11. If the wheel is going to be taken off for any length of time, install the drive chain adjusters and axle spacer along with the axle nut to avoid misplacing them.

12. Install by reversing these removal steps. Note the following.

13. Correctly position the rear caliper mounting bracket groove onto the swing arm stop.

14. Adjust the drive chain as described in Chapter Three.

15. Tighten the rear axle nut to the specification in **Table 9**.

16. Spin the wheel several times to make sure it rotates freely and that the brake works properly.

REAR SWING ARM

Removal/Installation

Refer to **Figure 15** and **16**.

1. Park the motorcycle on the centerstand.

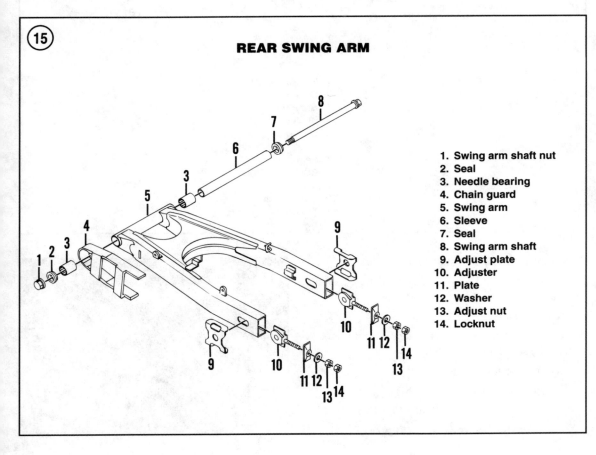

REAR SWING ARM

1. Swing arm shaft nut
2. Seal
3. Needle bearing
4. Chain guard
5. Swing arm
6. Sleeve
7. Seal
8. Swing arm shaft
9. Adjust plate
10. Adjuster
11. Plate
12. Washer
13. Adjust nut
14. Locknut

14

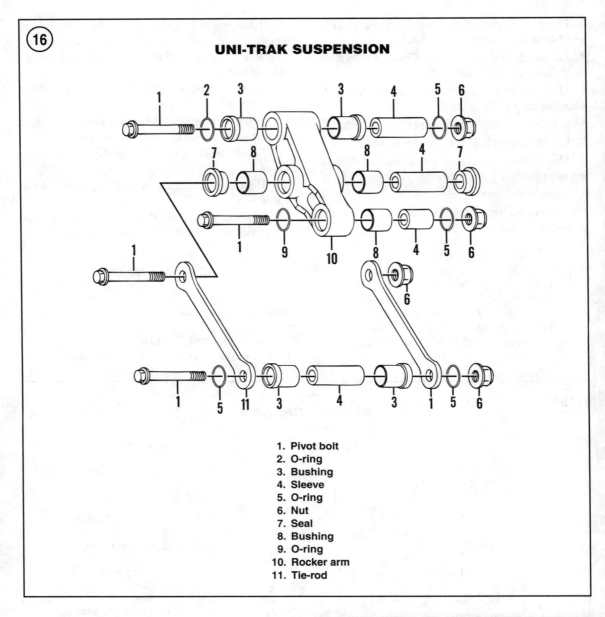

UNI-TRAK SUSPENSION

1. Pivot bolt
2. O-ring
3. Bushing
4. Sleeve
5. O-ring
6. Nut
7. Seal
8. Bushing
9. O-ring
10. Rocker arm
11. Tie-rod

2. Remove the seat and side covers.

3. Remove the mufflers as described in Chapter Seven.

4. Remove the chain guard.

5. Remove the rear wheel as described in this section of the supplement.

6. Remove the following:

    a. Swing arm pivot bolt nut (**Figure 17**).

    b. Uni-Trak upper tie-rod nut (**Figure 18**).

    c. Lower shock absorber nut (**Figure 19**).

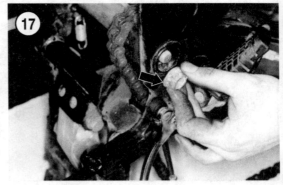

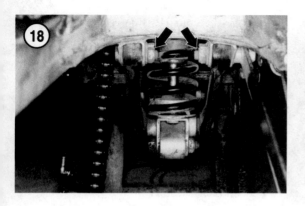

7. Remove the shock absorber bolt, tie-rod bolts and swing arm pivot shaft and pull the swing arm toward the rear and remove the assembly.

8. Remove the drive chain, if necessary.

9. Installation is the reverse of removal. Note the following:

a. Tighten the swing arm pivot bolt nut to the specification in **Table 9**.

b. Tighten the lower shock absorber nut and upper tire-rod nut to the specification in **Table 9**.

c. Adjust the drive chain as described in Chapter Three.

Table 9 REAR SUSPENSION TIGHTENING TORQUES

Item	N•m	in.-lbs.	ft.-lbs.
Rear axle nut	110	—	81
Shock absorber nuts	59	—	44
Sprocket nuts	59	—	44
Uni-track			
Rocker arm nut	59	—	44
Tie-rod nut	59	—	44

CHAPTER TWELVE

BRAKES

All U.S. and Canada models are equipped with a single disc brake on the front wheel. Some models other than U.S. and Canada models are equipped with dual front disc brakes. All models are equipped with a rear disc brake.

Brake specifications are in **Table 10** and **Table 11** at the end of this section.

FRONT BRAKE PAD REPLACEMENT

Front brake pad replacement is identical to prior years with the exception of models equipped with

dual front calipers. To maintain even brake pressure on the disc, always replace both brake pads in each caliper at the same time.

REAR BRAKE PAD REPLACEMENT

1. Remove the rear caliper as described in this supplement.

2. Lift the inner brake pad out of the caliper.

3. Push the caliper holder toward the piston and remove the outer brake pad from the caliper.

4. Lift the anti-rattle spring out of the caliper.

5. Check the caliper holder (A, **Figure 20**) to make sure the clips (B) are installed. **Figure 20** shows the caliper holder removed to better illustrate the step.
6. Remove the side covers as described in this supplement.
7. Remove the cap, diaphragm plate and diaphragm from the rear master cylinder.
8. Use a shop syringe and remove about 50 percent of the brake fluid from the reservoir. Do not remove more than 50 percent of the brake fluid, or air will enter the system. Discard the brake fluid properly.
9. Slowly push the piston into the caliper while checking the reservoir to make sure it does not overflow.
10. Install a *new* anti-rattle spring into the caliper.
11. Align the holes in the outer brake pad plate and install it into the caliper holder.
12. Install the inner brake pad into the caliper.
13. Hold the brake pads in place and install the caliper onto the brake disc as described in this supplement.
14. Support the motorcycle with the rear wheel off the ground. Spin the wheel and pump the rear brake pedal until the pads are seated against the disc.
15. Refill the rear master cylinder reservoir, if necessary to maintain the correct, fluid level. Install the diaphragm, diaphragm plate and top cap.

> *WARNING*
> *Do not ride the motorcycle until the rear brake is operating correctly with full hydraulic advantage.*

REAR CALIPER

Removal/Installation

1. Drain the master cylinder as follows:
   a. Attach a hose to the brake caliper bleed screw.
   b. Place the end of the hose in a clean container.
   c. Open the bleed screw and operate the brake pedal to drain the brake fluid from the brake line and master cylinder reservoir.
   d. Close the bleed screw and disconnect the hose.
   e. Discard the brake fluid properly.
2. Remove the banjo bolt and copper washers (A, **Figure 21**) securing the brake hose to the caliper. Cap the end of the brake hose and tie it to the frame. Be sure to cap or tape the end of the brake hose to prevent the entry of debris.

3. Remove the bolts (B, **Figure 21**) securing the caliper (C) to the mounting bracket.
4. Carefully slide the caliper up and off the brake disc. Remove the brake pads from the caliper.
5. Installation is the reverse of removal. Note the following:
   a. Tighten the mounting bolts to the specification in **Table 11**.
   b. Install the brake hose using *new* copper washers.
   c. Tighten the brake hose banjo bolt to the specification in **Table 11**.
   d. Bleed the rear brake as described under *Bleeding the System* in Chapter Twelve.

Caliper Rebuilding

Refer to **Figure 22**.
1. Remove the rear caliper and remove the brake shoes as described in this supplement.
2. Pull straight out and remove the holder from the caliper body.

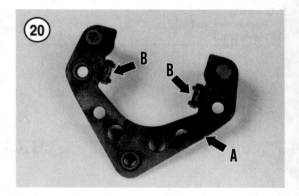

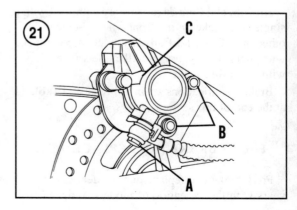

WARNING
Keep fingers and hand out of the caliper body are when removing the piston in Step 3.

Compressed air will force the piston out of the caliper body under considerable force.

3. Pad the piston with shop rags or wood block as shown in **Figure 23**. Apply light compressed air though one of the caliper ports and blow the piston out of the caliper.

4. Remove the dust seal and the piston seal (**Figure 24**).

5. Clean all caliper parts (except brake pads) in new DOT 3 brake fluid. Place the cleaned part of a lint-free cloth while performing the following inspection procedures.

6. Check the caliper bore (**Figure 25**) for cracks, deep scoring or excessive wear.

7. Check the caliper piston (**Figure 26**) for deep scoring, excessive wear or rust.

8. Replace the caliper body or piston if necessary.

9. The piston seal maintains the correct brake pad-to-disc clearance. If the seal is worn or dam-

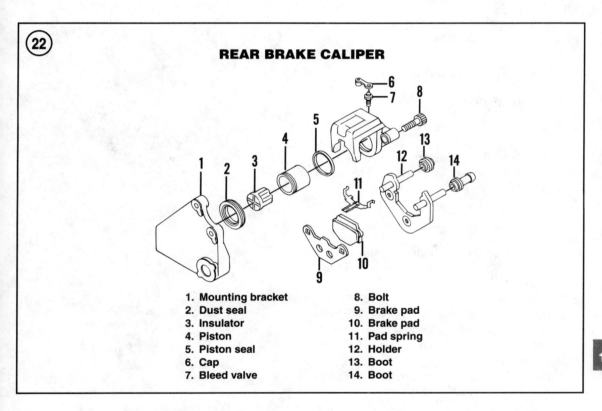

REAR BRAKE CALIPER

1. Mounting bracket
2. Dust seal
3. Insulator
4. Piston
5. Piston seal
6. Cap
7. Bleed valve
8. Bolt
9. Brake pad
10. Brake pad
11. Pad spring
12. Holder
13. Boot
14. Boot

14

aged, the brake pads will drag and cause excessive brake pad wear and brake fluid temperature. Replace the piston and dust seals if the following conditions exist:

    a. Brake fluid leaks around the inner brake pad.

    b. The piston seal (**Figure 24**) is stuck in the caliper body groove.

    c. There is a large difference in the inner and outer brake pad wear (**Figure 27**).

10. Measure the brake pad material with a ruler or caliper (**Figure 28**) and compare to wear limits in **Table 10**. Replace both brake pads if one pad is too thin.

11. Check the caliper holder (**Figure 29**) for damage. Replace the holder if necessary.

REAR MASTER CYLINDER

Removal/Installation

> *CAUTION*
> *Cover the frame with a heavy cloth or plastic tarp to protect the area from accidental brake fluid spills. Wash any spilled brake fluid off any painted or plastic surfaces immediately as it will destroy the finish. Use soapy water and rinse completely.*

1. Drain the rear master cylinder as follows:

    a. Attach a hose to the rear brake caliper bleed screw.

    b. Place the end of the hose in a clean container.

    c. Open the bleed screw and operate the brake pedal to drain the brake fluid from the brake line, the master cylinder reservoir and the master cylinder.

    d. Close the bleed screw and disconnect the hose.

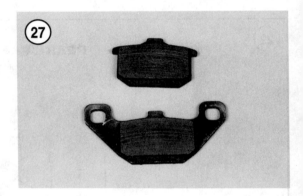

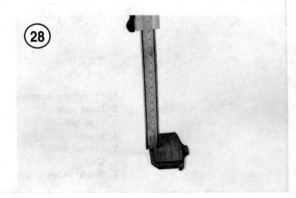

e. Discard the brake fluid properly.

2. Loosen the clamp and disconnect the reservoir hose from the master cylinder fitting.

3. Remove the banjo bolt and copper washers securing the brake hose to the top of the master cylinder. Cap the end of the brake hose and tie it up to the frame. Be sure to cap or tape the end of the brake hose to prevent the entry of debris.

4. Disconnect the rear brake light switch connector.

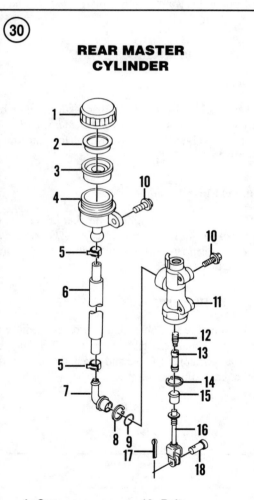

REAR MASTER CYLINDER

1. Cap
2. Diaphragm plate
3. Diaphragm
4. Reservoir
5. Hose clamp
6. Hose
7. Fitting
8. Snap ring
9. O-ring
10. Bolt
11. Housing
12. Spring
13. Piston assembly
14. Snap ring
15. Cover seal
16. Pushrod
17. Cotter pin
18. Joint pin

5. Remove the cotter pin. Slightly depress the brake pedal and withdraw the joint pin. Disconnect the brake pedal from the master cylinder pushrod.

6. Remove the bolts securing the master cylinder caliper to the footpeg mounting bracket.

7. Adjust the rear brake as described under *Rear Brake Pedal Height Adjustment* in this supplement.

Reservoir
Removal/Installation

1. Remove the rear portion of the fairing as described in this supplement.

2. Use a shop syringe and remove all of brake fluid from the reservoir. Discard the brake fluid properly.

3. Loosen the clamp and disconnect the reservoir hose from the reservoir fitting. Plug the end of the hose to prevent the entry of debris.

4. Remove the mounting bolt and remove the reservoir from the frame.

5. Installation is the reverse of removal. Note the following:

   a. Connect the reservoir hose onto the reservoir and tighten the hose clamp.

   b. Bleed the rear brake as described under *Bleeding the System* in Chapter Twelve.

Disassembly/Assembly

Refer to **Figure 30**.

1. Remove the rear master cylinder as described in this supplement.

2. Remove the snap ring and remove the piston stop and pushrod assembly.

14

CAUTION
Do not remove the secondary cup from the piston assembly in Step 3. Removing the secondary cup will damage it.

3. Remove the piston assembly and spring from the housing.

4. Inspect the master cylinder as described in this supplement.

5. Assembly is the reverse of these steps. Note the following:

   a. Soak the new cups in fresh brake fluid for at least 15 minutes to make them pliable. Coat the inside of the housing bore with fresh brake fluid before installing the parts.

CAUTION
When installing the piston assembly, do not allow the cups to turn inside out as they will be damaged and allow brake fluid to leak within the cylinder bore.

b. Install the master cylinder piston assembly in the order shown in **Figure 30**. Make sure the dust cover is firmly seated against the master cylinder.

Inspection

1. Clean all caliper parts in new DOT 3 brake fluid. Place the cleaned part of a lint-free cloth while performing the following inspection procedures.
2. Check the cylinder bore and piston contact surfaces for signs of wear or damage. If either part is less than perfect, replace it.
3. Check the end of the piston for wear caused by the piston stop. Replace the piston assembly if any portion if requires replacement. If the piston assembly is replaced, also replace the primary cup.
4. Check the primary and secondary cup on the piston for damage, softness or swelling. Replace the piston assembly if any of these conditions are found.
5. Inspect the piston stop and pushrod assembly for damage or bending. Replace if necessary.
6. Make sure the passages in the bottom of the brake fluid reservoir are clear. Check the reservoir cap and diaphragm for damage and deterioration. Replace if necessary.
7. Inspect the threads in the master cylinder body where the brake hose banjo bolt screws in. If the threads are damaged or partially stripped, replace the master cylinder body.

REAR BRAKE HOSE REPLACEMENT

Replacement of the rear brake hose is identical to the front brake. Refer to *Front Brake Hose Replacement* in Chapter Twelve.

REAR BRAKE DISC

Inspection

Inspection of the rear brake disc is identical to the front brake. Refer to *Front Brake Disc Inspection* in Chapter Twelve. Refer to **Table 10** for rear brake specifications.

Removal/Installation

Removal and installation of the rear brake disc is identical to the front brake. Refer to *Front Brake Disc Removal/Installation* in Chapter Twelve and remove the rear wheel.

BLEEDING THE SYSTEM

Bleeding the system with a rear disc assembly is identical to the front brake. Refer to *Bleeding the System* in Chapter Twelve and attach the bleed hose to the rear caliper assembly.

Table 10 BRAKE SPECIFICATIONS

	Standard mm (in.)	Wear limit mm (in.)
Brake disc thickness		
Front		
Single disc	3.8-4.2 (0.149-0.165)	3.5 (0.137)
Dual disc	4.8-5.2 (0.189-0.205)	4.5 (0.177)
Rear	4.8-5.1 (0.189-0.200)	4.5 (0.177)
Brake pad thickness		
Front		
Single disc	4.35 (0.171)	1.0 (0.04)
Dual disc	4.3 (0.169)	1.0 (0.04)
Rear	4.5 (0.177)	1.0 (0.04)

Table 11 BRAKE TIGHTENING TORQUES

Item	N•m	in.-lbs.	ft.-lbs.
Banjo bolts	25	—	18
Rear brake disc bolts	23	—	17
Rear brake reservoir bolt	7	62	—
Rear master cylinder			
Mounting bolt	23	—	17
Bracket locknut	18	—	13
Rear brake caliper mounting bolts	32	—	23

CHAPTER THIRTEEN

FAIRING COMPONENTS

SIDE COVER

Removal/Installation

Refer to **Figure 31**.

1. Remove the seat.

2. Remove the mounting bolts and the rear grab rail.

3. Remove the front lower and rear upper mounting screws and nylon washers.

4. Below the tail/brake light lens, remove the mounting screws and nylon washers.

5. At the upper front portion of the side cover, carefully pull out on the side cover and release the

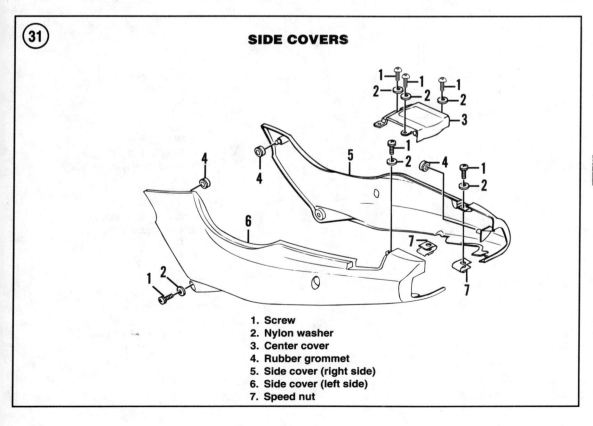

31

SIDE COVERS

1. Screw
2. Nylon washer
3. Center cover
4. Rubber grommet
5. Side cover (right side)
6. Side cover (left side)
7. Speed nut

14

mounting post from the rubber grommet in the frame mounting receptacle.

6. Carefully spread out on the front of the side cover assembly and remove it from the frame.

7. Installation is the reverse of removal.

MIRRORS

Removal/Installation

1. Hold onto the mirror and remove the nuts securing the mirror to the upper fairing and the mounting bracket.

2. Remove the mirror, collar and gasket from the upper fairing.

3. Installation is the reverse of removal. Be sure to install the gasket between the collar and the upper fairing.

UPPER FAIRING

Removal/Installation

Refer to **Figure 32**.

1. Working below the headlight assembly, remove the bolts, collars and nylon washers securing the upper fairing to the mounting bracket.

2. Remove the rear lower corner mounting screws and nylon washer on each side.

3. Remove both mirrors as previously described in this section.

4. Carefully pull the upper fairing forward and have an assistant disconnect the headlight and front turn signal electrical connectors from each component.

5. Carefully pull the front fairing and headlight assembly forward and off the mounting bracket and remove it from the motorcycle.

6. Install by reversing these removal steps.

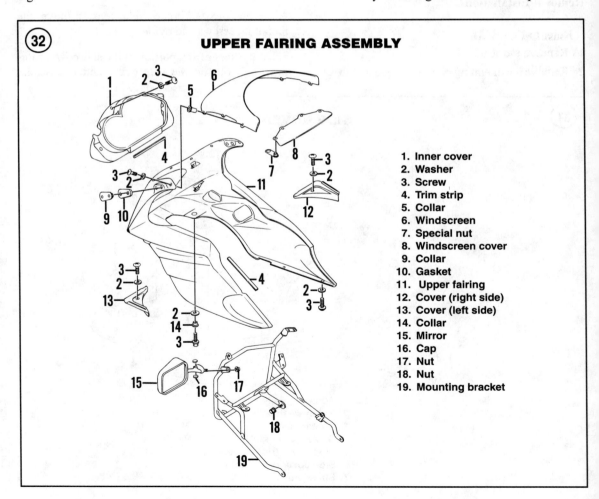

32 **UPPER FAIRING ASSEMBLY**

1. Inner cover
2. Washer
3. Screw
4. Trim strip
5. Collar
6. Windscreen
7. Special nut
8. Windscreen cover
9. Collar
10. Gasket
11. Upper fairing
12. Cover (right side)
13. Cover (left side)
14. Collar
15. Mirror
16. Cap
17. Nut
18. Nut
19. Mounting bracket

INDEX

15

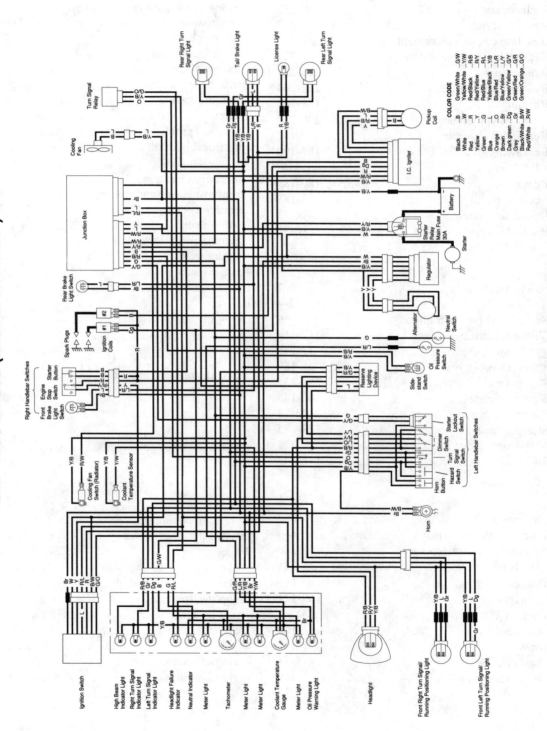

1987-1993 EX500 (U.S. & CANADA)

COLOR CODE

Black ...... B	Green/White ...G/W
White ...... W	Yellow/White ....Y/W
Red ...... R	Red/Black ......R/B
Yellow ...... Y	Red/Yellow ......R/Y
Green ...... G	Red/Blue ......R/L
Blue L	Yellow/Black ....Y/B
Orange ...... O	Yellow/Red ......Y/R
Brown ...... Br	Blue/Yellow ....L/Y
Dark green ...Dg	Blue/Red ......L/R
Grey ...... Gr	Green/Yellow ...G/Y
Black/White ...B/W	Green/Red ......G/R
Red/White ...R/W	Green/Orange...G/O

1987-1993 EX500 (AUSTRALIA & SOUTH AFRICA)

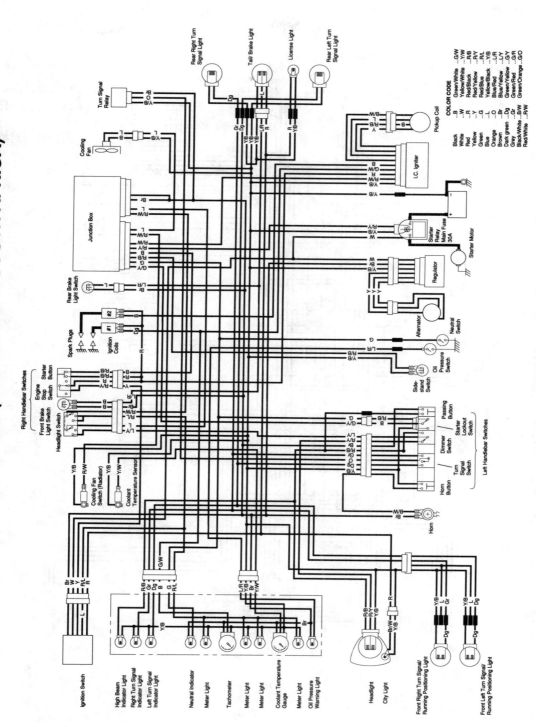

COLOR CODE

Black	B	Green/White	G/W
White	W	Yellow/White	Y/W
Red	R	Red/Black	R/B
Yellow	Y	Red/Yellow	R/Y
Green	G	Red/Blue	R/L
Blue	L	Yellow/Black	Y/B
Orange	O	Blue/Yellow	L/Y
Brown	Br	Green/Yellow	G/Y
Dark green	Dg	Green/Red	G/R
Grey	Gr	Green/Orange	G/O
Black/White	B/W	
Red/White	R/W	

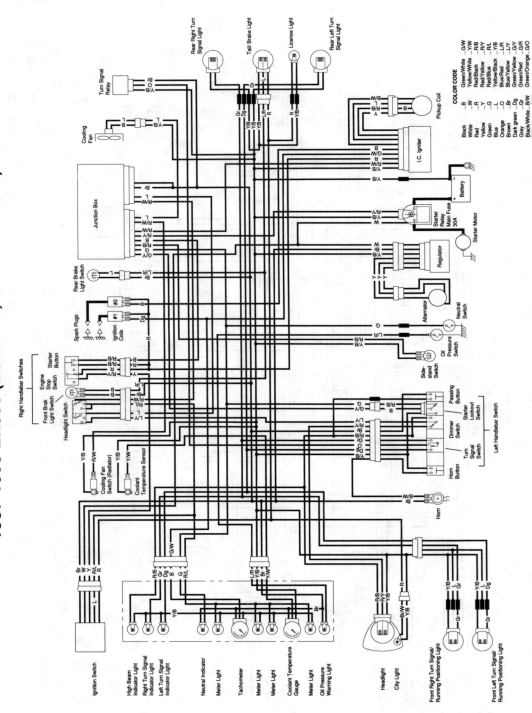

1987-1993 EX500 (EUROPE, EXCEPT ITALY)

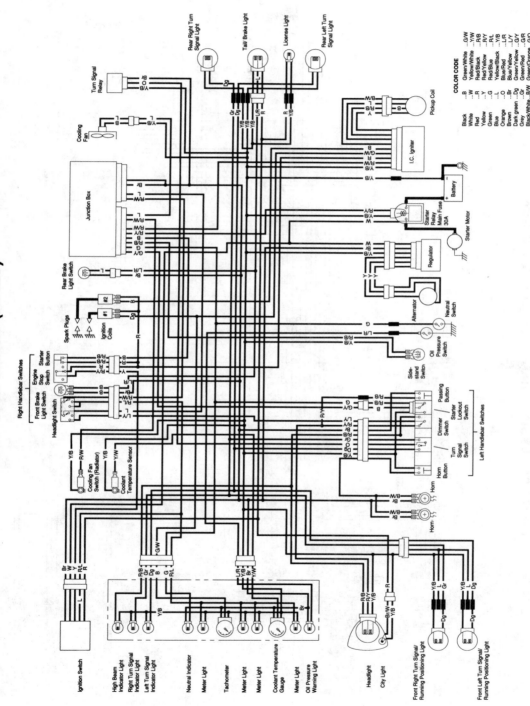

1987-1993 EX500 (ITALY)

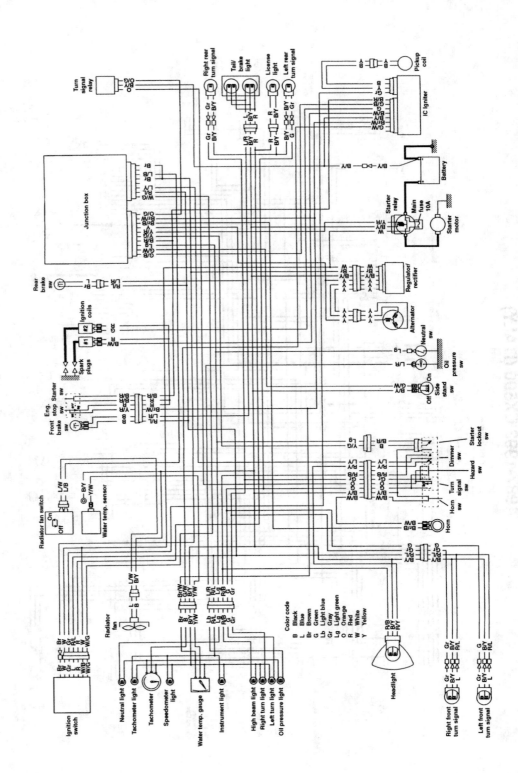

1994-2002 EX500, NINJA 500R (U.S. & CANADA)

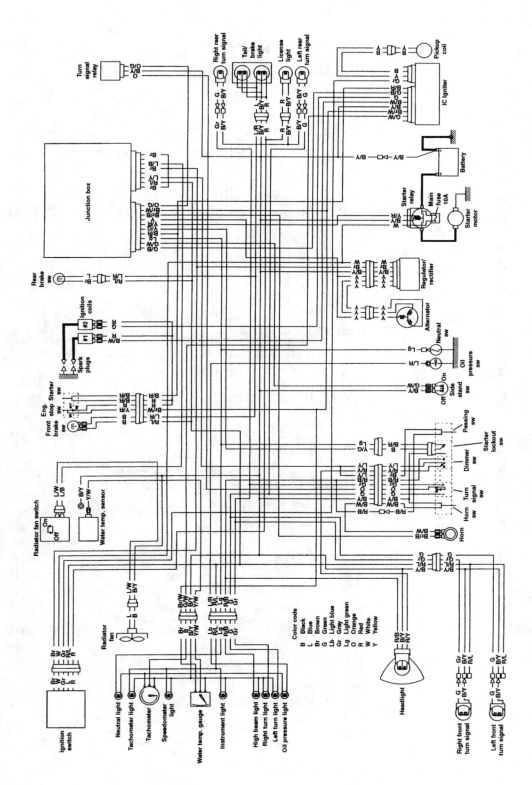

1994-2002 EX500, NINJA 500R (AUSTRALIA)

1994-2002 EX500, NINJA 500R (OTHER THAN U.S., CANADA AND AUSTRALIA)

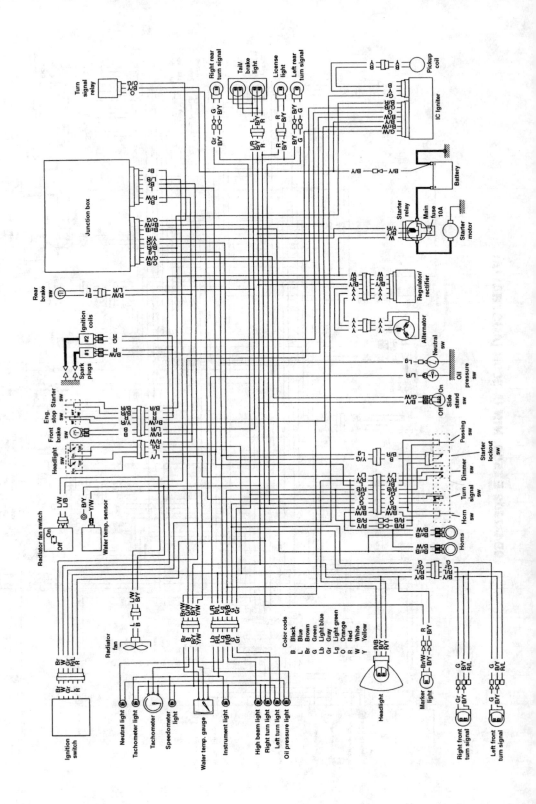